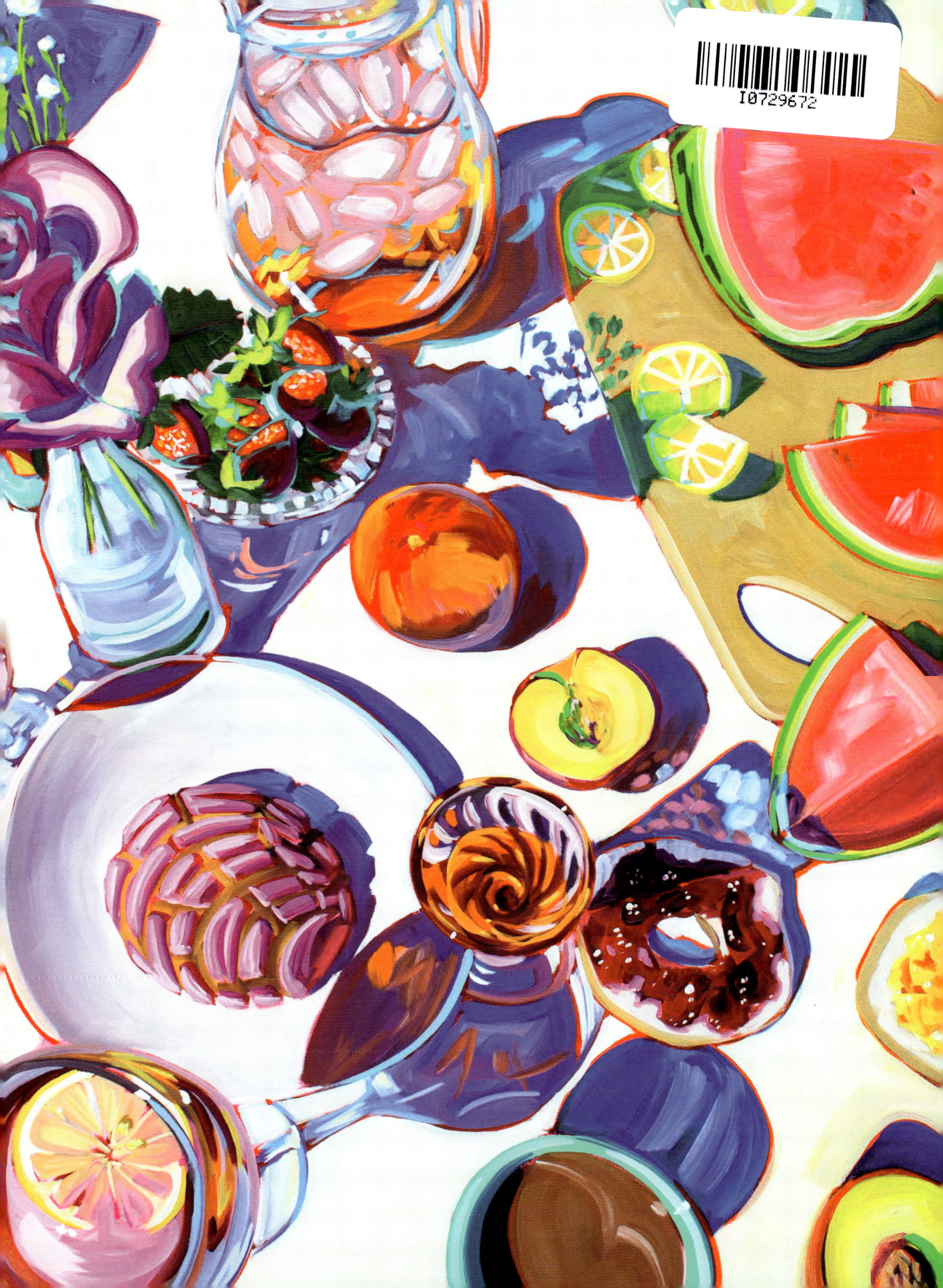

I0729672

MODERN STILL LIFE

From **Fruit Bowls** *to* **Disco Balls**

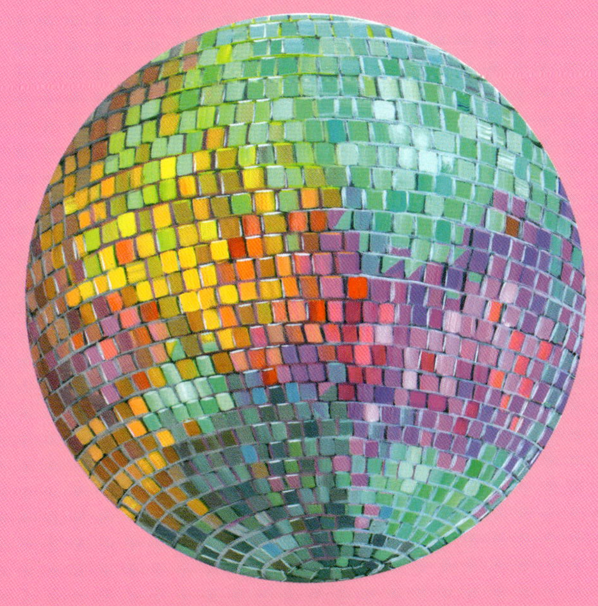

A Beginner's Guide to Painting Fun, Fresh Still Lifes in Oil and Acrylic

SARI SHRYACK

Walter Foster

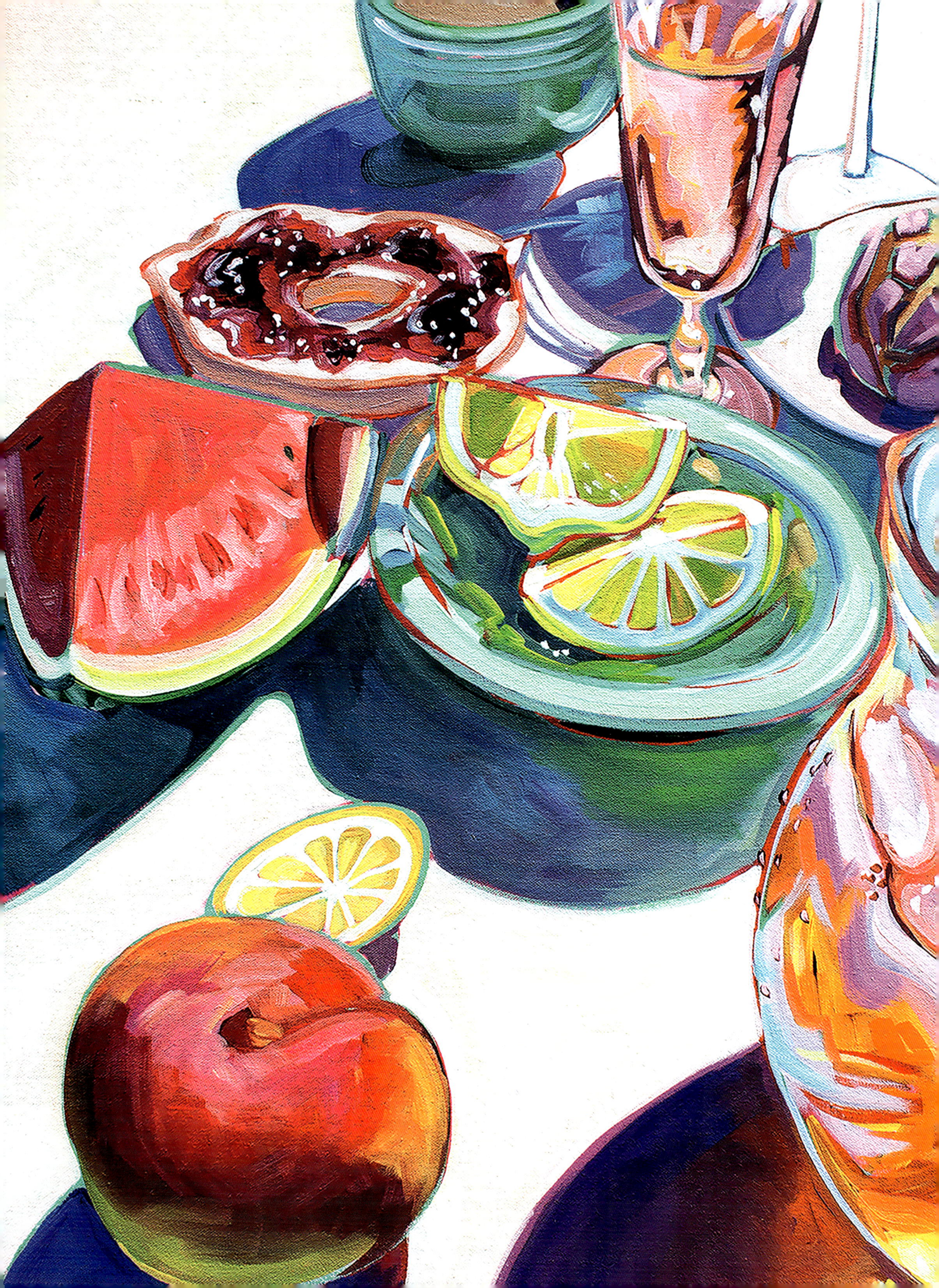

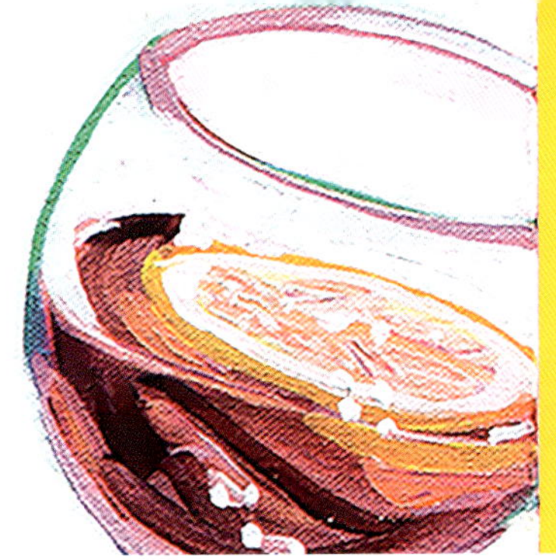

CONTENTS

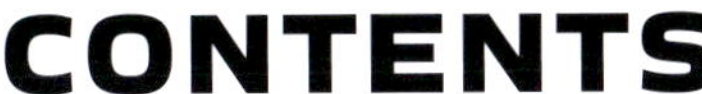

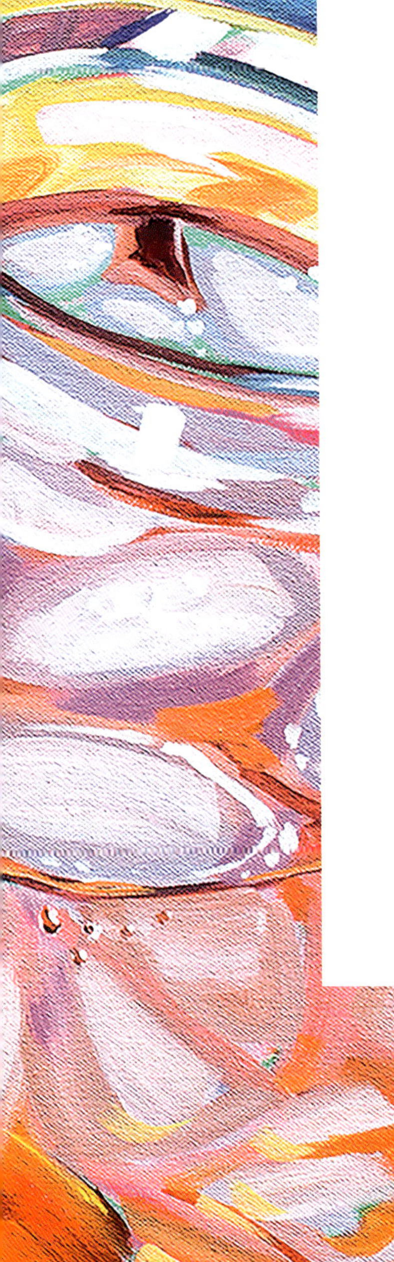

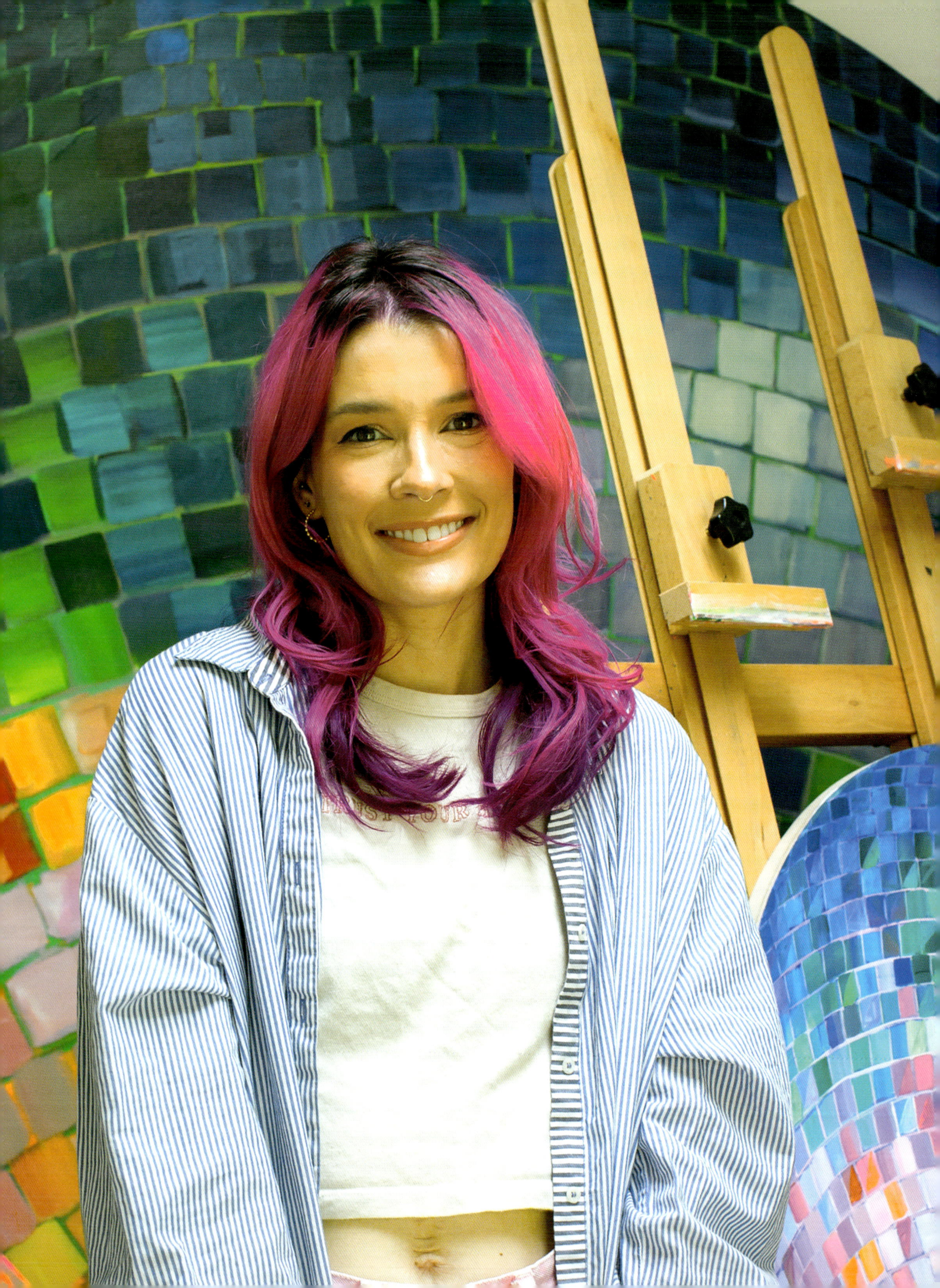

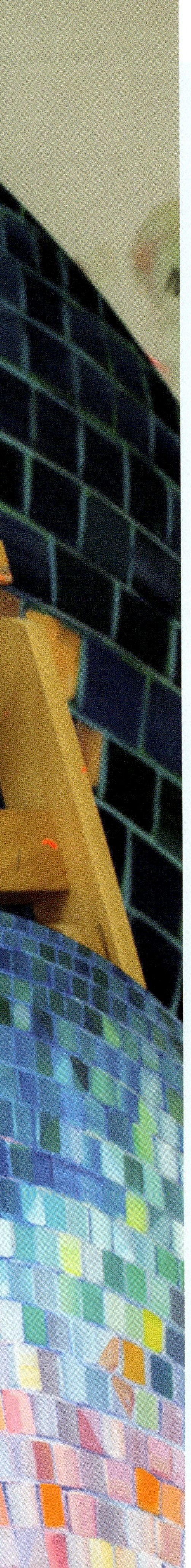

Meet the Artist

HEY Y'ALL! My name is Sari Shryack, and I am an artist and creator living in Austin, Texas.

Welcome to my painting book! I hope you're excited to be here with me. I'm thrilled to be able to share my representational painting knowledge and insights with you over the course of these pages.

The existence of this book is definitely a "pinch me" moment in my career. Since I started my painting journey as a college freshman in art school nearly fifteen years ago, I have dreamed of writing a book that blends my style and technique with the lessons I've been fortunate to learn from professors, fellow artists, painting masters, and many other creators that have helped me become the painter I am today. As I've developed over the years as an artist and created thousands of paintings, I've found that I have a deep love for sharing my process and skill through teaching. From teaching online courses, in-person workshops, and retreats both in the United States and abroad, I've honed my painting instructor muscles, and just as importantly, I've shared in the joy of making art with artists all around the world.

Although my painting repertoire encompasses many subjects and mediums, I chose to focus this book on the place where it all started back in college: still life in acrylics. Funny enough, I didn't really care for still life when we were learning by painting cones and boxes at my university, and I honestly didn't think I'd ever paint another one upon graduation. But once I was able to choose more stimulating objects to include in my pieces post-college, I fell in love with the subject. Still life has not only helped me strengthen my drawing and compositional skills, but it has also proved an excellent method for me in exploring the conceptual topics—such as class awareness and femininity—that define my work.

No matter where you're at in your painting journey, still life can be an excellent tool for improving your skills. You'll find in these pages that both my style and still life painting in general are quite forgiving of mistakes and beneficial for artists of all levels. My intent with this book is to provide an instructional guide that can meet every painter where they're at, and my years of teaching artists of all levels have made me adept at instructing beginners and accomplished artists alike. So, get ready to flex your still life muscles while creating impactful paintings that tell your story in a unique and colorful way. Welcome to *Modern Still Life: From Fruit Bowls To Disco Balls*.

PAINTING REPRESENTATIONALLY

Learning how to paint representationally has been one of the most transformative—and challenging—experiences of my life. Painting has not only paved the way for my career but also led me to discover a better version of myself.

Even when it didn't bring immediate financial rewards, my art practice enriched my life in profound ways. My practice began as an unexpected detour. I initially chose art as my major because as a student-athlete with a part-time job, I thought it would be the path of least resistance. Little did I know that I'd soon spend as much time in the studio at the arts building as I did on the track and at my fast-food job.

In that process, I unearthed a hidden creative voice, a means to connect with my inner emotions, and a practice where dedication and time could drive personal growth. My college professor played a pivotal role in this journey. He challenged the notion that art was reserved for an exclusive elite, emphasizing that it's accessible to everyone. He taught us that surrendering to the process and embracing mistakes could transform us into skilled painters with a unique visual language.

Over the years, I've shared my creative process, tips, and tricks on Instagram, and I've been fortunate to reach a broad audience. I realized that painting isn't an elusive talent but a collection of insights and perspectives anyone can harness to become their desired self.

By sharing this information in book format, I hope to reach even more of you. As you explore these step-by-step exercises, you'll notice that my journey—setting lofty goals, encountering early mistakes, and investing time—parallels the path many paintings in this book follow. These artworks often have a messy middle, and they're not always perfect. Yet, with dedication and persistence, they evolve into exciting and enjoyable creations. May you discover the best version of yourself and gain valuable insights from this book. Remember, if you can pick up a paintbrush, you already have everything in you that you need to be an artist.

PHILOSOPHY ON PAINTING

Let's establish a truism: painting can be for everyone. One of my favorite stories is about a university art professor chatting with a young girl. When he mentions he teaches people to paint, the girl looks at him, puzzled, and says, "Do people forget how?"

This little anecdote always makes me smile and serves as a reminder that our perceived limitations as artists are just that, perceptions. Too often, artists fall victim to self-doubt by wanting their drawing or compositional skills to be "perfect," and they become discouraged from pursuing art altogether.

Insecurity is natural when it comes to creating, but I wholeheartedly believe everyone is creative and capable of making powerful art. The techniques and tips in these pages are here to help you improve as a painter—no matter what level you're currently at—so that you can use your inherent creativity to make paintings that reflect your vision and style, whatever that may be.

As naturally creative beings, we're driven to make our mark, literally, to say, "Hey, I was here, and I saw this." That's what painting is all about.

Another key to painting, especially with the style we're exploring in this book, is embracing our mistakes. For me, miscues aren't just tolerated—they're welcomed as a part of the process.

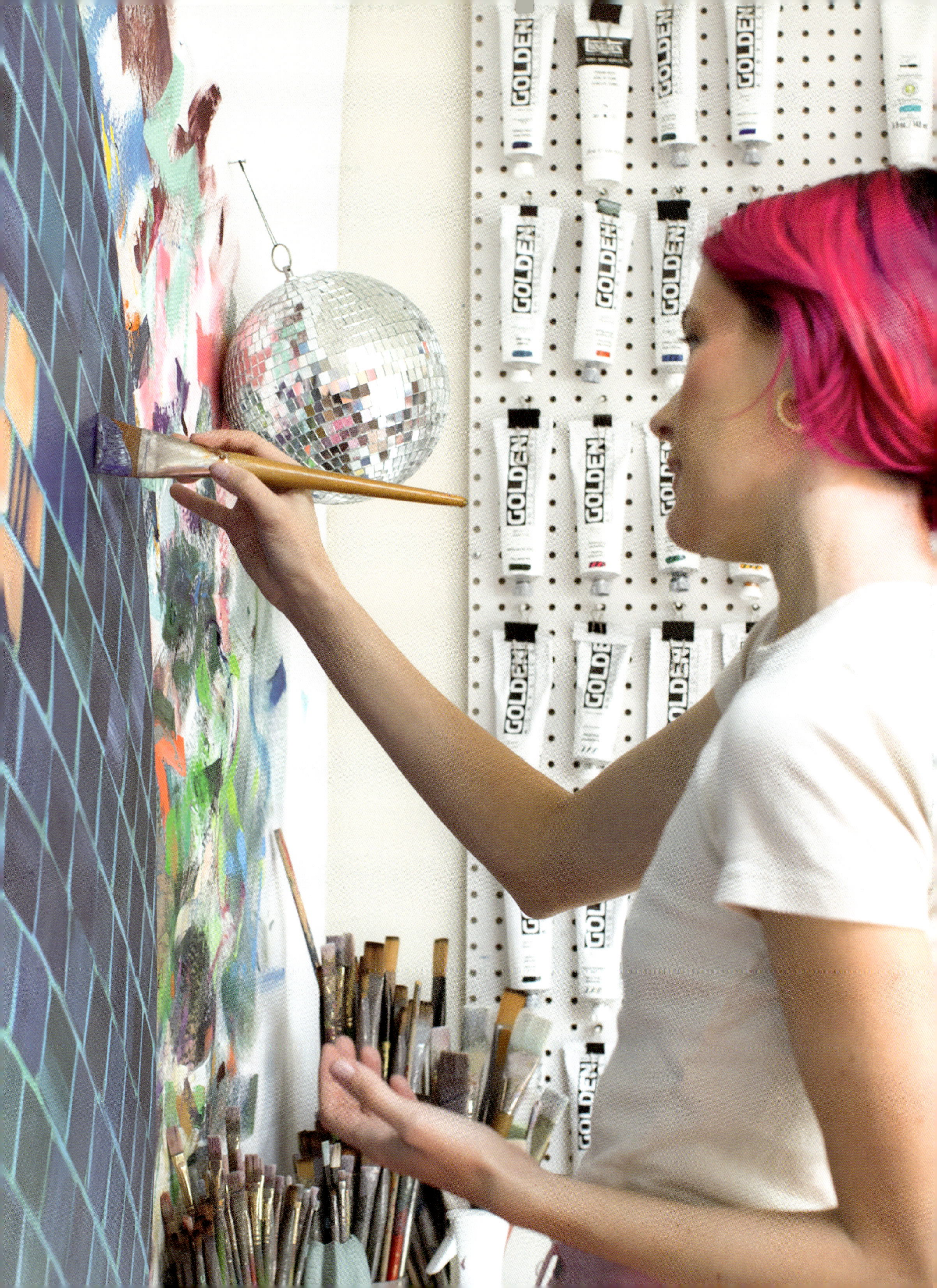

Mistakes have a funny way of spotlighting how uniquely creative we are. Mess up your sketch? Choose the wrong color? That's fine. When you paint over these "mistakes," you're not just smarter for the next round, but your "oops" moments might peek through, adding intriguing textures, colors, and patterns you never planned for. In my world, these unexpected twists often turn into my favorite parts of the artwork.

WHY WRITE A BOOK ABOUT STILL LIFE?

When deciding what topics to explore in a painting book, there are many considerations. One such consideration is deciding the subject that best conveys the techniques you're wanting to teach the student. For me, still life is the perfect jumping-off point because it's how I learned to paint, and it's the subject that I return to most frequently in my work. Even so, I'm aware of its complicated reputation within the art world.

Much like the hierarchical structure of Western art history, which often placed portrait painting at the top, followed by landscape, and relegated still life to the bottom, there's still a perceived hierarchy among subjects in art. This book aims to push back on that narrative while sharing with you the foundational tools that can be applied to all subjects in painting.

Still life, historically seen as an academic exercise or teaching tool, has often been over-looked. But I couldn't think of a better way to learn how to paint. Still life is tried-and-true for a reason, though it doesn't have to be limited to stuffy cardboard boxes and ancient Greek busts with decaying fruit. You can bring it to life in your own unique way.

While this book *does* include fruit, it's not limited to the traditional. You'll find the vibrant reds of a pomegranate, or the textured surface of an orange illuminated in sun-light. But your still life can be as personal and contemporary as you desire. Still life played a pivotal role in my early painting journey when I started sharing my work on Instagram. By updating this classic genre with contemporary objects from my own home, ones that resonated with my memories of the 2000s, I gave still life a fresh and modern twist.

Setting aside the nostalgia, if you want to master the interplay of light and composition, still life provides the perfect platform. It offers beginner painters the ease and control they need while honing their skills in drawing, composition, color, and lighting. You can create a still life from a photo or set it up in your studio using everyday objects. Even a coffee cup next to a paintbrush can constitute a still life, offering valuable lessons on light and color relationships. What's the best part? You don't need a model, and you're free from the con-straints of changing daylight as in *plein air* (outdoor) painting.

The insights you gain from painting still life translate to other subjects. While painting a face involves specific aspects like likeness and proportions, you'll find similar insights when painting something like a bunch of bananas or a bag of potato chips. And for those who doubt the contemporary appeal of still life, you've likely never experienced the joy of painting a niche and unique object. When someone recognizes their own Lisa Frank binder from 1997 and eagerly shares or purchases your painting, you'll understand the power of specificity and connection. So, I encourage you to embrace this painting style. Enjoy the process of selecting objects to paint, starting weeks or days before you set up your composition. Don't limit yourself to just candles and fruit. Let your creativity run wild. I hope you savor the journey that your still life practice takes you on.

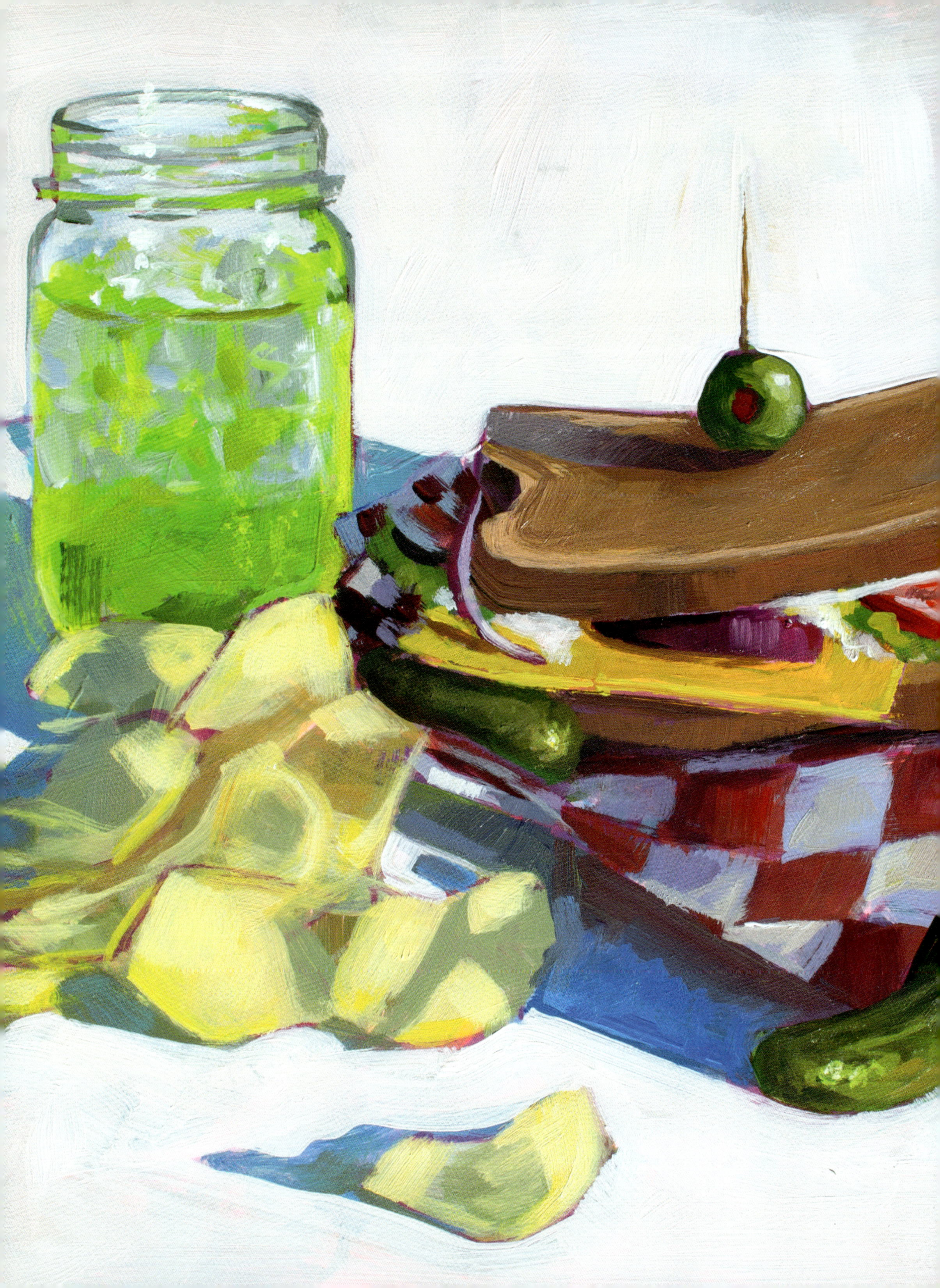

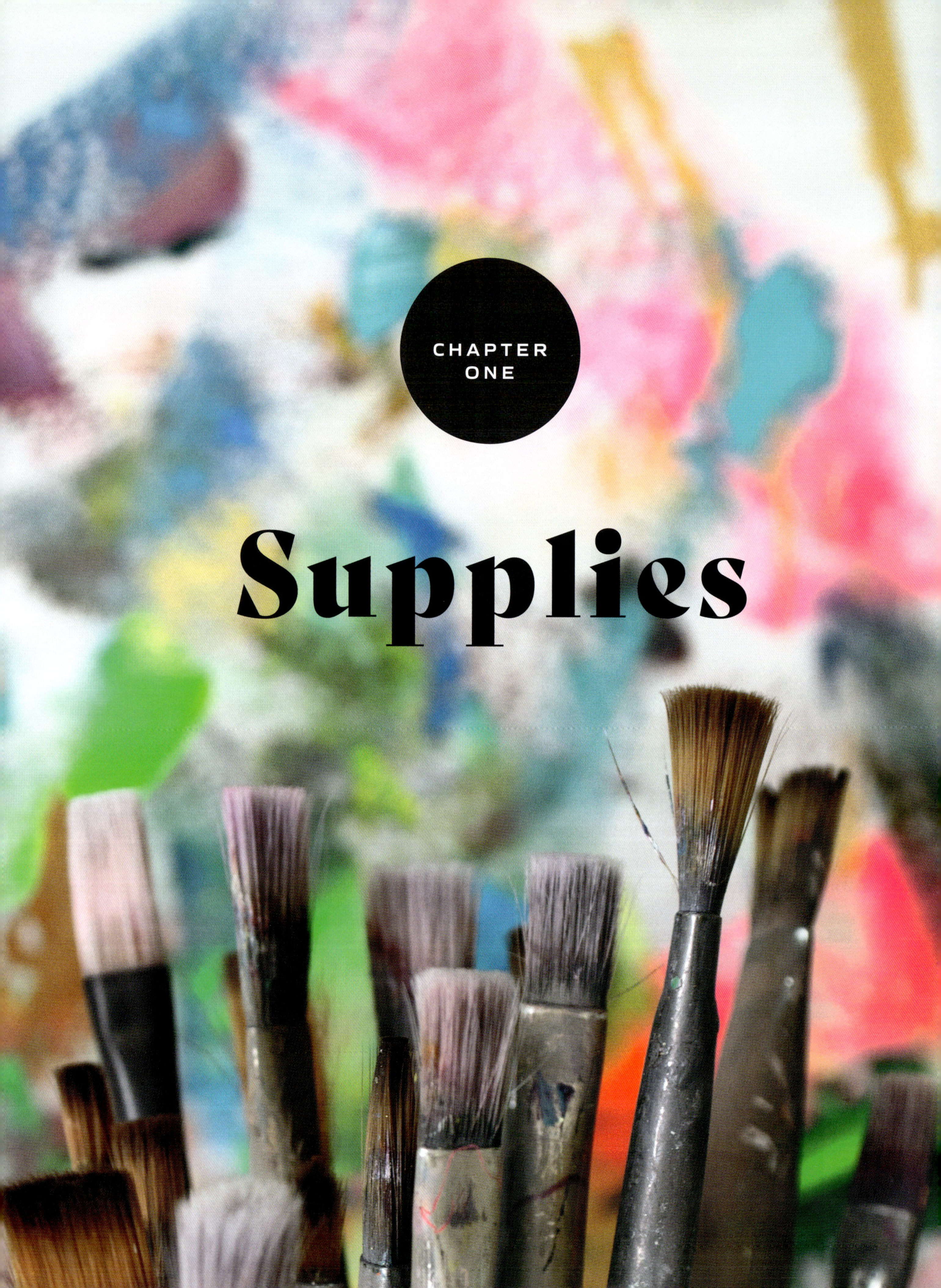

Supplies

...& the Mindset of an Artist, for Beginners

IN DECIDING WHAT TOOLS to use as a painter, the most important factor is using what works best for you. I strive to maintain a neutral stance on tools and assets that might aid artists. Often, in the realm of art education, well-meaning instructors may inadvertently establish false hierarchies or complicate the morality of using tools designed to enhance representational painting.

This includes practices such as painting from photographs, utilizing grids, or employing apps to match colors. Here's the crux of the matter for every artist: tools, in themselves, are neutral. They aren't inherently good or bad.

When you display your artwork, there isn't a descriptor alongside detailing how long it took, which references were used, the tools employed, or any help you might have received. In essence, the artwork stands independently, making the creative journey uniquely yours. I'm an advocate for painting from life and nurturing the innate ability to draw and discern value. Yet, everyone's learning curve varies. While some may be deeply engrossed in honing their drafting skills over years, others may not prioritize this at all. Their primary intent is to express their thoughts, nothing more.

The decision to use tools should be a personal one. I'd advise starting without them to gauge your proficiency and then assessing if a tool might enhance your process. For instance, in college, I was adamant about painting from life, a sentiment my professor shared. This approach has its merits. Yet, post-college, I lacked the space and time for such setups, resulting in an artistic hiatus for over a year. My shift to painting from photographs taken during walks near my home in Austin, Texas, revived my passion.

Nowadays, I enjoy a mix of painting *en plein air*, from life, and primarily from curated reference photos. At the end of each of my chapters on drawing, value, and color, I'll provide a list of potential tools and their applications. You can choose to follow or ignore these suggestions. However, if you find your current limitations stalling your painting passion, remember that these tools exist to assist you. They're at your disposal, and ultimately, it's all about finding what works for you in your art journey.

Tiling & Style

My approach is all about "value blobs"—we won't be blending. Don't get me wrong, blending isn't the bad guy here. In painting and artmaking in general, there is no incorrect way to do it, just different styles creating different effects.

But for the style we're learning in this book and to analyze color and form, it's all about laying down these blobs of color value. This method is also known as *tiling in*.

Grab your flat brush—we're going to master the art of painting blocks of color and mixing gradients to create shadows, form, and volume. Instead of blending smooth transitions on the canvas, we'll be *tiling* our way to a vibrant painting.

My style is representational, but with a twist. It's like I'm winking at realism without fully embracing it. At the risk of sounding cliché, I didn't choose this style, it chose me: my paintings can best be described as me striving for realism and falling slightly short in a way that embraces inevitable mistakes. My forgiving approach has allowed me to make playful and expressive work that is both familiar and unique.

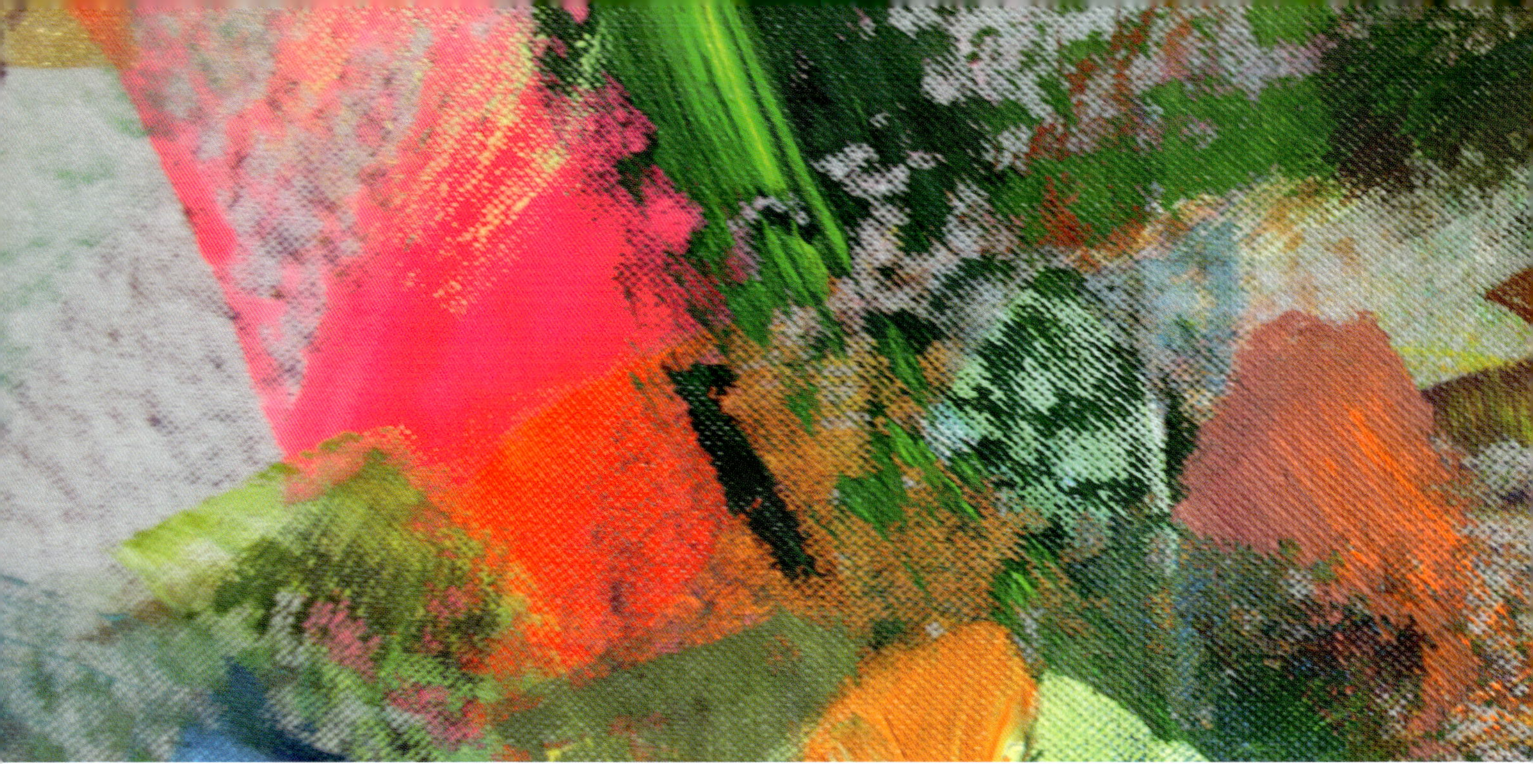

My style invites viewers to play a game of artistic catch. I throw them hints of the picture, not the entire scene. I'm not into spoon-feeding. I love when my audience paints their own picture based on my gestures. It's this playful approach that gives my work its distinctive appeal.

This style isn't just for still lifes. It shines in my disco ball paintings, where hundreds of colorful squares cascade across the canvas. Have you ever looked closely at a mirror ball? It's like a mosaic of tiny reflecting stories. But I don't paint every single mini reflection. Instead, I opt for averaged colors, resulting in a shimmering, stylistic disco ball.

In this book, I'm weaving all these elements together, creating a vivid tapestry of art that's as unique as it is informative.

SUPPLIES

First things first: let's talk about paint. To be honest, I'm quite particular when it comes to the paints I use, both in terms of brand and viscosity. I firmly believe that the quality of your paint can transform your artwork, and finding the tubes that work best for you will go a long way towards a fulfilling painting experience.

Low-quality paints often lack color payoff and opacity. Depending on the pigment, they can feel like a whole different substance. I've lost count of how many times people told me they struggled with acrylic paint, only to discover they were wrestling with a paint so translucent it needed two or three coats before reaching full opacity.

Are you trying to create the style within these pages with a thin, semi-transparent paint? It's like trying to play basketball with a lopsided ball—it might be possible, but it's oh so tricky. And yet, I'm not claiming that no one should ever use semi-transparent paint. If you're up for the challenge of layering several more times to get the same effect, go for it! Use what's accessible to you.

Personally, I'm a fan of GOLDEN and Liquitex Heavy Body Acrylic Paints. But really, any professional-grade acrylic paint should serve you well.

We'll dive into color palettes in greater depth in chapter 5, so don't worry about the details too much for now. My go-to colors are Titanium White, Cadmium Yellow Light, Yellow Ochre, Cadmium Red Medium, Alizarin Crimson Hue, Quinacridone Magenta, Ultramarine Blue, Phthalo Blue (Green Shade), Phthalo Green (Blue Shade), and Jenkins Green.

If you're painting on a budget, here's a pro tip: consider house paints. House paints are generally quite opaque—after all, nobody wants

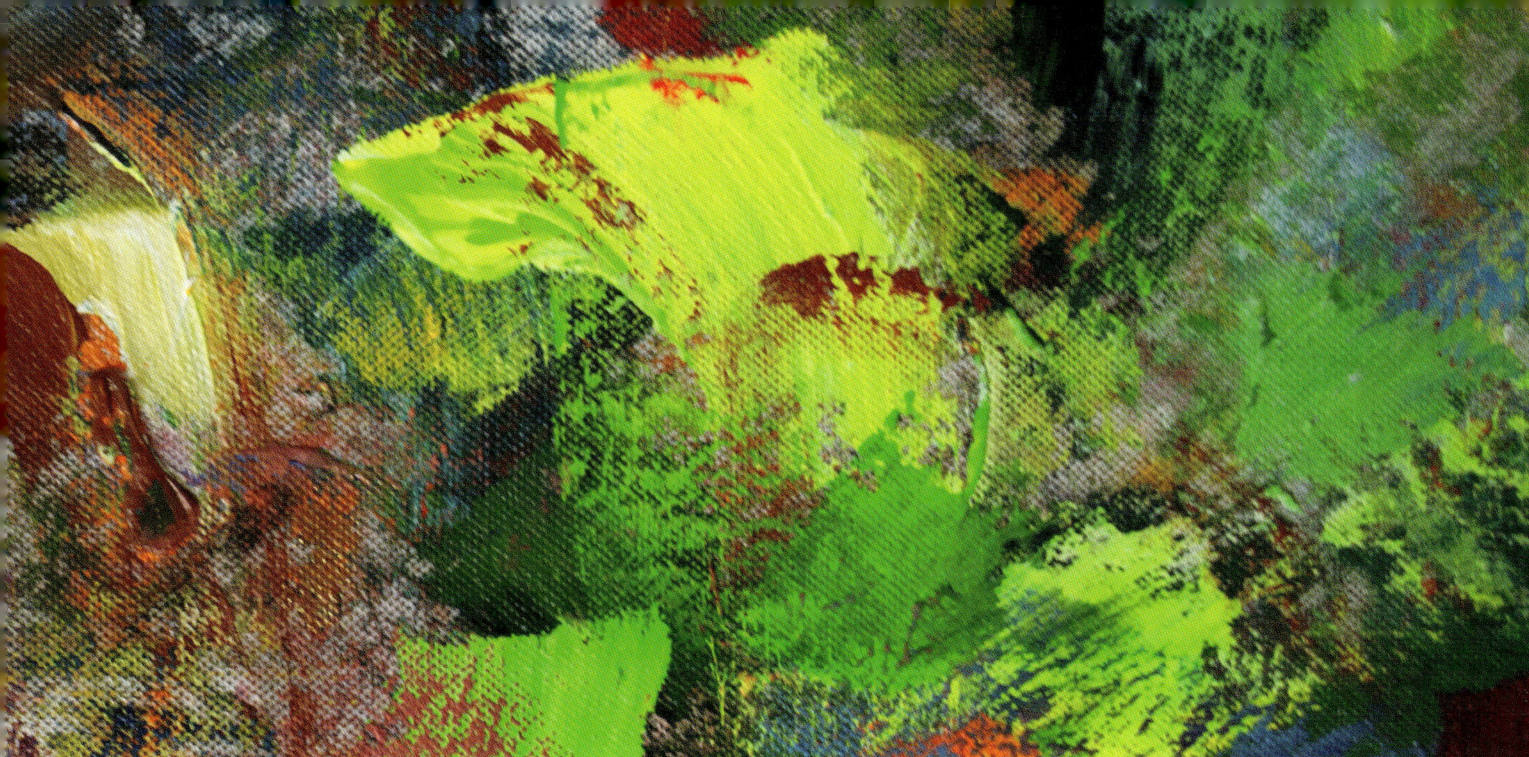

to paint their living room three times—so they often use a hefty base of Titanium White. You can usually snag samples of house paint without breaking the bank. What's the downside? Thanks to that Titanium White base, the colors can get a bit chalky. But if a bit of chalkiness doesn't faze you and you're trying to save money, this could be a crafty solution.

Besides paint, all you really need are tools to apply paint, a mixing surface, and a painting surface, with a few extras to enhance your painting experience. Students often overcomplicate their painting setup, but there's always a creative solution.

I'm a fan of painting on paper, particularly acrylic-friendly types due to its water-based nature. Affordable paper pads, perhaps an accessible 9- x 12-inch (23 x 30 cm) size, can take the pressure off being too precious with your work and encourage small studies.

Gessoed panels are another favorite. Cost varies here: the premium Da Vinci wood panels are pricier, while a humble pine wood board might need more prep to prevent the acrylic from pilling. Often, a budget-friendly option just means investing a bit more labor on your part.

And let's not forget the classic canvas. Whether you prefer a textured "tooth" or a smooth finish, it's all about what feels right for you. Listen to your instincts and find your ideal surface. There's no wrong choice as long as your materials hold up!

There are numerous suitable surfaces for mixing your paint. One option is freezer paper, which features a waxy, water-resistant side great for mixing. Plus, you can reuse the dried palette paper for collages or other crafts.

Another cost-effective choice is the glass from a thrifted or spare picture frame. Tape a piece of medium gray paper to one side, so the gray shows through the glass. Remember to round off the sharp edges and make sure the glass is thick enough to withstand scraping.

A long-term investment option is a Sta-Wet Palette. This comes with a sponge and semi-permeable paper. To preserve your acrylic paints, use a Sta-Wet Palette and a spray mist bottle to keep your paints damp. Be cautious since overwatering can break down acrylic paints. Spray sparingly when your paints start to form a skin or film and you'll extend their usability.

If you don't have a Sta-Wet Palette, Glad Press'n Seal Cling Film can be a good alternative to preserve your paints between painting sessions.

Brush choice is highly personal, but for the purposes of this painting style, which is focused on layering and tiling rather than blending, I suggest primarily using bright brushes and flat brushes. These can seem somewhat unwieldy initially but their versatility is surprising. They allow for various strokes: the sharp edge can yield a thin, straight line; the side of the brush can block in squares and shapes; and the corner can create dabs and dots. These basic marks can be used to create a complete painting. In this book, only bright and flat brushes are used.

Also, try using larger brushes than you might initially think necessary. The goal is to make broad value choices, and larger brushes can help in achieving that. In college, we occasionally used house painting brushes to prevent us from getting too detailed too early in the process. For example, if you're painting on a 9- x 12-inch (23 x 30 cm) surface, I suggest starting with a size 10 or 12 bright or flat brush. My rule of thumb is always to go one size larger than what I feel inclined to pick. This encourages bold color value choices and helps with tiling in your work.

Another helpful tool for this painting style is a dowel rod. It's a straight edge tool, typically available at low cost at stores like Walmart. We'll use it mainly for drawing and measuring our objects, focusing more on proportions than exact measurements.

Additionally, you'll need rags or paper towels, as well as a water bucket. I personally repurpose old towels and shirts as rags to remove excess paint from my brushes, mop up leftover paint, and keep my workspace tidy. Paper towels can also serve this purpose.

As for the water bucket, one or two containers will do. You can use mason jars or water buckets with multiple compartments from craft stores. I prefer having two or three separate containers to clean my brushes: one for the initial, messy clean; a second one to remove most of the remaining paint; and a final container with clean water to thoroughly rinse the brush.

Additional tools that might prove beneficial include an easel, a misting spray bottle, good lighting, and a designated area to dispose of your dirty paint water.

An easel can be of various types: a desk easel, a standing easel, or a wall-mounted setup. I've used simple nails in wall studs to hang my paintings in the past. Although rudimentary, it was effective. While I've painted in my lap before, a comfortable setup can make a huge difference.

It should be as easy and seamless as possible to avoid any discomfort or strain, as painting requires considerable mental and physical energy.

A misting spray bottle is particularly useful in hot, dry climates to prevent your paints from drying out.

Good lighting is essential. A large window with diffused lighting is ideal, but if that's not an option, aim for an indoor light with a natural light bulb that's neither too warm nor too cool.

When it comes to disposing of dirty paint water, it's critical not to pour it down the drain or on the ground as it can contaminate water supplies. I use an evaporation method, but there are other options like using the GOLDEN Crash Paint Solids Waste Water Cleaning System, paint hardener, or even cat litter to solidify the water before disposing of it in the trash. Always aim to minimize the amount of dirty water by cleaning off your brushes with rags to remove excess paint.

About Acrylics

Let's talk about acrylic paint and why I'm so enthusiastic that it's a fantastic medium for students learning how to paint. Maybe I'm biased because this is the medium I started with, but I'd argue that it's incredibly beginner-friendly. It challenges newer students in ways that are excellent for learning essential painting techniques. For instance, it teaches you how to mix distinct colors and values to create form, rather than relying on the blending that slower-drying mediums permit. But don't worry, I'm going to walk you through all of this.

Acrylic paint is generally considered a less toxic medium for novice painters to begin their painting journey with. As long as you're not turning dried paint into dust or drinking your paint water, the act of painting with acrylics is safe and requires much less ventilation than standard oil painting. Because acrylic is water-soluble, you'll clean your brushes in water, which easily breaks down the paint. In

contrast, oil painting often requires a paint
thinner, like odorless mineral spirits or even
turpentine, both of which have strong fumes.
Proper ventilation is essential with these fluids
to avoid harmful exposure that can be immediately irritating and potentially cause long-term
health issues.

A crucial point to consider about acrylic paint
is its composition. While it contains pigment,
similar to gouache, watercolor, and oil paint, its
binder consists of a blend of water and acrylic
polymer, rather than the gums found in gouache
and oils used in oil paint. Though normally safe
for handling, acrylic's environmental impact is a
concern. As of this writing, the full environmental implications of these plastics remain a topic
of research. Hence, it's crucial to devise a method
to dispose of your paint water responsibly before
buying acrylic paints.

Later in this book, I'll share the cleanup tips
and methods I employ. As long as you have
a responsible cleanup routine, ensuring no
paint-contaminated water reaches the water
supply, I believe acrylic remains a remarkable
medium. That said, there are some practical
challenges associated with acrylics, challenges
I personally view as teaching assets.

For one, acrylic paint dries incredibly fast. On
hot Texas summer days, it's near instantaneous. In
cooler, damper climates, while the paint may not
dry instantly, it does experience a more extended
"gummy" phase. This fast drying can be challenging for students expecting a buttery, blendable
paint. With acrylics, I advocate for a layering
approach, abandoning the notion of on-canvas
color mixing. Instead of blending a shadow and
highlight to create a mid-tone, as is common
with watercolor, gouache, or oil, you might have
to distinctly mix and apply each shade. This
method can seem more labor-intensive, but it's in
this nuanced color differentiation that profound
learning occurs.

Moreover, with acrylics, you might find yourself repeatedly mixing the same shade unless you
prepare a large batch. As trying as this sounds,
mastering color mixing is fundamental to painting. In my view, it's essential to pick your battles.

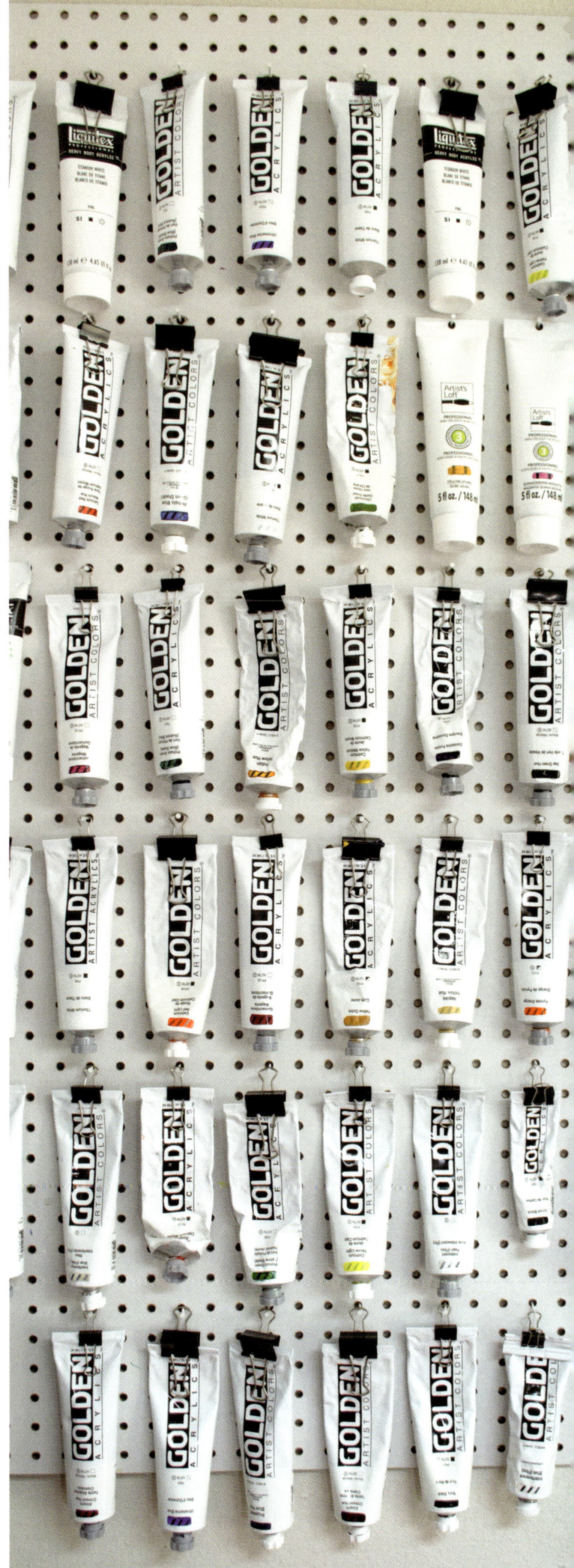

While navigating a chaotic setup doesn't impart any significant skills, the continuous challenge of color mixing refines your ability to achieve the exact shade you envision, forming the core of your painting expertise. Given these insights and viewing challenges as learning opportunities, you can understand my enthusiasm for acrylics as a foundational learning medium.

About Oils

It's important to note a key difference between oil and acrylic paints: oil dries significantly slower. There are countless methods for applying oil paint, each unique to the individual. This subject could easily fill its own book, detailing the myriad ways to utilize oil paints. For the purposes of this book, I will guide you through my preferred setup.

When I first experimented with oil paints, I sought a setup that mirrored the qualities of acrylics that I enjoy. The method I've settled on, which I believe complements this book best, focuses on the texture and drying time.

Unlike acrylics, which dry almost instantly, oil paints might take up to a week to dry to the point where you can add a layer of paint on top. This is where your choice of medium is crucial. A medium is an oil or gel that you mix into your paint to create a more workable viscosity or texture. Linseed oil is a standard medium; however, it doesn't speed up dry time. I prefer Galkyd and Liquin gels for their ability to create a soft peak and sour cream-like consistency with a resin finish. These mediums also accelerate drying, potentially reducing the wait to just a day or two, depending on climate and paint application thickness. To achieve the right viscosity, use a palette knife to mix your medium until you reach that soft peak consistency.

Regarding safety, oil paints differ from acrylics because they require a solvent for brush cleaning. You can also use solvent to thin out your oil paint. If you do this, remember to follow the fat-over-lean rule. This means you don't want to put a thin, inky layer of paint over a thick layer of paint, because the thin top layer will cure faster than the layer below it and cause structural damage to your painting. If you want to thin your paint with solvent and/or medium to a thin, inky texture, make sure it's under the thicker paint layer. And if you want to apply a thick, viscous layer of paint with visible brush marks, make sure it's above all of the thinner layers of paint. Specific to this book, your thinnest layer should be your initial block in, and your opportunity to paint in thicker, more textured brushstrokes will appear in the last two to three steps.

When it comes to oil paint safety and proper paint disposal, it's important to note that solvent fumes can be harmful, so good ventilation in your workspace is essential. Wearing gloves is also recommended to prevent skin irritation from solvents.

For disposal, I recommend reaching out to your local waste municipalities to learn where and when you can safely dispose of your solvent waste. There is also a fire-safety risk that comes with painting with oils. The solvent is flammable and should be kept in a temperature-controlled environment, and you should have a fire extinguisher in your painting space to be extra cautious. Spontaneous combustion can happen due to the flammability of the solvents and the heat created from the oxidation process of the oil paint. Unlike acrylic paint, which evaporates, oil paint cures through the chemical process of oxidation. This process takes in oxygen and expels heat. The risk here is that bunched-up paint rags with solvent and oxidizing oil paint can be a fire hazard. I recommend disposing of oily rags in a waste can that is designed to be fire-safe. At the very least, I recommend laying out your oily rags on a flat surface in a temperature-controlled room until the oil paint has fully cured.

Other Paint Mediums

What other mediums might benefit from the lessons in this book?

While this book was written with acrylic and oil painters in mind, any medium that is both opaque and able to be layered can easily be adapted to the lessons and insights in this book. I

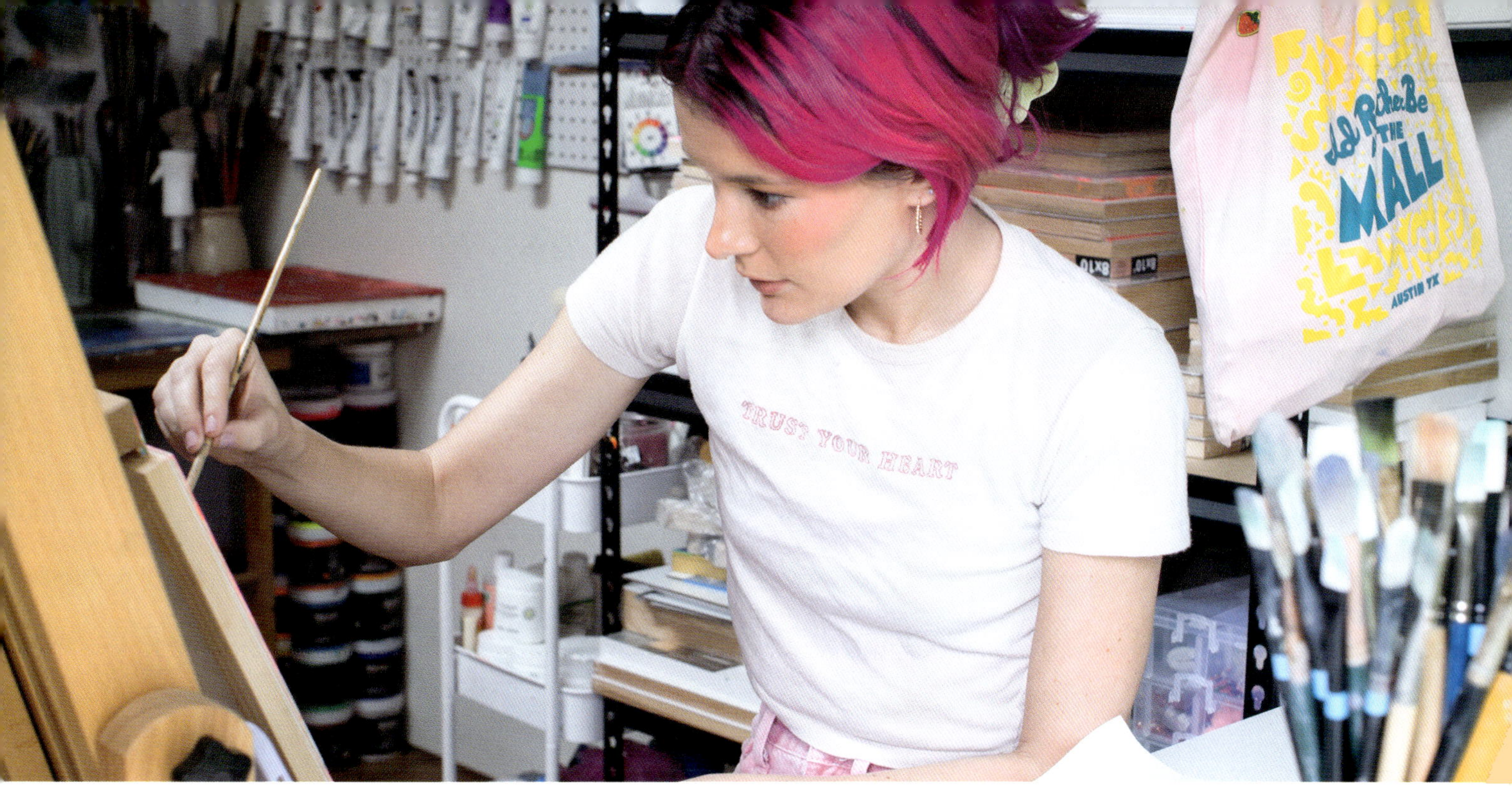

have used these techniques with water-soluble oil, acrylic gouache, and traditional gouache paints.

In the same way that an oil painter using this book will have to account for the longer dry times between layers, a painter using another medium will have to adjust for the characteristics of their chosen medium. For example, someone using traditional gouache with gum as a binder might have to contend with the fact that their layers become reactivated by the moisture in the top layer. However, the gouache painter can lean into this blending as something they anticipate and work around or embrace into their painting style.

My over-arching philosophy on medium is this: use whatever is accessible that you're comfortable with. You can be as creative in your choice of medium as you are in your painting practice.

MINDSET & APPROACH

Mindset plays a critical role in the art of painting. Just as the right paints and brushes are necessary for creating a painting, the right mindset is equally essential. One can't expect to create a successful piece with unsuitable materials, like ketchup, mustard, and a feather, any more than

one could produce quality work without an open, curious mind and a determined spirit.

Just as you could technically go through the motions of creating a painting using condiments and a feather, your end result wouldn't match your expectations or aspirations. The painting wouldn't turn out well, no matter how meticulous or dedicated you were during the process.

The same concept applies to your mindset when painting. You could attempt to execute the painting with the right materials, but without a positive mentality, the result would likely be unfulfilling. The right mindset is just as important a tool in your artist's toolkit as your brushes and paints. Approaching your work with a positive and ready-to-learn attitude is critical to developing as an artist and producing work that meets your expectations.

When I teach painting workshops, I always allocate a significant amount of time at the beginning to discuss expectations. It's important to understand what we hope to achieve and how to handle those inevitable moments when we fall short. Embracing the learning process, including the successes and failures, is key to developing as an artist. So, approach your painting practice with openness, curiosity, and determination and see it as an essential tool, just like your paints and brushes.

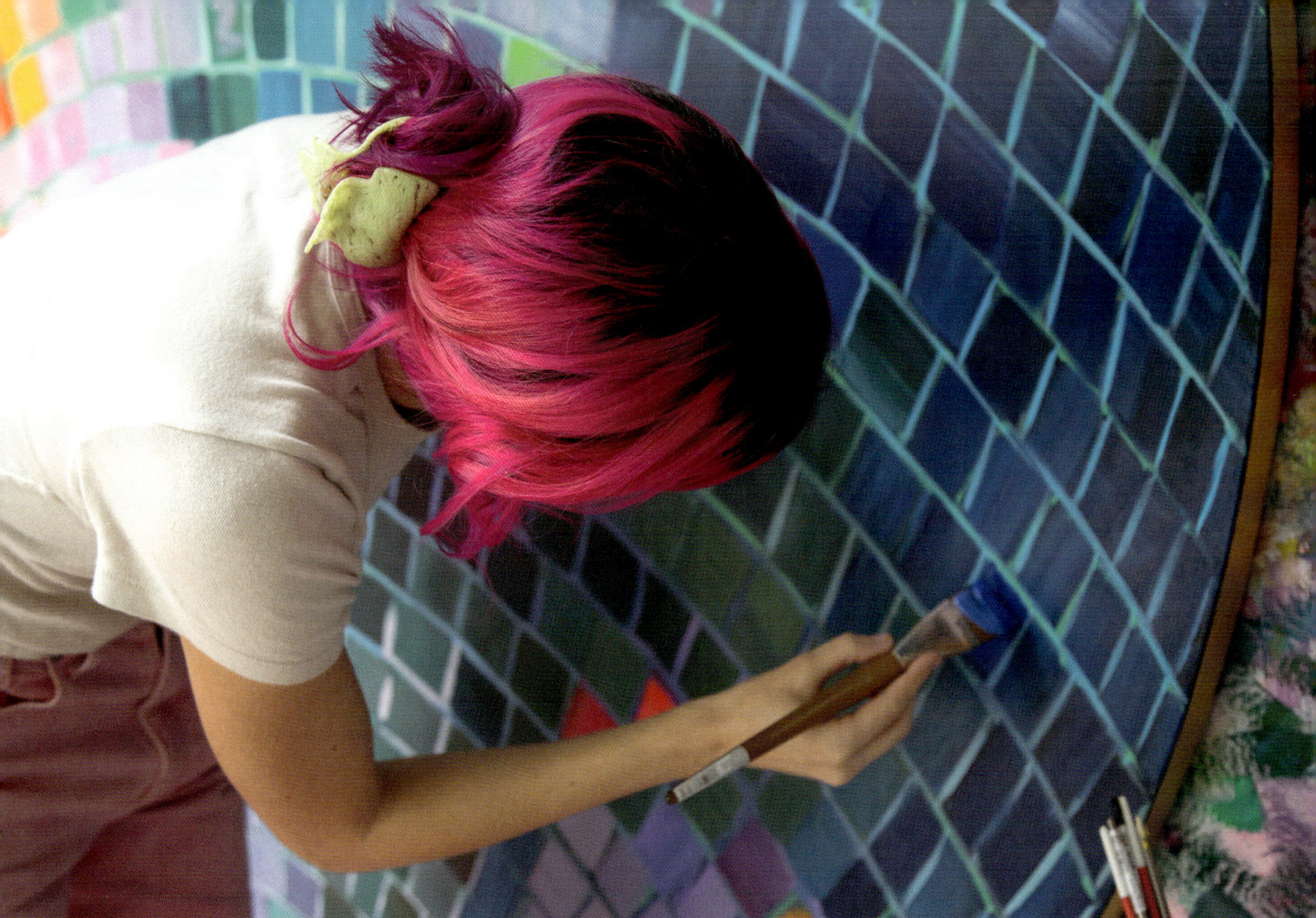

Openness

The personality trait of openness plays a crucial role in the creative process. Openness, in this context, refers to a person's proclivity toward new experiences, ideas, and diverse stimuli. In essence, it's a willingness to explore, to step beyond familiar grounds, and to make connections where they might not immediately seem apparent.

Scientifically, openness to experience is one of the five major domains in the Five-Factor Model of personality, which is a robust and widely accepted model used to explain differences of personality. This trait has been consistently linked to various facets of creativity.

A study published in the *Journal of Personality and Social Psychology* found a strong correlation between the trait of openness and creative achievement, as well as creative potential. This research indicates that individuals high in openness tend to produce more creative work, often because they are more inclined to take intellectual risks and think outside the box.

Another study in the *Journal of Research in Personality* found that openness was related to cognitive exploration, further fueling the creation of novel and useful products or ideas. By being more willing to delve into new cognitive territories and entertain various perspectives, people with high openness tend to be more adept at synthesizing unique combinations that can lead to creative insights.

In short, the trait of openness enriches our creative processes by allowing us to venture into the unknown, embrace novelty, and perceive connections that others might miss. It's an essential component of the creative personality, fostering an intellectual curiosity and a boldness that, when coupled with other traits and skills, can drive the innovation and originality at the heart of creativity.

Curiosity

Curiosity is a cornerstone of the creative process. It's the spark that propels us to ask questions, seek answers, and explore new possibilities. It allows us to approach our work, not from a perspective of right or wrong, but with an open, questioning mind.

In the context of painting, approaching your work with curiosity rather than rigid expectations can free you to explore and learn. Instead of viewing a painting as a failed attempt if it doesn't match a preconceived picture in your head, curiosity encourages you to ask, "Why did this outcome occur?" "What can I learn from this?" and "How can I adjust my techniques or materials to create different results?"

Curiosity can transform your painting practice from a task-oriented process into an exploratory journey. It helps you to detach from the fear of making mistakes and allows you to embrace unpredictability, thereby nurturing your creative growth.

Determination

Determination is an essential factor for success in any endeavor, including creative practices such as painting. It's the driving force that keeps you going, helping you to overcome obstacles and persist even when things get tough.

Applying this to your painting practice, it is determination, not just raw talent, that can guide you in consistently showing up at your easel, refining your skills, and persisting through challenging paintings.

A study in the *Journal of Happiness Studies* links self-compassion, which includes being kind to oneself, recognizing one's shared humanity, and maintaining a balanced awareness of one's emotions, with resilience and optimism. This self-compassionate determination can translate into patience with your painting development, an understanding that growth takes time, and an ability to bounce back from disappointments or perceived failures.

So it's determination—fueled by self-compassion and consistency— that is indeed the engine of your creative practice. By committing to show up, being patient with your progress, and extending kindness to yourself along the journey, you are not only enhancing your painting skills but also enriching your overall well-being.

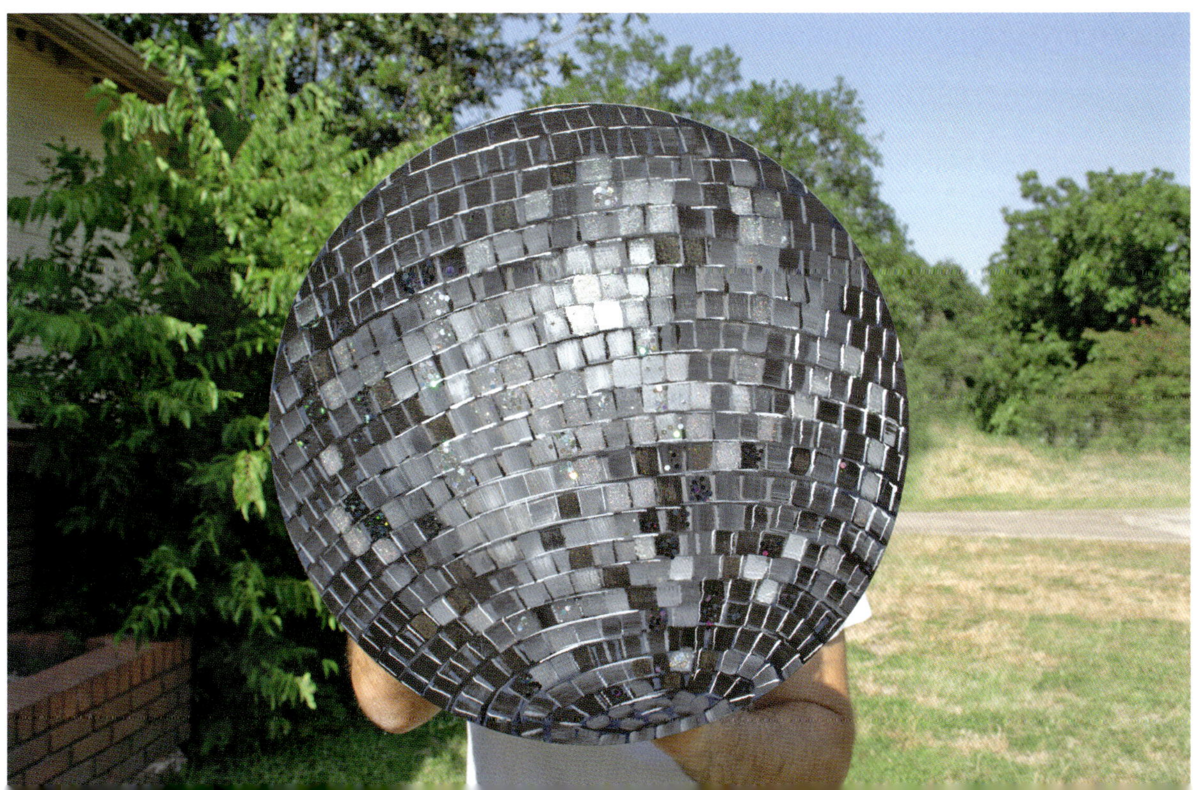

Still Life Setup

AT THE OUTSET of writing this book—a step-by-step painting instructional guide—the topic of conversation naturally veered towards the subject matter the book would explore. I recall my college art history survey classes where I learned about the hierarchical nature of four categories of painting: religious paintings reigning supreme, followed by portraits, landscapes, and lastly, the humble still life. At that time, I thought this knowledge was only important for an exam.

Yet, the understanding of these categories and their hierarchy has significantly aided me both as a painter and throughout this book-writing journey. Still life painting has not only been a pivotal part of my career, but it resonates deeply with our materialistic culture.

As you drive down highways, the sight of storage units scattered around is a testament to this. What enchants me about still life is the arranging of objects, especially those embedded with marketing narratives. When you pick up objects from a thrift store or your bathroom, they often carry a visual history, a story—we might already have notions about the type of person who would buy this, the gender who might use it, or the class of person who might prefer those beauty products.

Meeting people at whatever level they are at is something I cherish. Not everyone has had the privilege of attending art classes, yet the beauty of still life is that by using everyday objects, people can tap into a rich reservoir of visual knowledge they already possess. It's about connecting the dots, making art feel accessible, and leveraging the information ingrained in us through years of being marketed to and incorporating it into the painting process. These facets of accessibility, among others I'll delve into, fueled my resolve to advocate for a book on still life in contemporary times. I hope you relish this chapter as much as I do.

WHY STILL LIFE?

Why still life painting, you ask? If you're skeptical, I get it—in college, I painted so many fruit bowls and potted plants that I vowed to never paint them again. It's understandable for me when artists are hesitant to dive head first into a subject we commonly associate with academia.

But for me, still life has transformative power as a tool for technical improvement and a vehicle for communicating shared narratives that enrich our understanding of cultures past and present. Still life painting is older than you may realize. Its roots sink deep into the soil of ancient Egypt, where artists created wall paintings of food offerings. Fast forward to the Middle Ages, and you've got the church using symbolic objects in artwork.

But it was the Dutch in the seventeenth century who said, "Hey, let's make this a thing." They took everyday objects, like shiny apples and reflective metal goblets, and turned them into something extraordinary. And so, the humble still life took the art world by storm.

Jump to more recent times, and you'll see artists like Cézanne and Picasso expanding on their predecessors' still life approach by bending and breaking the rules to bring the legacy of the practice into the modern canon. The story of still life painting, from ancient offerings to modern-day masterpieces, is the story of ordinary objects with extraordinary stories to tell.

Still life's rich potential for storytelling is particularly poignant in our current era, with its characteristic of a consumer culture and the significance attached to objects. In the West, especially in the United States, we can't ignore our relationship with things. Our surroundings are filled with objects, from the clutter in our homes to the storage units that line our streets. Despite attempts at decluttering, possessions seem to constantly accumulate, indicating our materialistic tendencies.

Moreover, the things we purchase are often embedded with narratives carefully crafted by marketers. The objects we own can hint at our identity, lifestyle, and status. When we explore painting a portrait of a person through still life, the selection of objects, such as the brand of gum they chew or the type of makeup they use, can reveal intimate details about the subject. These objects can hint at their gender, socio-economic status, and even the era they were born into, with remarkable accuracy.

Given these fascinating aspects, still life deserves a new appreciation and a modern approach. It's a potent tool for depicting narratives, particularly in our object-centric culture. As we delve deeper into this topic, we'll explore how a contemporary take on still life can reflect our identities and society, shedding new light on this traditionally undervalued genre.

Still life is indeed a wonderful gateway into painting, offering both accessibility and an opportunity to master the skill of composition. While it's understandable that many new painters may feel drawn towards painting portraits or landscapes—subjects traditionally associated with the art form—these can often be challenging to access, particularly for beginner artists.

On the other hand, still life allows for the exploration of objects that are readily available in our immediate environments. Your bedroom, bathroom, or kitchen, for example, are likely filled with objects that can be used to create captivating still lifes. These objects, which you are presumably already attracted to on a visual level, offer a wonderful starting point for your painting journey.

What sets still life apart is the control it gives you over the composition. As an artist, you have the power to arrange and rearrange objects as you see fit, enabling you to create compelling compositions that can tell a multitude of stories. This level of control is often overlooked by new painters, who tend to focus more on developing their technical painting skills.

However, mastering composition is an essential skill in painting, and still life provides an excellent platform to learn and refine this ability. Given its inherent accessibility and the unique opportunities it presents for artistic exploration, it's no wonder that I am thrilled to create a book

dedicated to contemporary, colorful still life paintings, rendered in my own distinctive style.

PRACTICING THE SETUP

Formal elements in art refer to the visual tools that an artist uses to create an artwork. These elements include shape, color, line, texture, space, and form. They are concerned with the physical qualities or the *form* of an object. These can be measured, quantified, and are not subject to individual interpretation. For example, if you group objects based on their round shape or their blue color, these are formal characteristics.

Conceptual elements, on the other hand, relate to ideas or themes that inform the artwork. These are elements that are dependent on individual or cultural interpretation, background knowledge, or context. For example, grouping objects because they all are kitchen utensils, come from the 1990s, or because they are considered "cute," is based on a conceptual commonality.

Understanding these different ways of grouping can enrich your still life compositions. For an exercise, try gathering around fifteen to thirty objects. Start by grouping them based on formal elements: their color, shape, texture, size, and so on. Then, reshuffle and regroup them based on conceptual elements: their function, era, cultural significance, and so on.

Once you've done that, experiment with arranging these groups in different compositions. See how the relationships between the objects change as you adjust the groups and the arrangement. This practice will give you a deeper understanding of how both formal and conceptual elements can be used to create engaging and meaningful compositions.

Composition is a vital aspect of creating visual art, much like drawing and understanding color. It's the way you arrange elements within a piece to create a balanced, engaging work. While there are some general rules to composition, it's also about using your intuition and personal aesthetic.

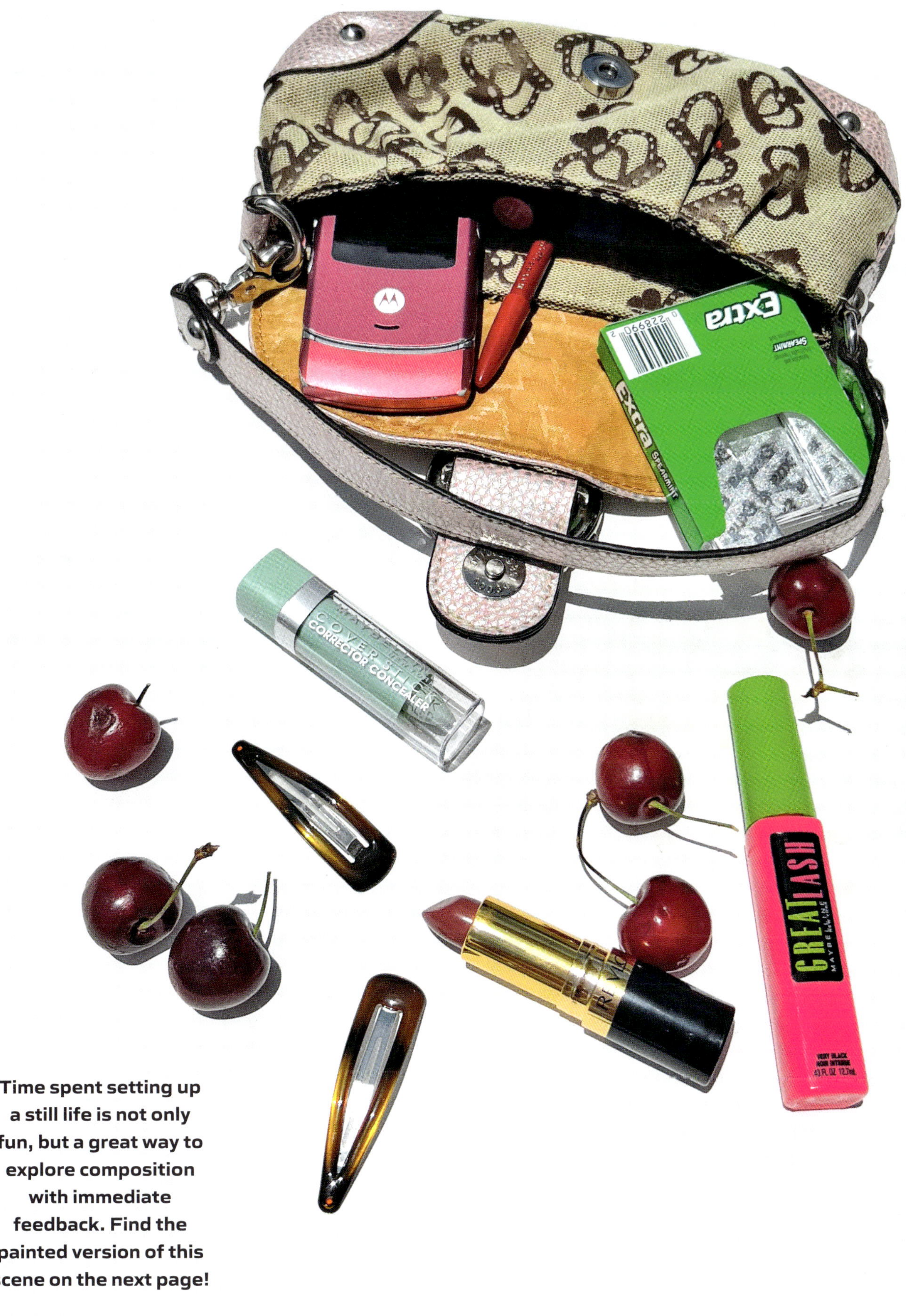

Time spent setting up a still life is not only fun, but a great way to explore composition with immediate feedback. Find the painted version of this scene on the next page!

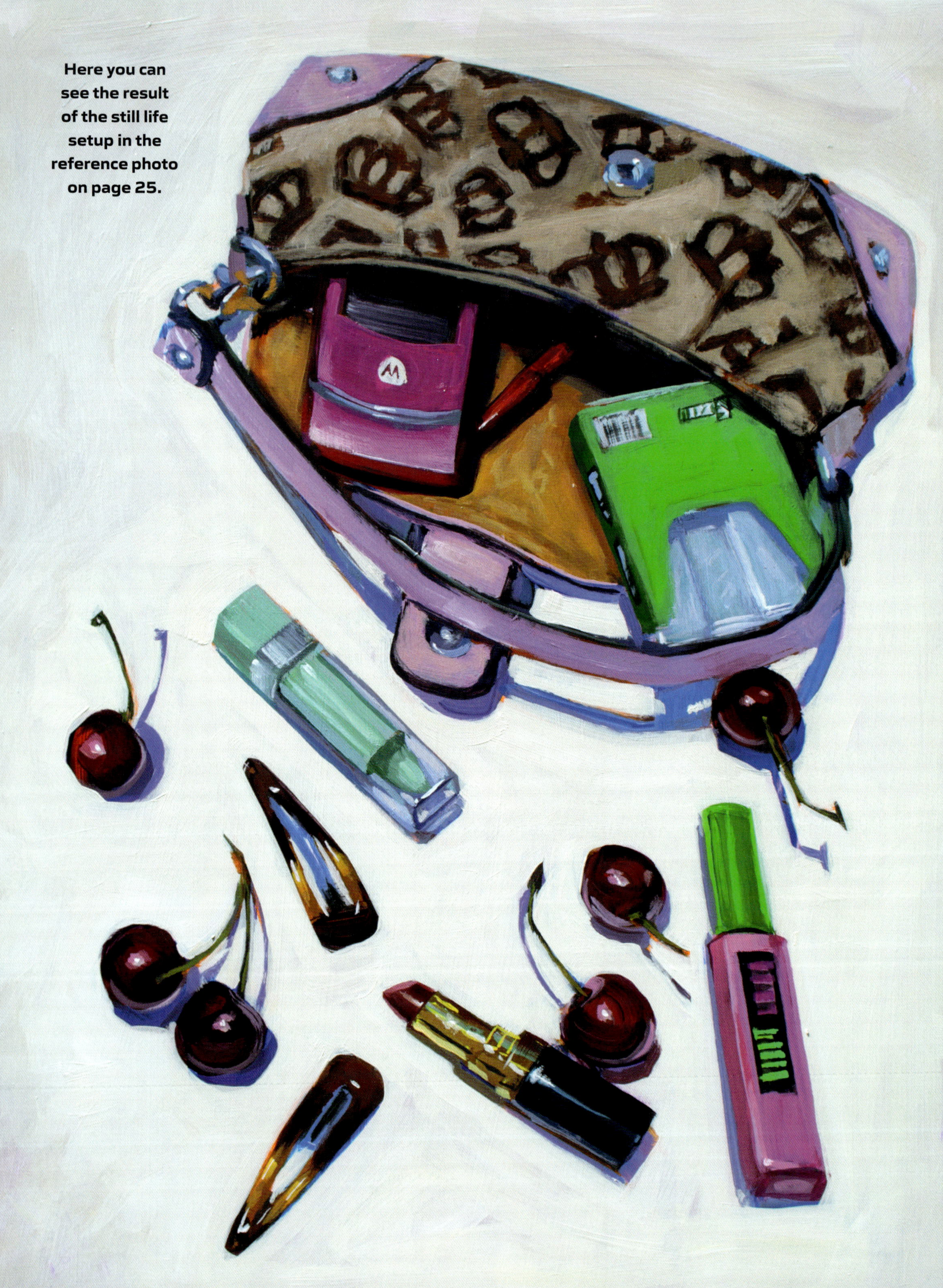

Here you can
see the result
of the still life
setup in the
reference photo
on page 25.

COMPOSITION

Let's discuss a few basic principles of composition I use most frequently when setting up a still life:

- **Active vs. Static Composition** Active compositions give a sense of motion, as if the objects are ready to move or change. On the other hand, static compositions give a sense of stillness and stability. It's a balance you can play with to achieve the desired mood in your painting.

- **Optical Center** The optical center of a piece, where the viewer's eye is naturally drawn, is slightly above the geometric center, the actual center. This is because our eyes tend to perceive the center of an image a little bit higher than the actual middle. This phenomenon is tied to our perception of gravity and how we project it onto a two-dimensional surface.

- **Eye Movement** Our eyes tend to scan an image from left to right, much like reading a page in English. We usually enter the painting at the top left and move in a semi-circular motion across and down the canvas. You can take advantage of this natural tendency when arranging your composition to guide the viewer's gaze through the artwork.

- **Edge Tension** This refers to the intensity of interaction between the objects in your painting and the edge of the canvas. An object that intersects the edge can create tension and draw the viewer's attention. If this isn't your intention, you might adjust your composition to avoid such intersections. However, repeating this intersection multiple times can make it look intentional and become a deliberate part of your composition.

- **Repetition** Using repetition in your composition can strengthen your visual message and create a sense of harmony or rhythm. Repeating shapes, colors, or patterns can guide your viewer's eye across the artwork and make your composition more cohesive.

- **Positive and Negative Space** Positive space is occupied by your main objects, such as a teacup and a donut in your example. In contrast, negative space is the area surrounding these objects, including any "holes" or empty areas within the objects themselves, like the donut's hole. Paying attention to both types of space is crucial for a balanced composition. Skilled artists use negative space to enhance the impact of their main subjects and create more interesting compositions.

Incorporating these elements into your compositions allows you to guide the viewer's gaze, create balance, and make your artwork more engaging. Remember, these aren't rigid rules, but tools that you can adapt to your style and the message you want to convey in your art.

Studying the work of master artists and painters is an invaluable way to gain insight into the effective use of compositional tools and techniques. This can certainly be applied to still life painting as well.

The Raft of the Medusa by Théodore Géricault, for example, showcases dynamic composition and the use of diagonals and triangular structures to guide the viewer's eyes throughout the canvas. It's a great example of how to keep the viewer's gaze engaged and moving around the artwork.

Edgar Payne, known for his landscape paintings, uses compositional structures like the *S* curve, radiating lines, and other geometric forms to add visual interest and guide the viewer's gaze through the scene. His book *Composition of Outdoor Painting* provides many insights into his approach.

These techniques aren't exclusive to any one genre or style of painting. They're universal principles that can be adapted to any subject matter or medium. Studying various artists' compositions will surely enrich your own painting practice, helping you to see these principles in action and learn to apply them in your own unique way.

Active Composition vs. Static Composition

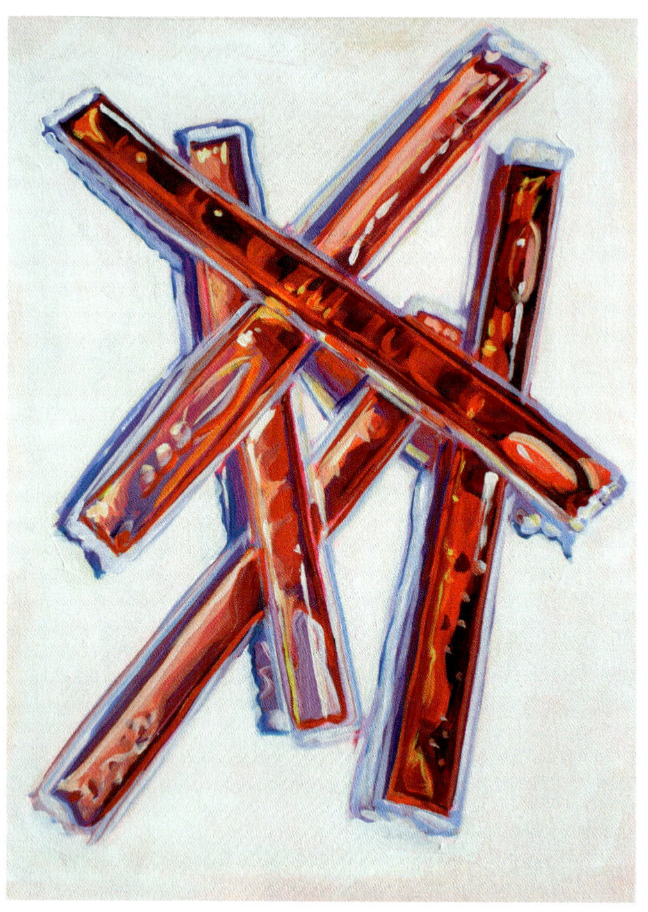

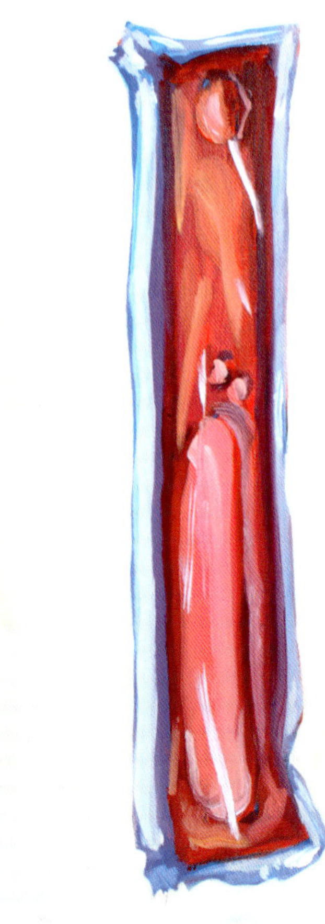

Edge Tension

Repetition

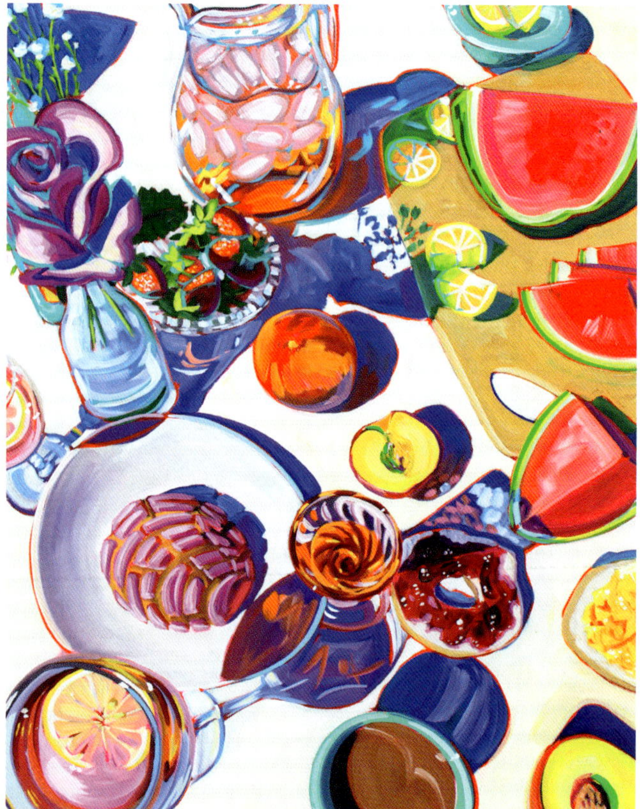

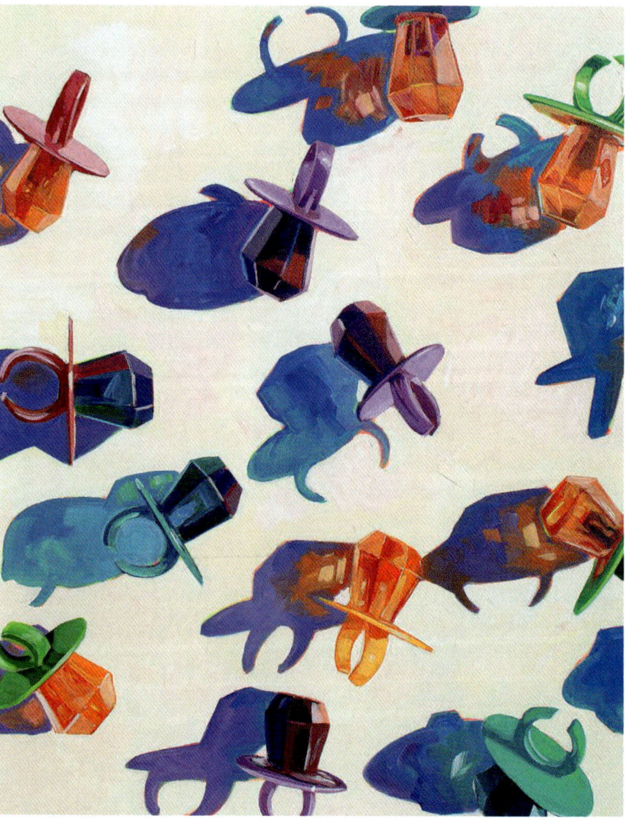

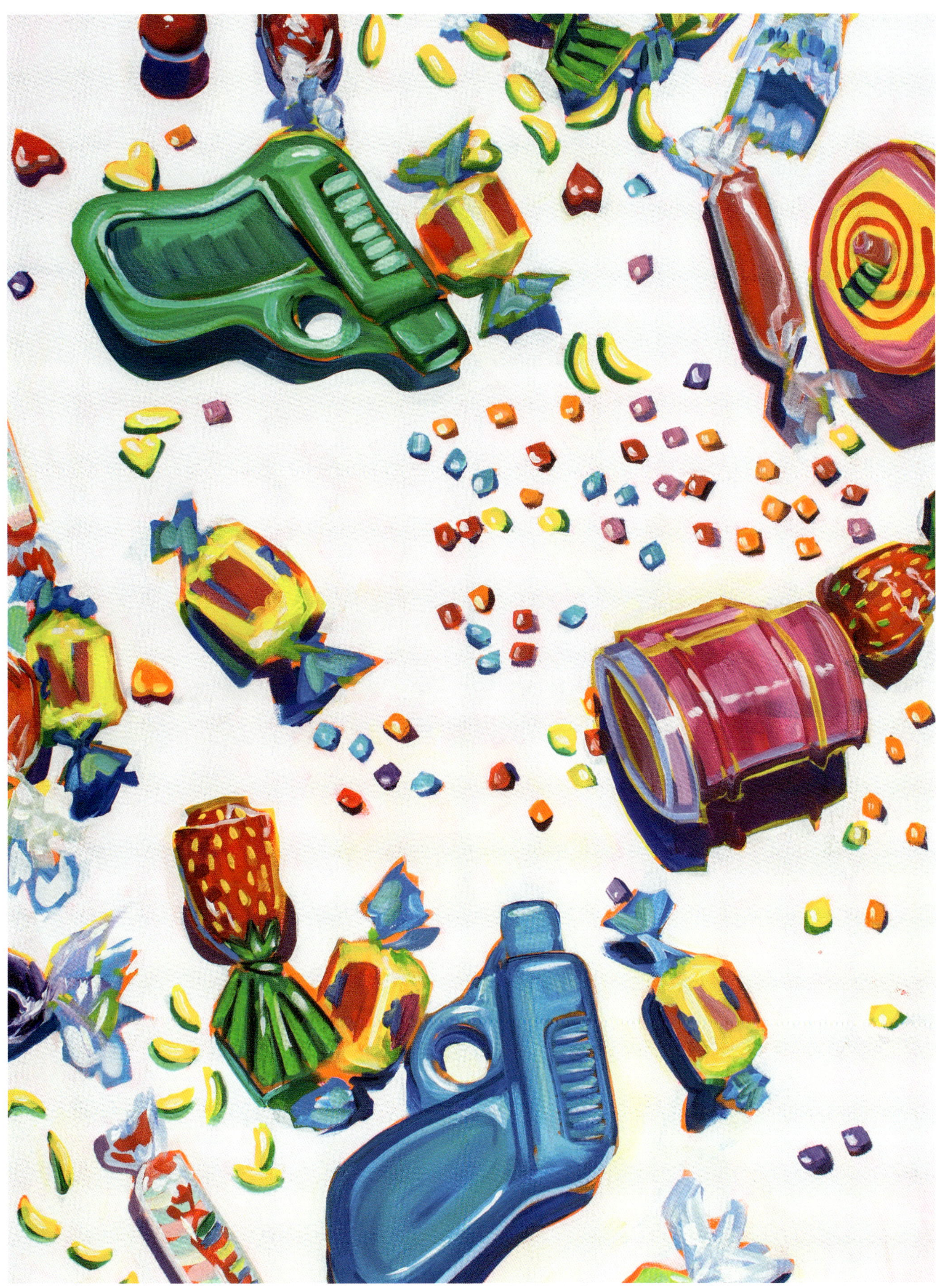

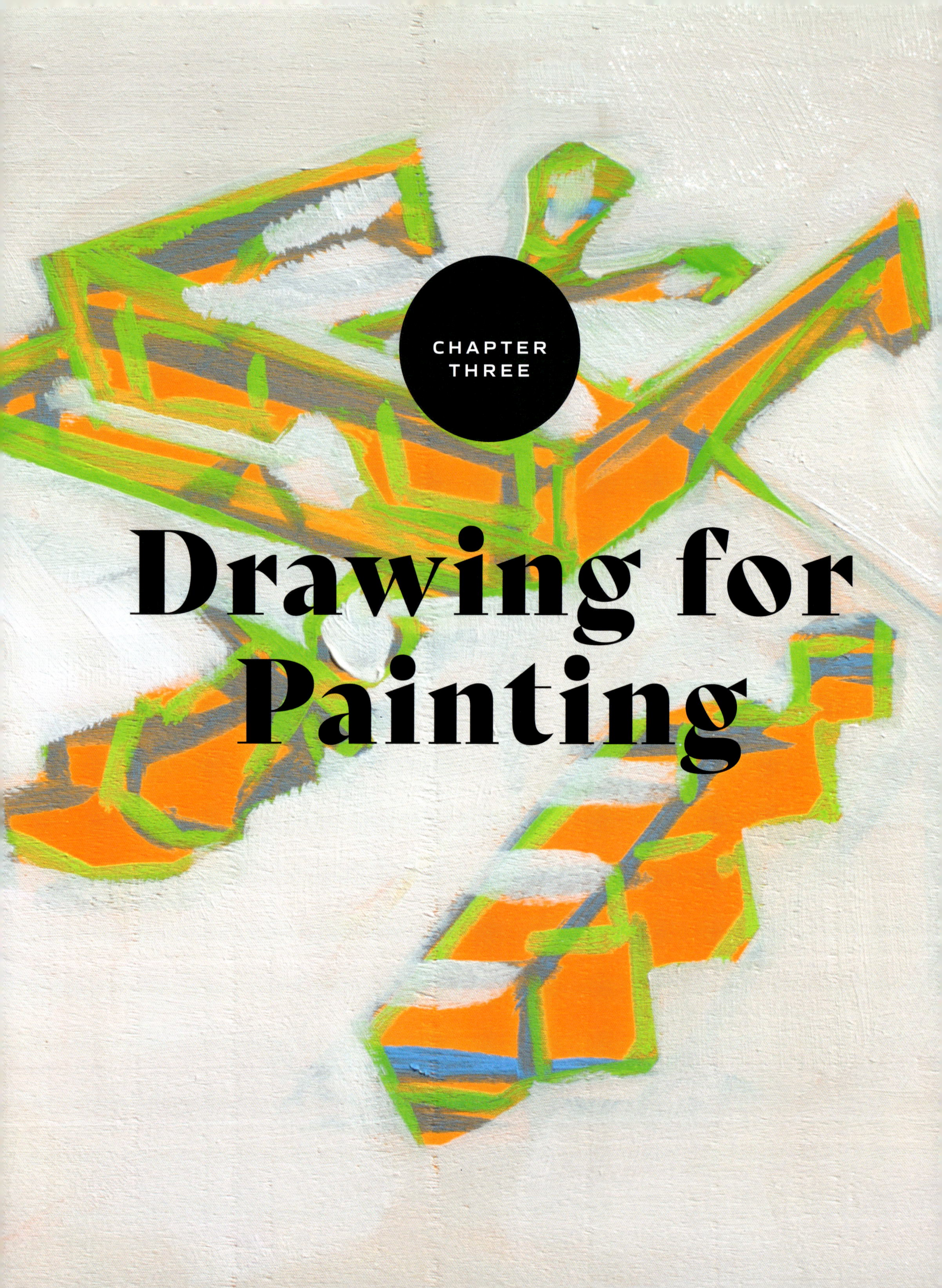

Drawing for Painting

DRAWING

I've encountered many gifted painters, both abstract and representational, who don't necessarily see themselves as adept draftspeople. In other words, drawing isn't their forte. This realization is actually reassuring. Being a master at drawing isn't a must-have to excel in painting.

Over time, as my painting took precedence, my doodling and cartooning skills waned. Yet, my capacity to gauge proportions and create drawings that complement a painting has grown remarkably. Drawing for the purpose of painting is different than drawing as an independent art form. While there are intersections and a solid grounding in drafting can be beneficial, they aren't identical. Recognizing this distinction is pivotal.

So, what does "drawing for painting" entail? It closely resembles the process of measuring and establishing a foundational framework for your art. Just as in my painting technique, you'll begin with broader shapes, gradually honing in on the intricacies. As I said previously, you don't need a meticulously accurate contour drawing to start painting.

Some styles, like grisaille, are grounded in detailed drawings overlaid with sheer paint washes to introduce color. However, in our approach, we're integrating three essential painting elements concurrently: drawing, value, and color. Our drawing may appear a tad chaotic initially, with a plethora of lines and boundaries. Yet, these serve as crucial markers, akin to bumper lanes in bowling, guiding our journey. They ensure that as we pursue color and value choices, we stay on course, preventing drawing and proportion inaccuracies from hindering our progress.

After priming my canvas, my usual next step is to draw. But, instead of pencils, I use my paintbrush to map in my initial draw lines. To me, pencils can tempt an artist into crafting intricate drawings that eventually get overshadowed by opaque acrylic layers, but a brush nudges you towards the looser strokes apt for painting. This choice was influenced by a great piece of advice I received at a workshop. The instructor pointed out that if mastering painting with a paintbrush is your goal, then not only should you paint with it, but you should also draw, shade, and blend with it.

To master your paintbrush, put aside the graphite pencil and embrace drawing with paint. Opt for a paint color that contrasts with your background in terms of value. For instance, if you've primed with a dark color, use a lighter one to draw. In this step, I suggest using a surfactant (flow improver), such as GOLDEN Wetting Aid, to give your paint an ink-like consistency ideal for drawing. A flat or bright brush, as long as it's relatively new with a sharp edge, is perfect for the task. Before diving into your painting, practice with your brush on scrap paper.

Draw using larger muscle groups, such as your shoulders or back, rather than the smaller ones in your fingers or wrists. This technique, commonly seen among architects, offers greater control and precision. In this phase, we aren't chasing detailed contour drawings. Our aim is to set boundaries. Start by outlining the outermost points of your subject, like the highest, furthest left, furthest right, and lowest points. A strong drawing commences with thorough observation, so as you embark on your drawing, it's essential to determine if your composition leans more towards a landscape or portrait orientation. No matter one's expertise, it's common to sometimes misjudge a composition's orientation. A handy trick involves using a dowel rod, extending your arm fully, and adjusting the rod to match the top and bottom of your composition. Rotate the rod to compare with the left and right sides. This process helps in discerning whether you're working with a landscape, portrait, or even a square composition.

After you've determined the proportions of your drawing, the next step involves identifying what I term as the *marquee object*. This object within your still life setup or reference photo holds a somewhat central position in your painting. It's neither a minuscule detail nor overwhelmingly large, but somewhere in between.

The marquee object serves a pivotal role: it acts as a unit of measurement throughout your entire painting. To begin, extend your arm fully towards your reference photo or still life setup. Using the dowel rod, gauge how far this object is from the top, bottom, left, or right perimeter marks of your painting. Once you've plotted the marquee object on your drawing, ensure its size and placement are precise.

Remember, during the initial phases of honing your drawing skills, the process might be time-consuming. As you develop a better knack for proportions, this process should become easier. I, for instance, can now execute this step much faster than during my college days. So, patience is key and try to avoid being too hard on yourself.

To verify the object's size, extend your arm as you did with the overall layout and use the dowel rod to measure the marquee object's height. Rotate your arm to check its width. This measuring process—comparing the actual object to its representation in your painting—requires constant back and forth with the dowel rod. Once you're certain about the proportions of the marquee object, ensure its placement is correct. Use the dowel rod to measure how many "marquee object units" there are from the top, bottom, left, and right perimeters of your painting. For example, the distance might be equivalent to three marquee objects from the left and one and a half from the right. With the marquee object correctly sized and positioned, you can then utilize it as a reference to measure and plot the rest of your painting.

Much like how one would use a ruler to measure in inches or centimeters, the marquee object becomes your reference metric when measuring the height or width of elements in your painting. It might feel peculiar initially to measure items as "two or 2.5 oranges tall," but that's precisely the method you'll use.

Another invaluable technique is the act of *dropping a vertical* or *dropping a horizontal*. Novice painters and sketch artists, unfamiliar with this approach, might sometimes misjudge diagonals, either exaggerating or understating them. By dropping a vertical—essentially aligning a straight reference next to a perceived line—you can gauge its true orientation. This is an indispensable tool, as many times I've mistaken the tilt of an arm or a body contour in a portrait, only to realize it deviated only slightly from being a pure vertical or horizontal.

Additionally, the dowel rod can assist in comparing the relative heights of objects. For instance, by extending your arm and holding the dowel rod horizontally while observing your reference, you might discern that the top of your marquee object is just slightly taller than another object on the opposite side of your painting.

To summarize, you have two main tools to employ when drawing:

1. **Marquee Object Measurement** This is a method I strongly recommend. It employs the central object as a unit of measurement, creating a consistent scale throughout the artwork.

2. **Dropping Verticals and Horizontals** By superimposing these straight references onto both your painting and the reference photo, you can constantly verify the alignment and orientation of objects.

Lastly, always remember the "One Look, One Mark" rule, where you make one brush mark for each gaze at the subject. It's easy to get carried away when drawing familiar objects. Continuously cross-checking proportions is crucial. You aim to reproduce what stands before you, not a stylized, cartoonish rendition or a memorized version. This is especially true if your goal is a true-to-life, representational drawing.

Drawing Step-by-Step (3D Watercolors)

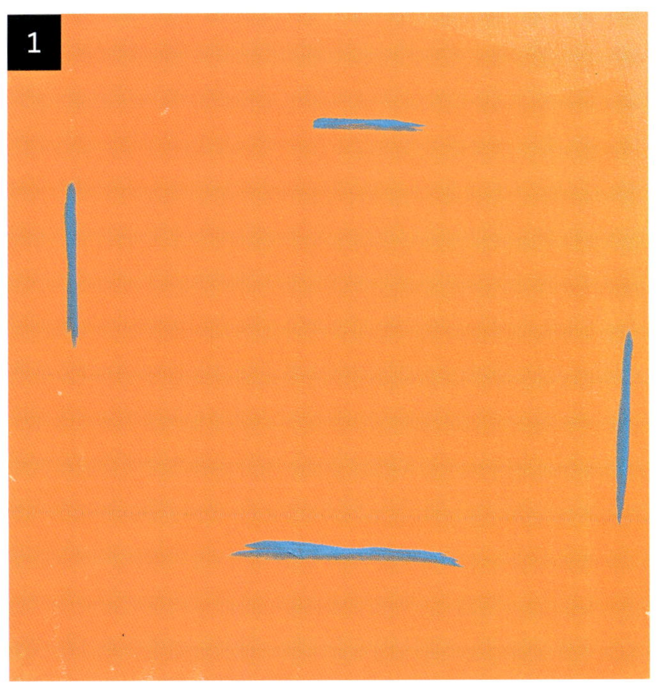

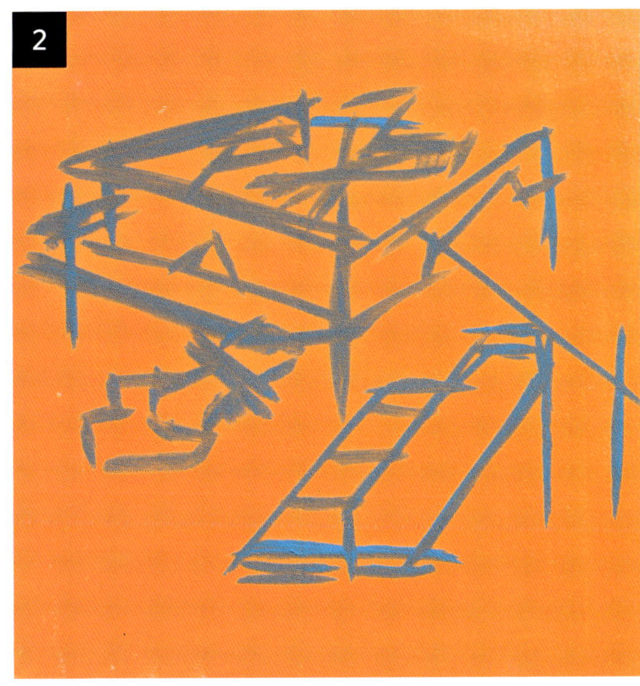

STEP 1

I start by priming my canvas with a bright orange color.

I mark the boundaries of the main forms I'm painting. Using a reference and dowel rod, I determine the furthest points of my composition: left, top, right, and bottom. Holding the dowel rod out, either horizontally or vertically, I align it with the most extreme points on the reference.

This simple technique, even with its imperfections, offers clarity. It helps ascertain if a composition is a more horizontal or landscape alignment and aids in centering the subject and gauging its main placement on the canvas.

STEP 2

Here, we're using straight lines to shape the painting's form and set its placement. Remember, this isn't just about drawing, but about observing and positioning objects relative to one another. Building on the last step, use the dowel rod to pinpoint the extreme edges of objects. For instance, when aligning the rod with the bottom of the 3D glasses, note where it intersects with other items, like the top of the Ring Pop. Small details, even a millimeter's difference, matter. In my painting, the 3D glasses were a central reference. I gauged how other objects interacted with its boundaries.

This drawing approach, focused on relationships and proportions rather than detailed outlines, means constantly checking your work. Using the dowel rod helps verify alignments. Complex setups can often be more beneficial than simple ones. Without tools like grids or projectors, this method sharpens your observational skills and spatial judgment. Some imperfections may arise, but don't worry because upcoming steps will help you refine your work.

(continued)

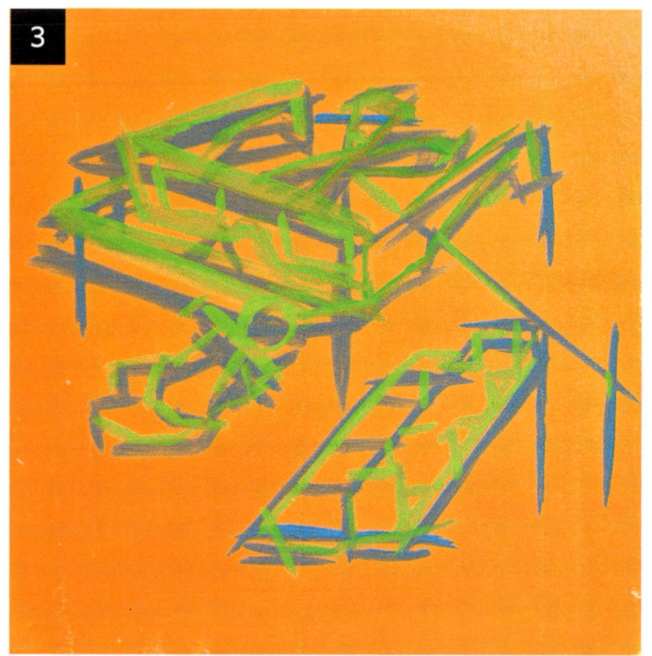

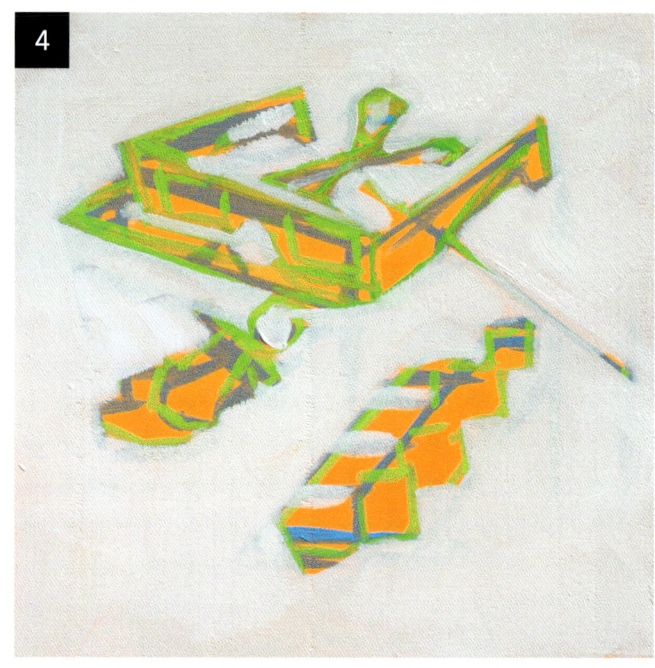

STEP 3

Now, we'll improve our initial sketch. Don't dwell too much on perfecting it from the start. If you're about 80% sure your proportions are accurate and there's no significant oversight, go ahead and move forward. Any adjustments can be made as you progress. However, if glaring issues become evident after your initial sketch—which happened to me often as I honed my drawing skills—you can make corrections. If, for instance, the 3D glasses were drawn too large, there's no need to start over. Simply choose a different color and adjust the parts that are off, using the dowel rod for guidance. Here's a tip: Once you've confidently nailed down an object's placement and size, use it as a reference point—your *marquee object*— to check and adjust the positioning and size of surrounding items.

STEP 4

I emphasize the power of using negative space, like the background's off-white color, as a drawing tool. This technique is prevalent in my works and helps refine drawings. Often, I find greater control using the edge of a flat brush to define an object's boundary by shaping the space around it, rather than detailing the object directly. Practically, this involves a dance between painting the object, refining, and then using the negative space to shape it. With this approach, busy draw lines are simplified, and the object's form becomes clearer. While I switched up the order in this example to demonstrate, the method can simplify intricate drawings. But a word of caution: avoid using the purest white. Choose a slightly muted shade, ensuring you have room later to enhance both color saturation and value.

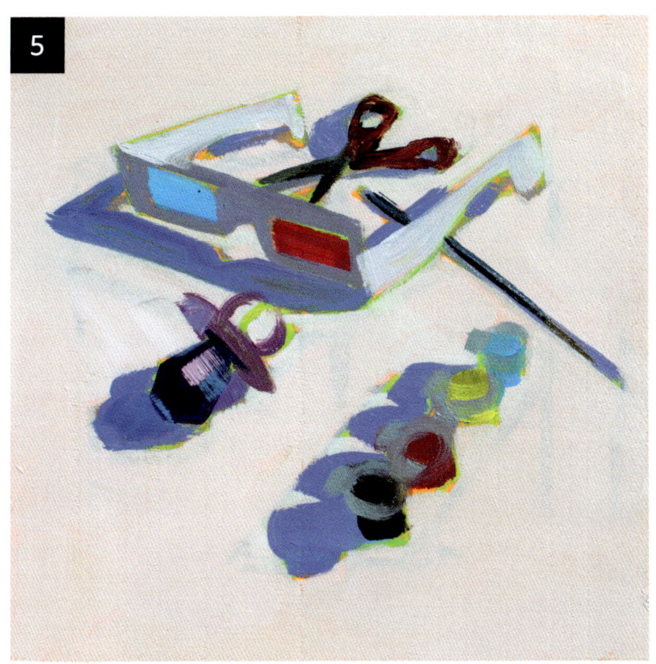

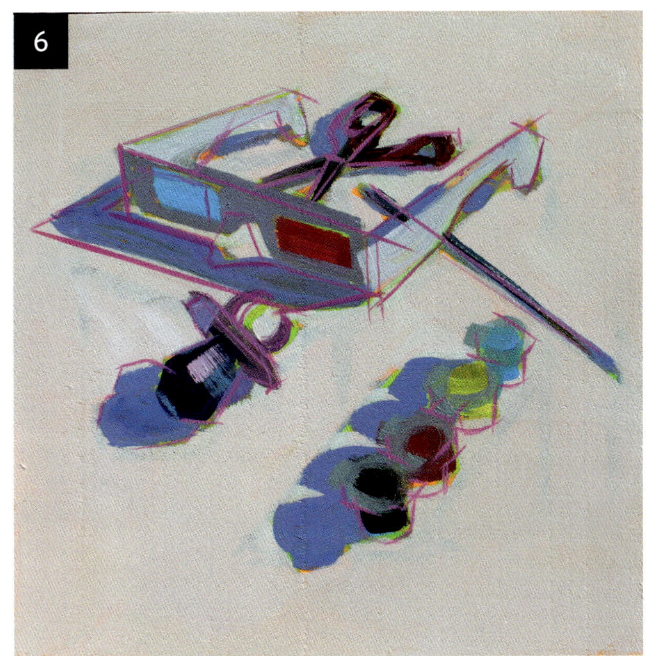

STEP 5

I've mapped out the general shapes, values, and color blocks, guided by my previous drawings. Using a slightly larger brush for this task provided speed, but also introduced some inaccuracies. A notable error is where the arm of the 3D glasses doesn't connect with the front, especially on the red side. Here's a key insight: during this phase, even though our focus is on blocking colors and values, we're still essentially drawing. Don't rush to make it look "finished."

For instance, when working on the arm of the 3D glasses, I noticed an alignment issue with the front, but prioritized staying true to my reference over achieving a "realistic" look. If this painting ended here, connecting the 3D glasses might have been understandable. But given the multilayered process, I left the misalignment as a reminder to re-evaluate that section later. Remember, even when not directly "drawing," keeping an eye on accuracy can be invaluable in subsequent stages.

STEP 6

I utilize Quinacridone Magenta, thinned for precision. As the painting evolves, achieving thin, exact lines becomes crucial for detailing. This redraw serves two main purposes: 1) correcting drawing errors made during block-ins and 2) introducing more detail, like the edge of the Ring Pop, the scissors' intricacies, and the paint containers. While this step mirrors earlier drawing phases, drawing becomes easier with the accumulated information on the canvas.

Even if some parts were slightly off, like the arm intersection of the 3D glasses, much of the composition is on point, making refinements simpler. You aim for higher accuracy with each phase, striving for 90–95% correctness now. And you can continually refine challenging parts, ensuring they align with the rest. Don't neglect to measure object intersections, even for non-touching elements. For instance, verify that the intersection of the 3D glasses aligns with the right parts of the scissors and paint. Ensure these interrelations remain consistent throughout the painting, even in the later stages.

(continued)

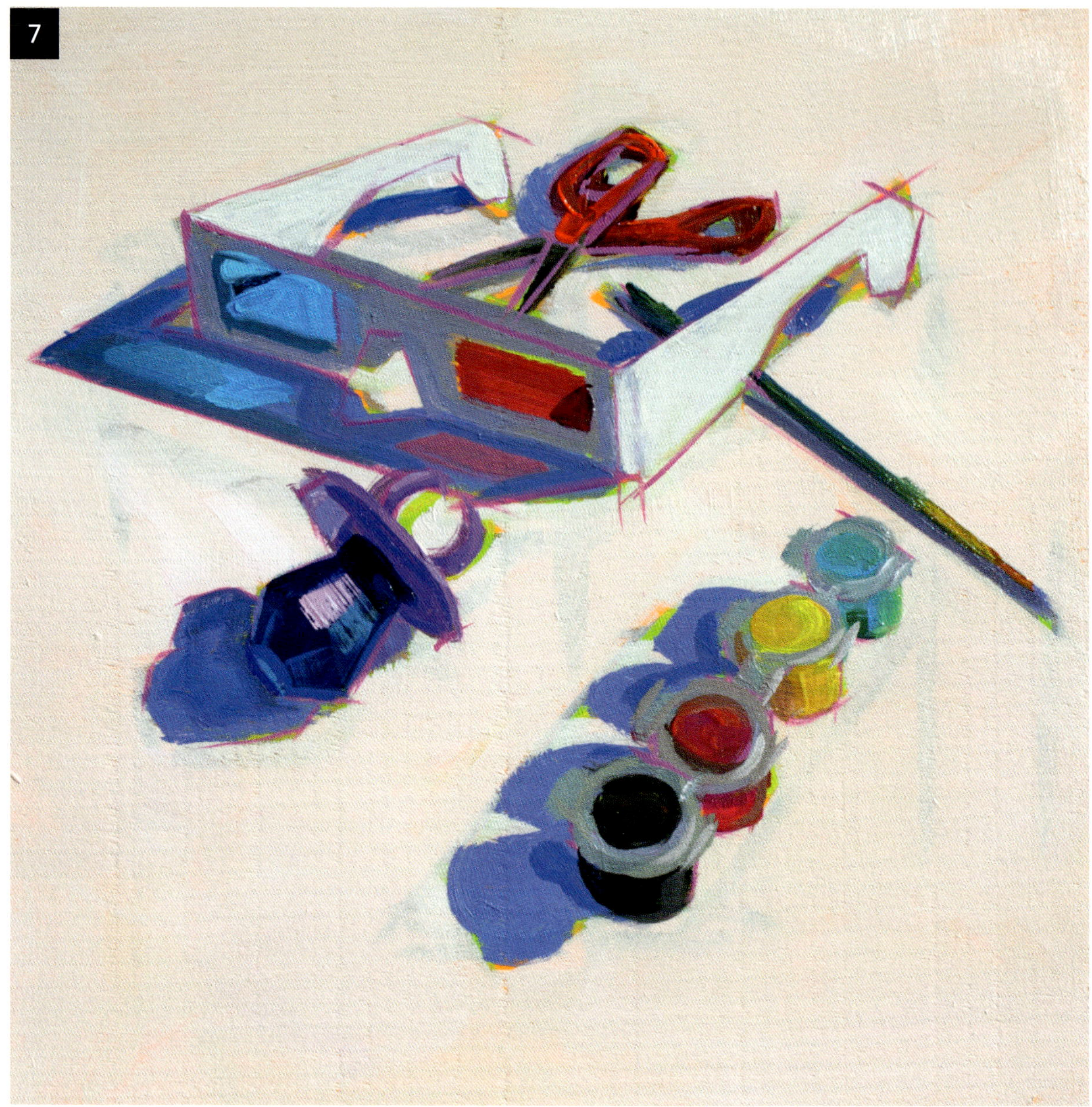

STEP 7

I corrected errors from earlier stages, enhancing areas like the red on the scissors, the arms of the 3D glasses, and deepening the shadows. This included adjustments for the translucent reflection from the lenses of the 3D glasses and adjustments to the brush and paints. Thanks to the corrections made in the previous step, pinpointing the accurate placement of colors and values became easier.

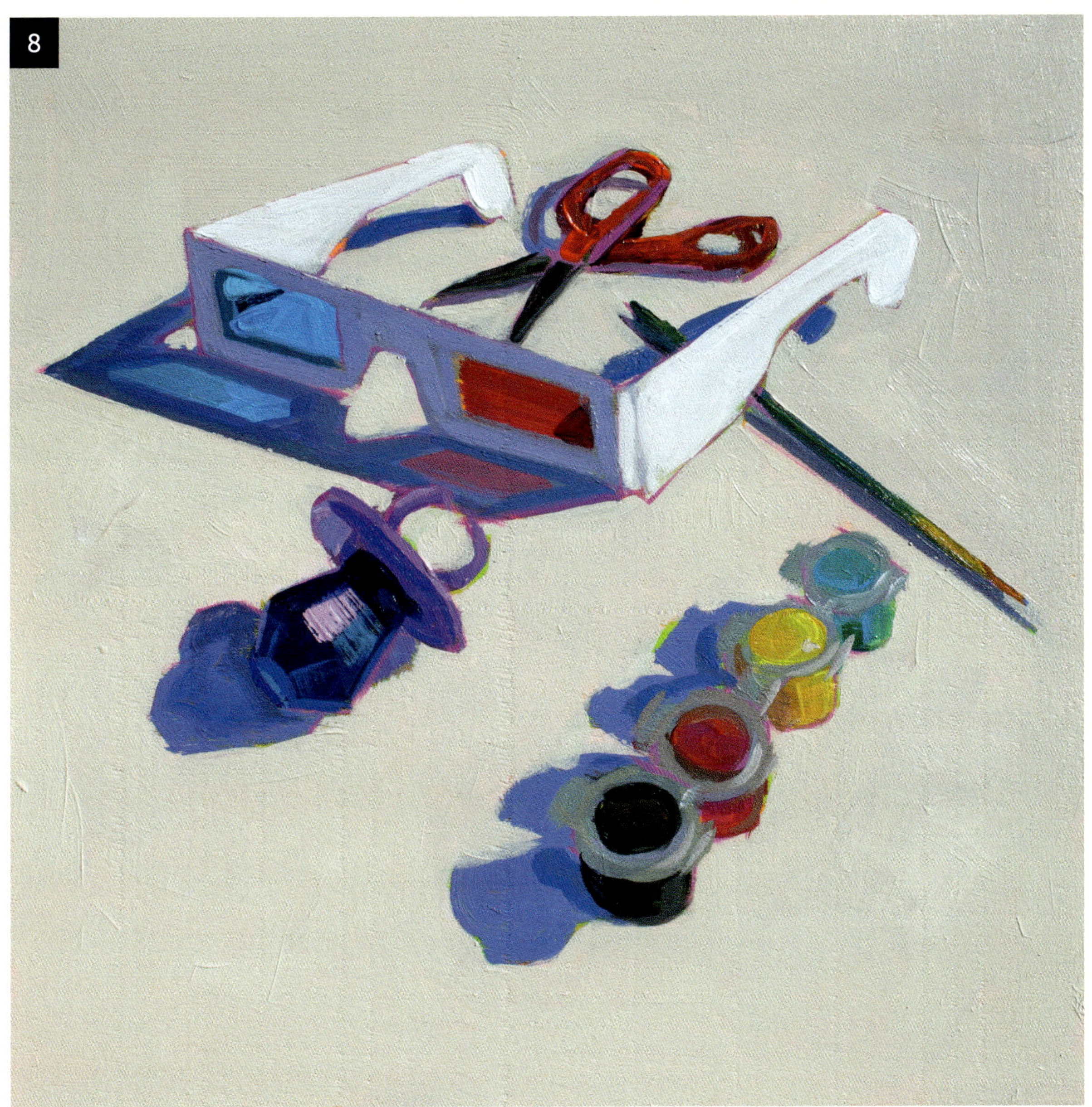

STEP 8

I utilized the background color as negative space to further refine and define the objects, cleaning up excess draw lines from prior stages. While I don't mind some draw lines showing, the goal was to respect the recent redraw from step 7. This technique helps in correcting drawing mistakes. Now, the painting appears functional, with only minor adjustments and highlights remaining.

(continued)

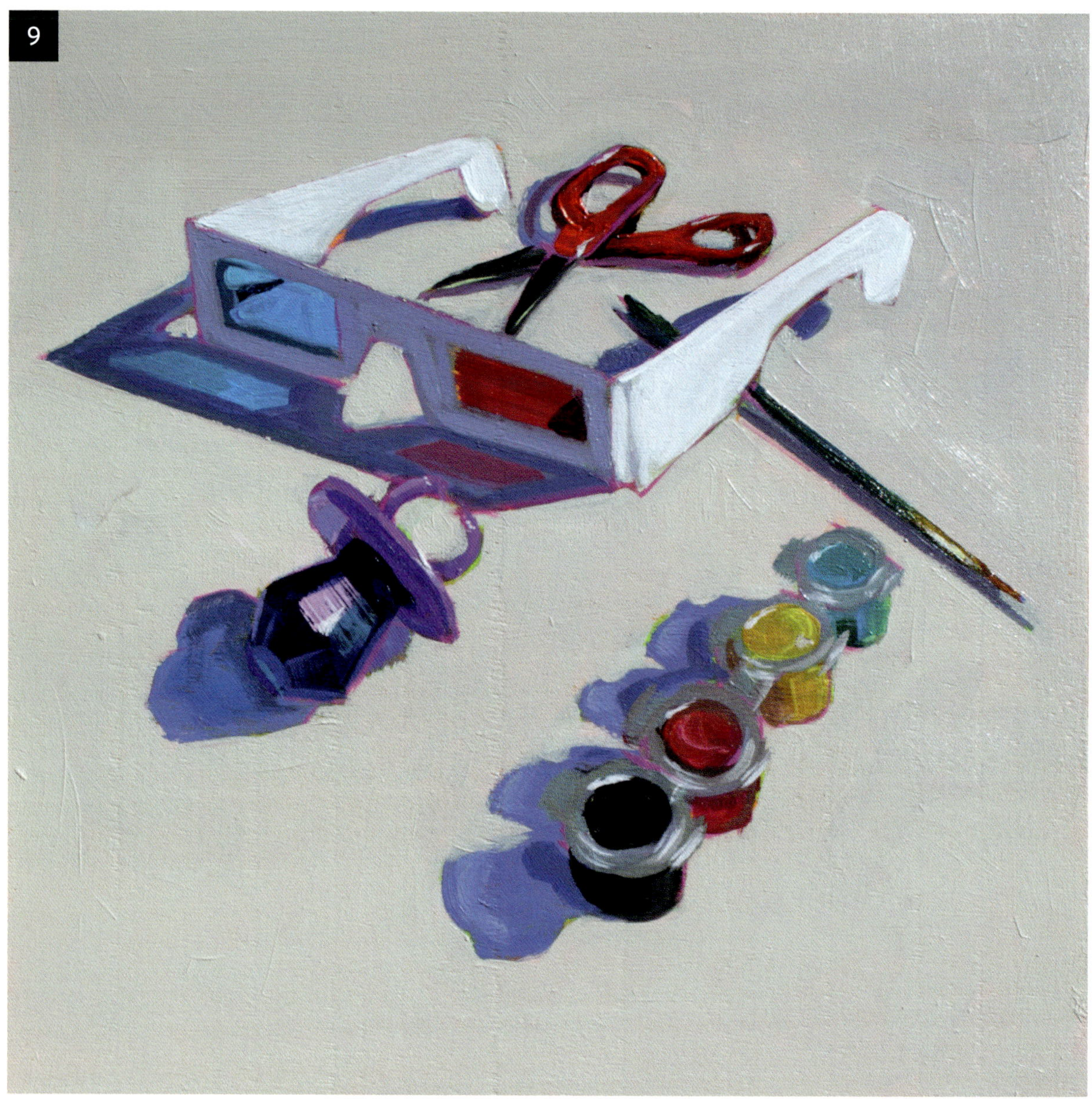

STEP 9

This is the final touch-up where I add the highlights, emphasizing the texture and material of the objects. Highlights reveal the shiny surfaces of the scissors and the reflective nature of the paint and the Ring Pop. While the painting should already convey its message without these details, the highlights provide depth, revealing the finer details of each object's surface. It's like putting the cherry on top, making the painting complete and more informative.

DRAWING TOOLS

- **Dowel rod** This is a simple yet effective tool for drawing. While some artists use their thumb to gauge proportions, a dowel rod offers a more extended reference point, making it particularly useful.

- **Proportional dividers or ratio tools** These tools, much like the dowel rod, aid in comparing measurements between your reference image and your drawing or painting on the canvas.

- **Gridding** While not a "tool" in the conventional sense, gridding involves creating a grid on both your reference photo and canvas.

  This technique is especially beneficial when painting from a photograph. To maintain accuracy, ensure that both your reference photo and canvas share the same ratio, such as 5:7 or 1:3. By using this grid system, you can keep your drawing proportional and avoid any distortions.

- **Hand mirror** By viewing the reflection of the subject and giving yourself a pair of fresh eyes, you can see—and correct—glaring proportional issues that you couldn't identify previously.

- **Projectors** Many artists, especially those working on larger pieces, opt for either a desk or wall projector. A projector simply casts the desired image onto your canvas, allowing you to trace it with ease.

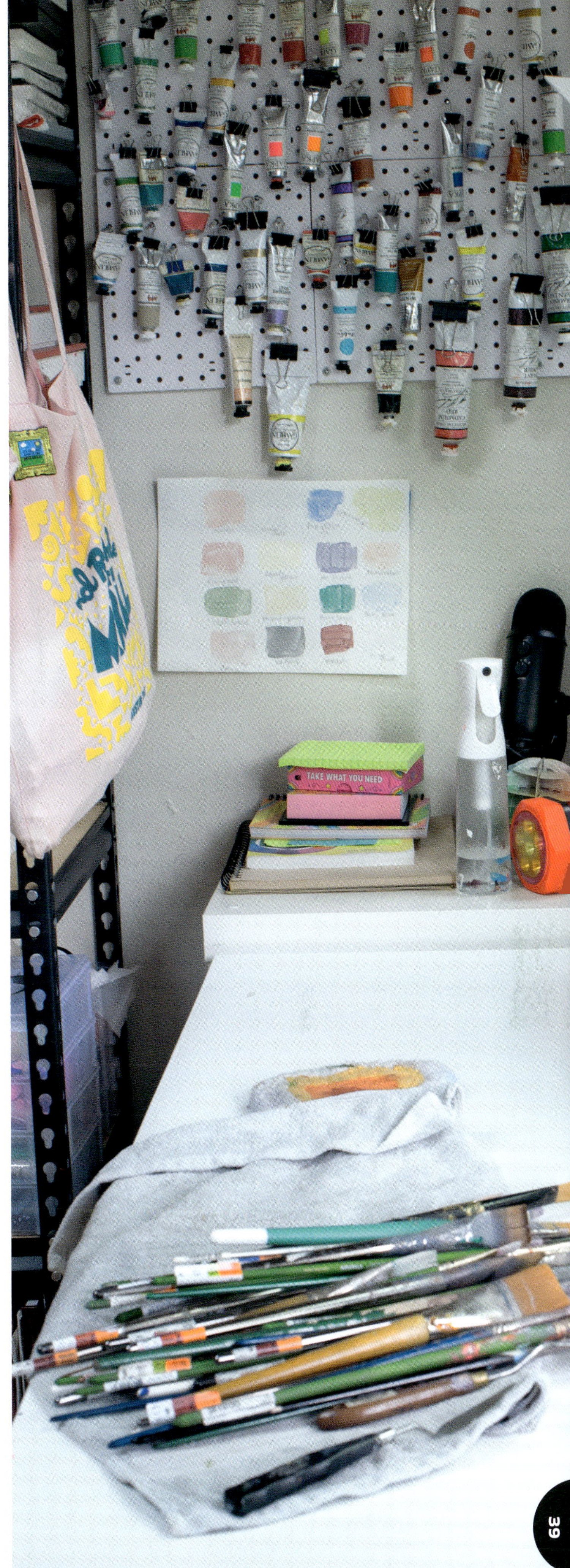

Value Study

WHEN I FELL IN LOVE with painting, looking at paintings, picking out paint colors, and mixing paint on my palette, I fell in love with color. I love the vibrancy, the way it can make you feel, the moods—everything about it. I still do. In fact, my love for color has only intensified through years of painting.

But when I set out to become really good at handling color, I was shocked to learn that so many of my lessons came from learning about value. Value is basically just how light or how dark a color is. That is, if you remove all the color, you're still left with a black and white image. That image is using value to describe form. Because I was singularly focused on color, I found myself overlooking value for many years. I loved using bright colors, but always felt frustrated when my paintings came out cartoony instead of realistic and saturated the way I had intended in my head. It was only after forcing myself to do many value studies that I started to understand the importance of navigating value in making your colors shine.

If you're drawn to painting because you like colors and you're skipping over all the graphite drawings and moody black and white photography just so you can play in a world of color, I implore you not to skip this chapter. In fact, I find that it's often very necessary work if you want to make your colors the star of the show.

THE IMPORTANCE OF VALUE STUDY

Think of value as the backbone of your painting. Color can be likened to the personality, the aspect that catches the eye and evokes emotion, but value is the structure, the foundation upon which that personality stands and shines.

Without the depth and dimension that value provides, even the most vibrant colors can appear lackluster. Why does value matter so much? Imagine a photograph without shadows or highlights, only mid-tones. It would look flat, without depth or dimension. This is what happens when you paint without considering value. No matter how bright or beautiful the colors are, without the right values, a painting will lack depth, contrast, and definition.

One of the key practices that helped me understand the significance of value was working with monochromatic paintings. By limiting myself to a single hue and playing with only its tints and shades, I was able to truly grasp how value can change the perception of an image. It forces you to see the world not in colors, but in lights and darks, helping you distinguish the subtle differences that bring a subject to life. The challenge with value, especially for newer artists, is that it's often overshadowed by the allure of color. It's like the unsung hero of a painting. But once you truly understand and master value, it's like unlocking a superpower. Your paintings will have a depth and realism that isn't achievable with color alone. So, as tempting as it may be to jump ahead to the chapters bursting with color, I implore you to spend time here, in the realm of black and white. Mastering value will not only refine your skills but will also elevate every hue and shade you lay down thereafter. Remember, value does the heavy lifting. Give it the attention it deserves, and it will transform your painting.

Not only does value make your paintings come to life, but it can also impart a distinctive signature style to your work. Values can vary from high contrast to low contrast. A painting with high contrast has sharp differences between its lightest lights and darkest darks. On the other hand, low contrast paintings feature values that cluster around the middle of the value scale, rather than ranging from extreme highs to lows.

Additionally, there are high-key and low-key paintings. High-key paintings predominantly feature values at the lighter end of the scale,

Once you truly understand and master value, it's like unlocking a superpower.

while low-key paintings gravitate towards the darker end.

To truly grasp these concepts, I'd recommend looking up examples of high-key and low-key paintings online. A potential pitfall when emphasizing contrast is that the painting might take on a more illustrative or flat appearance, leaning towards a cartoonish style. This isn't inherently bad. In fact, for some artists, this might be the desired effect. However, understanding and controlling this aspect is crucial.

My initial focus as a novice painter was solely on color, and as a result, when I amped up the contrast, my works, despite having appealing colors, appeared flat and lacked depth. It was only when I began discerning the nuances within the mid-ranges of the value scale that my paintings started to gain a more lifelike and three-dimensional feel. Value is pivotal in depicting realism. It describes form, indicating the direction of light in your piece. By assessing the values—how light or dark the contours of an object are in relation to the light source—you can interpret its shape and texture. Is it round? Is it shiny? Is it rough or smooth? Is the light source direct or diffused? All these details are communicated through value, providing context and narrative to the viewer.

To truly understand value, consider doing a value study. This involves creating a painting in monochrome, often using shades of gray, though occasionally I've used colors like Dioxazine Purple given its ability to achieve deep darks. In a value study, you distill your subject or reference photo into a set number of values, whether that's three, five, seven, or even ten, and then represent that on your canvas using your chosen grayscale. The practice compels you to condense and decide what elements are crucial in your composition, setting aside the allure of color to concentrate on the interplay of light and shadow.

While working on a value study, I've observed that initiating with a middle value and then gradually progressing towards the extremities of the value scale simplifies the process. Often, I start by priming my canvas with a middle gray. This sets the foundation, especially if I'm aiming for a three, five, or seven value study, as this middle gray essentially represents the median value.

From here, I either advance by adding a shade that is one step lighter or one step darker, refining my approach as I proceed. The beauty of value studies is that they challenge you to find identical values across different objects. This concept, often referred to as finding the "lost edges," arises when two disparate objects, like an item in the backdrop and another on a tablecloth, share a close match in both color and value. Though these exact matches in color are rare, when considering only value, such occurrences are surprisingly more frequent. There's an elegant sophistication in a painting when areas with identical values are discernible.

Imagine the shaded side of an orange having the same value as a tall glass behind it. Many budding painters tend to perceive each object as distinct in terms of drawing, color, and value. But through value studies, the realization emerges that the demarcation between objects can blur if their values align.

In the value study accompanying this chapter, observe sections where objects share equivalent values with their surroundings. The key lies in discerning the value of forms rather than distinct objects. By concentrating on blocks of similar value rather than outlining every individual object, your painting exudes a more realistic and lifelike aura. I gain immense enjoyment from identifying these subtle value matches in my work and truly cherish those moments of discovery.

VALUE PAINTING STEP-BY-STEP

Start with a canvas or piece of paper primed with an opaque layer of your middle value.

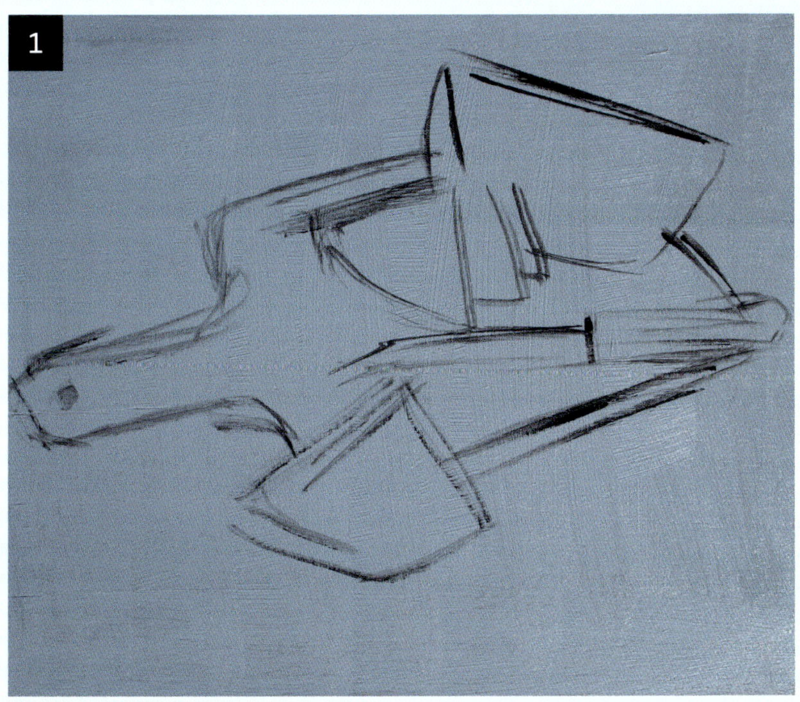

STEP 1

Initial Draw-In Begin by establishing the foundational structure of your painting. Unlike a precise contour drawing, this step involves identifying specific intersections on the canvas. Think of it as creating the scaffolding for your artwork rather than a formal sketch. To ensure visibility, select a color that contrasts with the background color used to prime the canvas. This will help your initial drawing stand out and guide your subsequent artistic process.

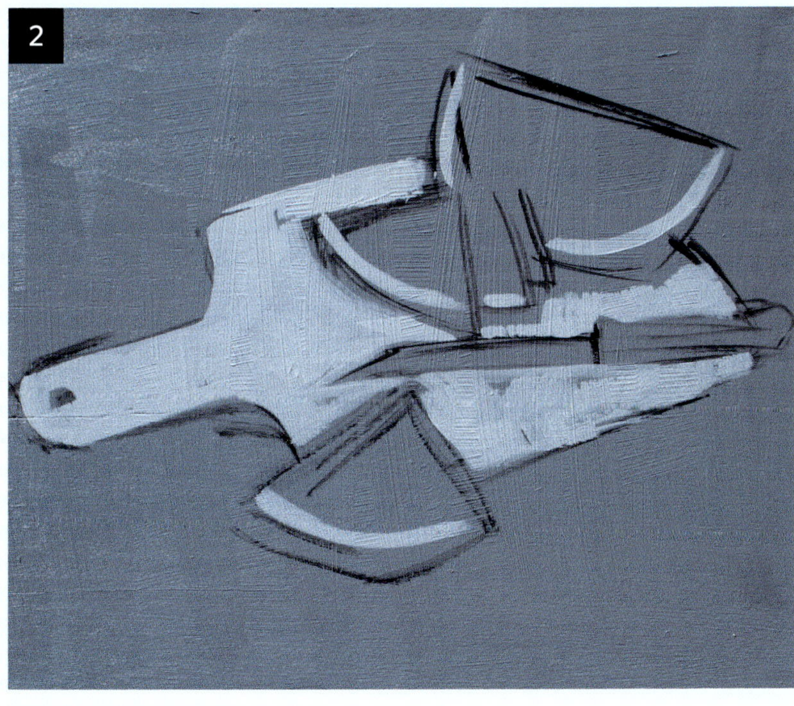

STEP 2

Choosing the Second Lightest Value Take a moment to observe the area where the second lightest value is located. Remember, your focus should not be solely on the subject but on honestly recognizing where the values in the painting align. This step is crucial for maintaining accuracy and capturing the nuances of light and shadow in your artwork. Stay attentive to the values present and make informed decisions about your color choices based on this evaluation.

(continued)

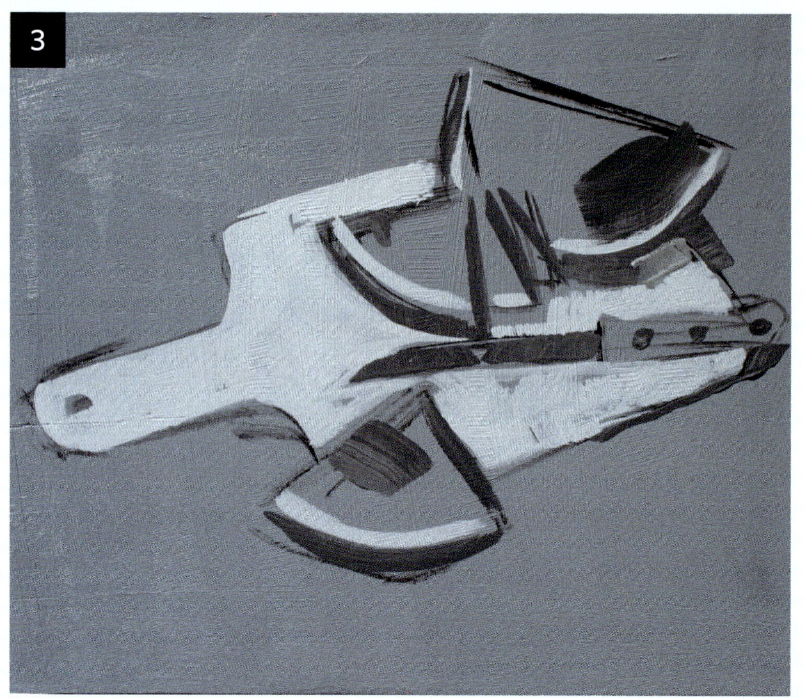

STEP 3

Selecting the Second-to-Darkest Value Determine the specific location on your painting where the second darkest value belongs. As you progress through this step, you'll start to gain clarity and a clearer sense of the image you're painting. This is an exciting stage where your artwork begins to take shape, and the interplay of light and dark becomes more pronounced. Continue to analyze your painting's values and make informed choices that enhance the overall composition.

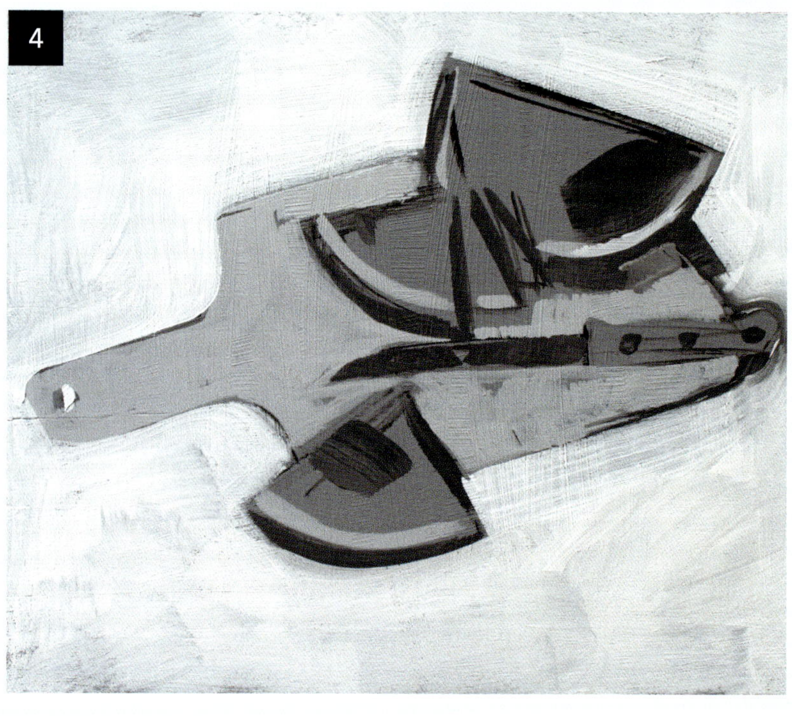

STEP 4

Identifying the Lightest Value In this step, your task is to pinpoint the location on your painting where the lightest value from your five-value color palette belongs. It's important to avoid fixating solely on highlights, as often they tend to blend with the surrounding values within the limited range of five-value distinctions.

Instead, maintain a broader perspective and carefully assess the overall composition. By doing so, you'll be able to accurately place the lightest value, ensuring a harmonious integration of tones in your artwork. This step contributes to the cohesive portrayal of light and shadow within your piece.

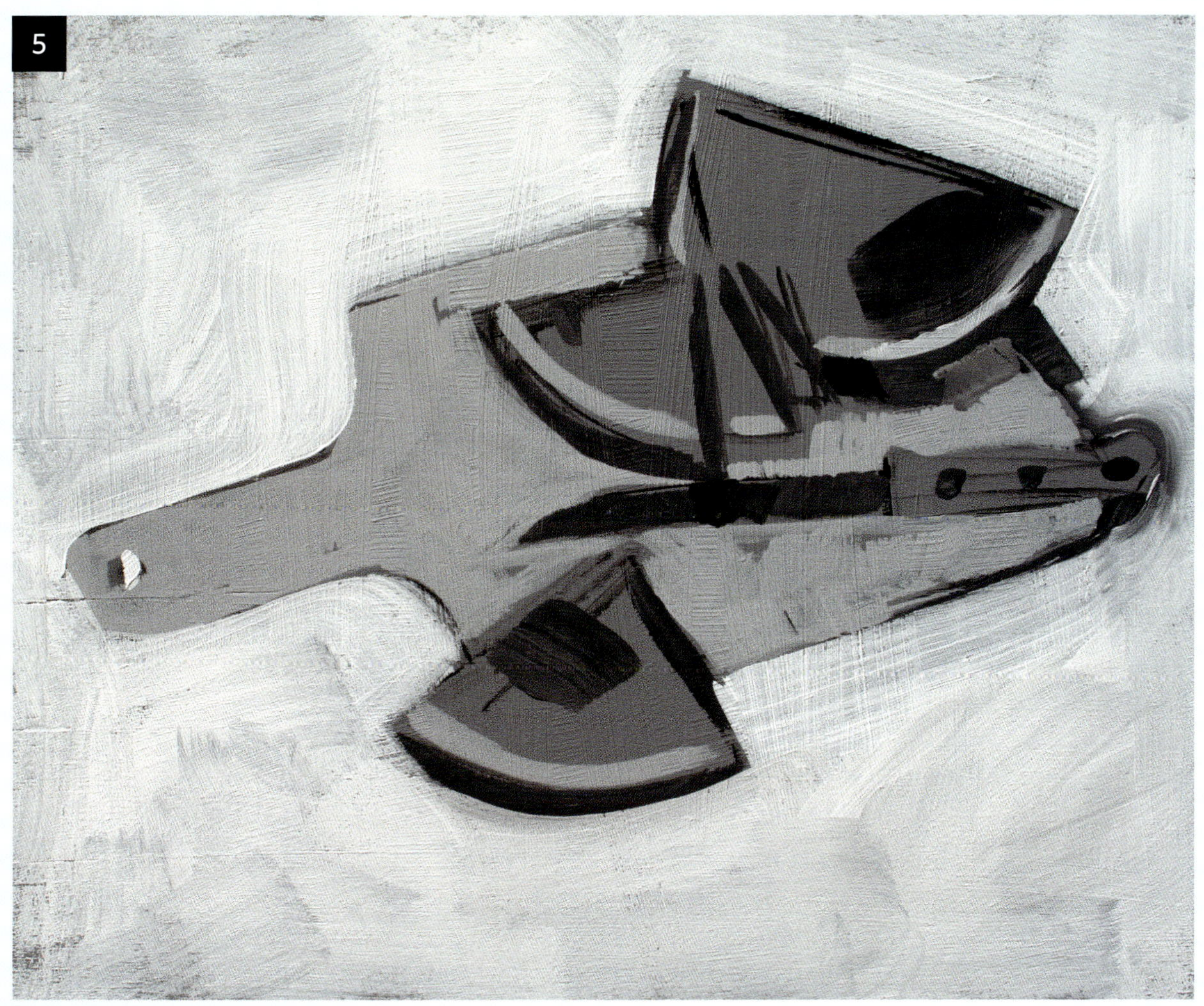

STEP 5

Adding the Darkest Value Now, let's introduce the darkest value into your painting. Keep in mind that in this particular drawing, the composition may not heavily rely on this darkest value, as it tends to lean towards a high-key approach with emphasis on the lighter three values of the value scale. Nevertheless, pay attention to the impact created by the addition of this darkest value. Notice how it provides context and enhances the effect of the second darkest value added in step 3. This strategic placement of values contributes to the overall visual narrative and adds depth to your artwork.

Take a moment to observe the interplay of values and appreciate the subtle transformations unfolding on your canvas.

(continued)

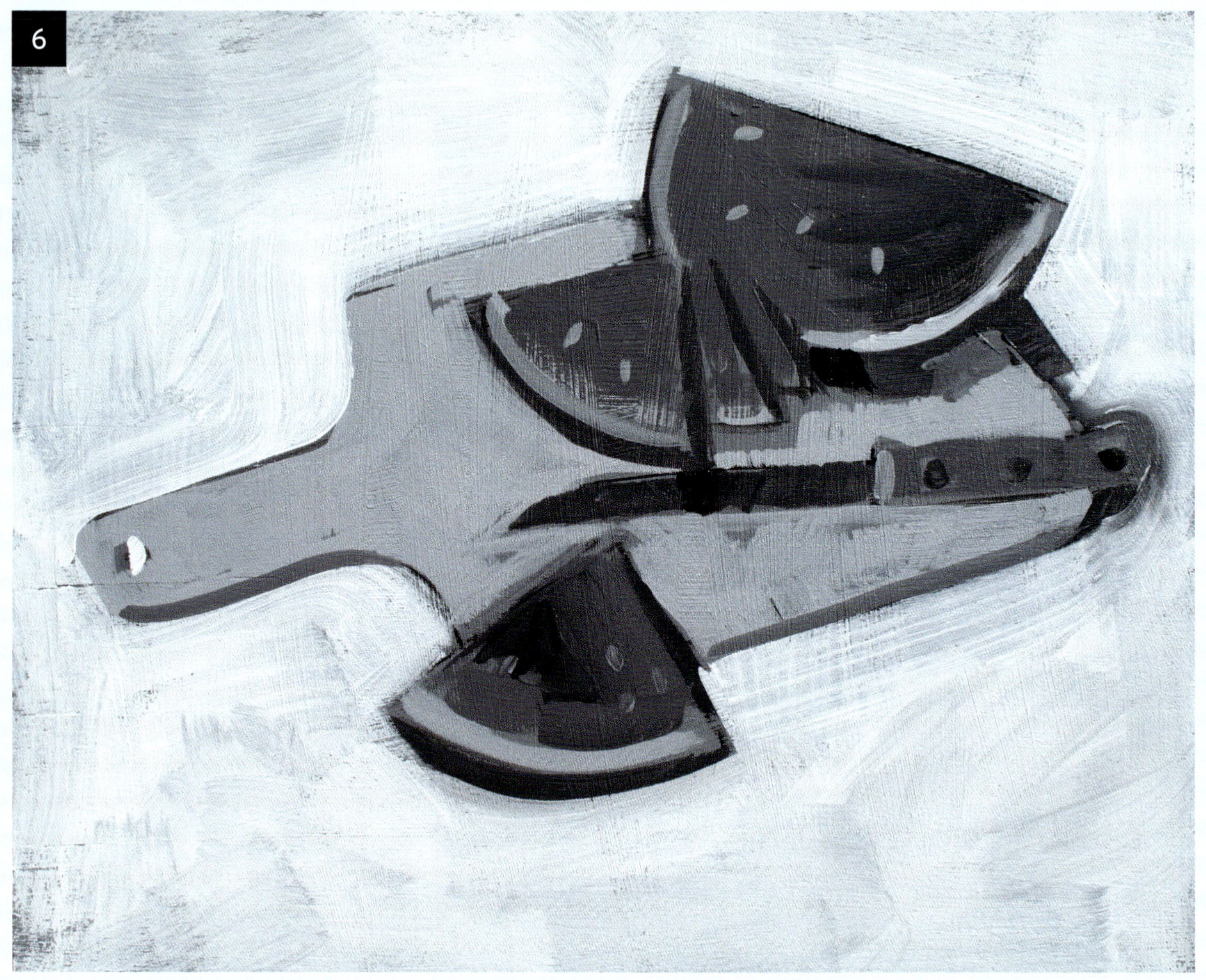

6

STEP 6

Adding the Middle Value and Final Touches We have reached the final step of our process, which involves adding the middle value to your painting. Although your canvas was initially primed with this value, there may be instances during the painting process where revisiting this color becomes necessary to achieve greater accuracy. Now is the time to consider incorporating the most prominent highlights.

If there are elements within your composition that possess sufficient strength and contrast to make their own distinct statement, this is when you should introduce them. However, I advise against adding highlights too early in the composition, as they typically lack the distinctiveness needed to be addressed earlier on. At this concluding step, you have gathered enough information from the previous stages to discern if highlights or specific details are essential to include in your final study. In the case of the watermelon seeds, they were deemed significant enough to be incorporated. Take this opportunity to evaluate the overall impact of your painting and make any necessary adjustments to achieve your desired outcome.

TWO VALUE STUDIES

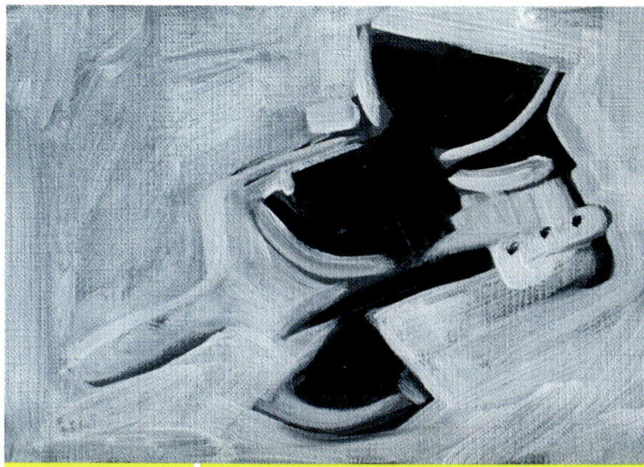

2 VALUES (NOTAN)

Use black and white paint in this study to isolate two value groups, with white representing the lighter 50% of the value scale and black representing the darker 50%.

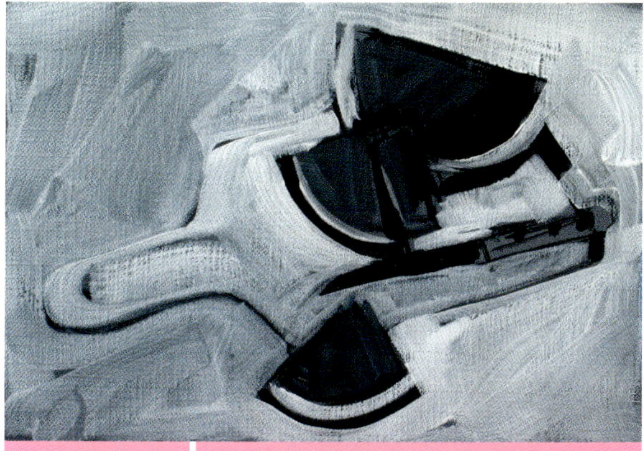

3 VALUES

In this value study, we're using black, white, and middle gray to capture the values in our reference photo.

VALUE TOOLS

- **Red viewfinder** This is arguably the most effective tool for discerning value. A simple red piece of plastic suffices, and it works by drowning out color, leaving only value visible. In a bind, even 3D glasses can be used—just look through the red lens. As a painter, I rely on this tool frequently, whether I'm referencing a canvas, a photograph, or painting en plein air.

- **Plastic viewfinder with value scale** This tool comes equipped with a 1–10 value scale. By peering through its clear plastic, you can gauge the value and attempt to match it. It's particularly useful when mixing colors on a palette.

- **Hand technique** Sometimes, simplicity is key. By forming an *okay* gesture with your hand, you can create a minuscule circular opening. Holding this up to a reference allows you to check color and value, using your hand's known value as a benchmark. While it might lack the precision of other tools, it's a handy method when others aren't available.

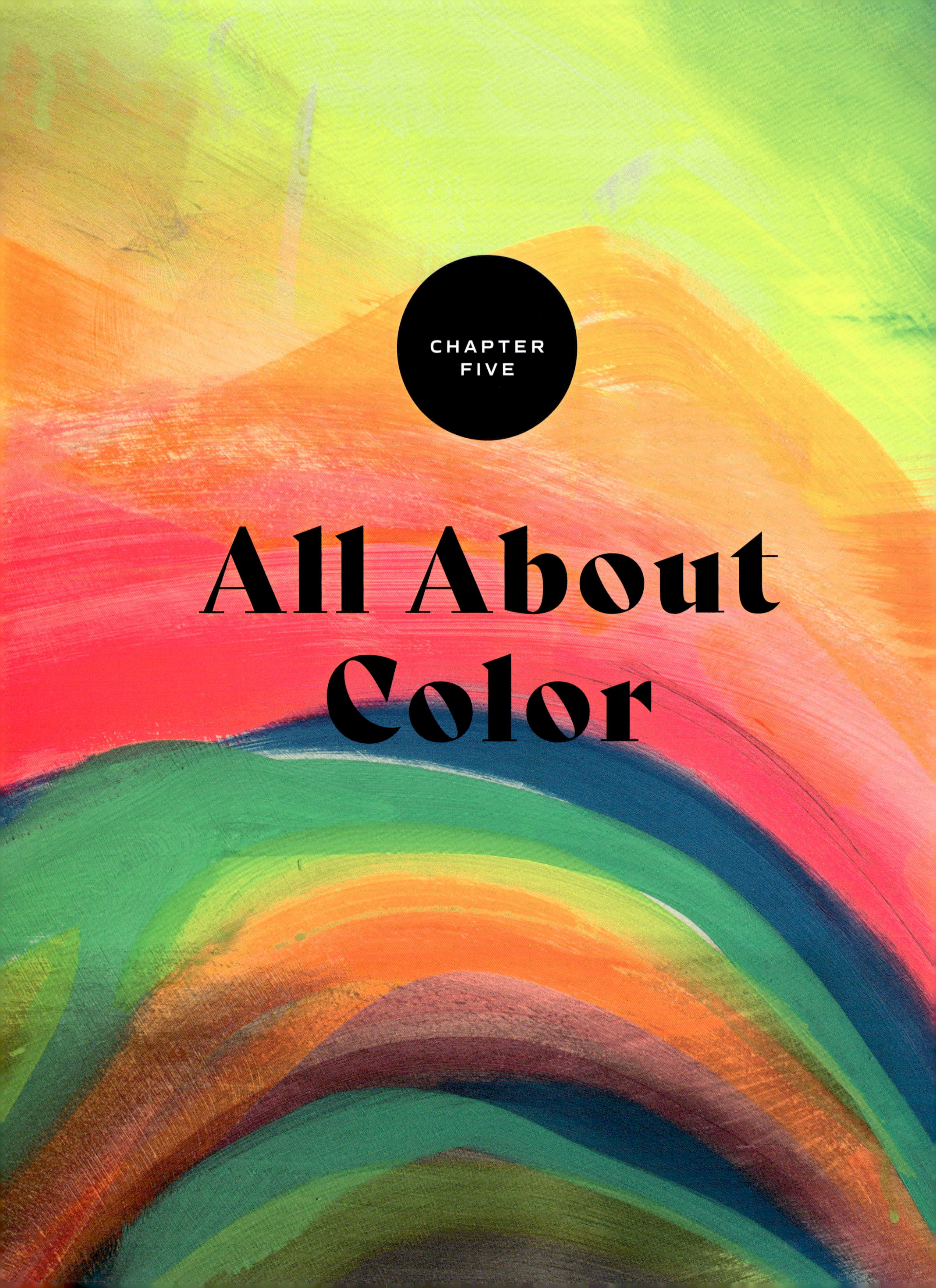

All About Color

COLOR IS MY FAVORITE aspect of painting. I often joke that I mastered drawing, setting up still lifes, and priming canvases just to indulge in the vibrant potential of color. The magic of taking tubes of paint, mixing them, and then constructing something ethereal and stunning on canvas never ceases to captivate me.

I once read a book titled *Full Spectrum*, which included an informative quote from a neuroscientist named Bevil Conway who specializes in the visual cortex. Conway points out that we don't actually require color to comprehend the world around us. Even the most advanced AIs that process visual data often rely on grayscale rather than color. Yet, the region of our brain that processes color sits adjacent to the part that interprets the world in black and white.

As Conway eloquently states, "There are two separate processes [in the visual cortex] 'What is that?' and 'Do you give a shit?' Color is doing the second." Yes! I love this sentiment. Although color might not aid in our understanding of the world, it undeniably evokes emotion. This is why I believe it's essential for me to provide a compelling chapter on color in this instructional book on painting.

Delving deep into color theory can be a daunting journey, with endless nuances to explore. But I've always believed that the best way to learn painting is by diving right in. This chapter will guide you through some fundamental terminology, navigation of the color wheel, and techniques for painting with a limited palette. By following these steps, I assure you that your skills in rendering color will be honed to the level required for you to blossom into an accomplished painter, with a keen understanding of color and light.

While I advocate for diving right in, embracing a hands-on approach, and learning through trial and error when it comes to color, I believe there are benefits to understanding a few basic terms and mastering the use of color coordinates to navigate color mixing.

There is a vast amount to grasp about color theory—just Google "color theory books" and consider the plethora of approaches and content to see my point. And yet, you don't need an exhaustive understanding of light physics or eye biology to excel as a painter. In fact, some of my favorite color theory books acknowledge that those who seem to have an intuitive grasp of color are painters. While they might not be able to explain the intricate physics causing colors to interact in surprising ways, they comprehend how these principles function through countless hours of painting. So, let's dive in.

The most critical terms to understand are *perceptual color* and *local color*. Typically, when we paint, we interpret perceptual color—color perceived with all lighting effects and optical illusions in play. This often contradicts our knowledge. For example, consider a plein air painter observing mountains in the distance that appear as a muted purple. While we recognize mountains aren't inherently purple, the interplay of their warm, reddish brown hue with the blue of atmospheric perspective makes them seem so. Focusing on perceptual color means not questioning *why* the mountains look purple but acknowledging and depicting them as they appear.

If painters only had to observe, this would be the end of the story. But painters mix their own colors, requiring an understanding of local color. Local color is the inherent color of an object under neutral, bright lighting.

A story from my art school illustrates the distinction between perceptual and local colors. I studied in the Missouri Ozarks, and my college was surrounded by many rural towns. A student from one such area took a mandatory semester of art, as required by his non-art major. In a painting class, he painted a distant barn for his plein air assignment. During a critique, the professor questioned the barn's vivid red, especially given its distance. The student defended his choice, revealing that he'd bypassed color mixing by directly using the paint from the barn's paint can.

While this was the barn's local color, in the painting, the distant barn should have appeared less saturated and more violet due to atmospheric perspective.

I love the anecdote about the barn because the red hue is significantly altered by factors like atmospheric perspective—literally tiny water droplets reflecting bluish wavelengths, creating a blue haze—and the barn's distance, which makes it appear less vibrant. Add to that the potential for *simultaneous contrast*, another essential term. Simultaneous contrast refers to how a color might appear differently depending on adjacent colors. This effect is especially pronounced when the colors are opposites.

For instance, the distant barn might appear more brown and muted if surrounded by vibrant orange autumn leaves, but it might seem more radiant amidst bright spring trees. In essence, simultaneous contrast illustrates how perceptual color can be deceptive. As painters, our role is to interpret the perceptual color in our reference, utilize local color knowledge and perceptual color understanding to mix new shades, and then re-engage with perceptual color to produce a cohesive artwork.

This interplay can make painting quite challenging. If you've ever chosen a paint color for a room, convinced of its perfection in the aisles of Home Depot amidst a sea of other hues, only to apply it at home and find it too bright, too saturated, and too warm, you grasp the intricacies of differentiating actual or local color from perceptual color. Because of these complexities, I stress the use of color coordinates, crafting your own color wheel, taking color notes, and understanding color complements to navigate the world of color mixing effectively for your artwork.

Understanding the relationship between language and color mixing is crucial. The key to grasping color is to simplify where possible. Just as I advise against buying a paint tube for every conceivable color—ending up with an overwhelming (and expensive) array of over 100 choices—having an overabundance of words for colors can also be confusing.

Streamlining our language can be beneficial. Historically, there's a deep connection between color and language. Linguistic relativism argues that the more words we have for colors, the more colorful the world we perceive.

While this is fascinating, language often falls short. For instance, what one person calls robin's egg blue, another might describe as seafoam green. Pantone, an entire industry, exists mainly to standardize color names for designers, underscoring the challenge of this task. Interestingly, we often call people with bright orange hair "redheads." This isn't due to a past inability to perceive orange. Rather, when the term *redhead* originated in Old English centuries ago, the word *orange* hadn't been established. In fact, the term *orange* in the context of color is relatively recent.

I prefer a simplified approach: a basic color wheel using red, orange, yellow, green, blue, and violet. I eschew terms like *orange* in favor of *bright orange*, facilitating navigation around the wheel by intensity or saturation. Saturation refers to a color's vividness: colors straight from the tube are typically at their peak vividness, while muted colors tend toward gray.

For instance, a nearly gray muted purple would be *low intensity*, whereas a vibrant grape color would be *high intensity*. Other useful terms include *light* or *dark*, indicating value, tint (color plus white), and shade (color plus black). Occasionally, *warm* or *cool* can describe colors. In terms of green, a warm green leans toward yellow, while a cool green is bluer. It's all relative, especially with colors like orange and blue. A *cool orange* means it's closer to red, a cooler color than yellow. These terms combined create a system of color coordinates, akin to plotting a map. If you understand this system, *low intensity dark green* will guide you to a specific spot on your color wheel. Instead of seeking an exact hue, you're finding a color relative to others. This approach aids in discerning both local and perceptual colors. I suggest identifying random colors in your surroundings and applying these coordinates. While it might feel awkward initially, with practice, it becomes intuitive.

HOW TO MAKE YOUR OWN COLOR WHEEL (& WHY IT'S IMPORTANT)

Now, I'd like for you to make a color wheel. It might feel elementary or overly basic, but trust me: it's not merely about listing rainbow colors in sequence.

The aim is to diagram color relationships. Remember, these relationships are vital for understanding perceptual color. When deeply engrossed in color mixing—navigating the intricate nuances of color coordinates—it becomes invaluable to have a visual aid. A quick glance at your color wheel, affixed to your easel, can promptly show you the complement of the hue you're mixing. This convenience, along with familiarizing yourself with the color dynamics of your chosen palette, justifies crafting a color wheel.

Begin with thick paper suitable for acrylic paint and stencil a circle on it. Next, place your primary colors. The primaries you select greatly influence the tone, range, mood, harmony, and values of your palette. Their unique combinations can produce varied results, as seen from the distinct palettes I've discussed in this chapter. Note: It's pivotal for colors within a painting to be harmonious only within that artwork's context.

The most vibrant red should simply appear as the most striking red to be perceived as such. Following that, mix your secondary colors: green, purple (or violet), and orange. Then, comes your tertiary colors: blue green, yellow green, yellow orange, red orange, red violet, and blue violet. Some hues may naturally be darker.

To appreciate each color's depth and range, introduce both tint (by adding white) and shade (by adding black) to each. The subsequent step involves mixing color complements. This principle is paramount in color theory. A complement doesn't merely enhance a color's appearance but completes it. When mixed, complements neutralize each other, producing a chromatic gray—a perfect neutral gray derived from colors. Achieving an ideal chromatic gray can be challenging, but strive for the closest approximation. I'd like you to craft three color spectrums: one spanning blue to orange, another from yellow to violet, and the last from red to green. Blend the complements until you produce varying shades of each hue, with gray ideally at the center and then transitioning back through the color spectrum.

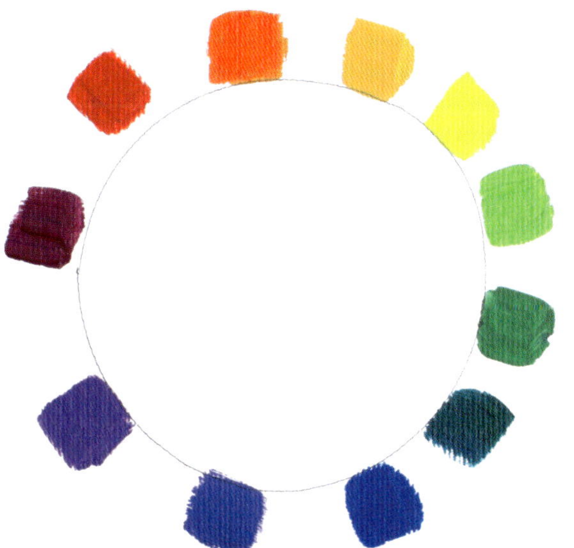

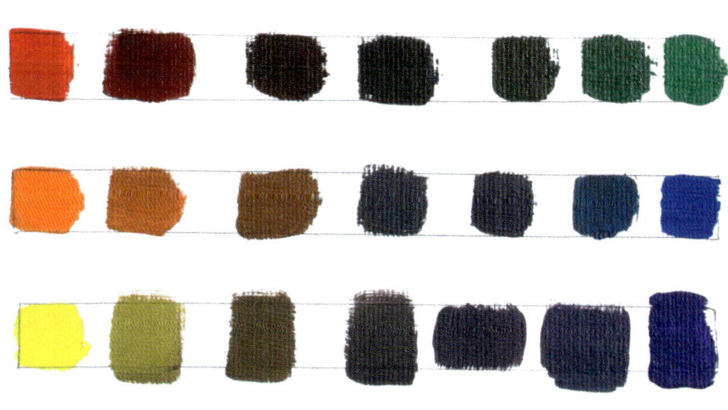

Tomatoes on Toast Step-by-Step

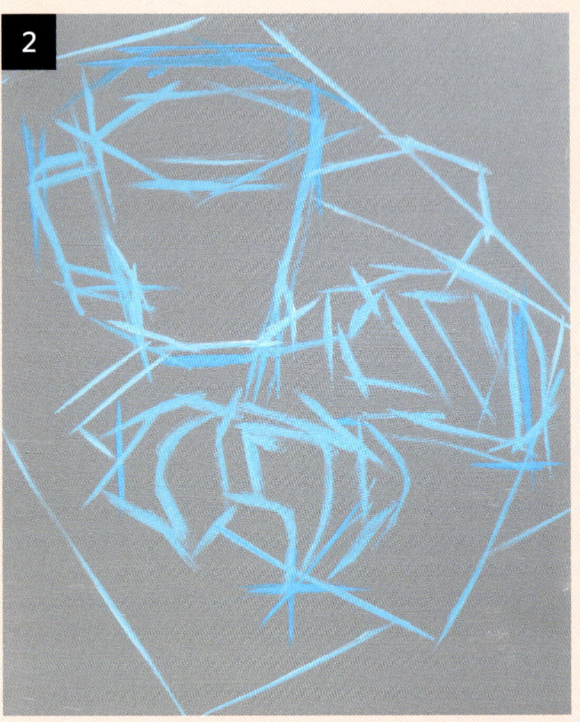

STEP 1

To start, I prime a wood panel with a coat of N5 Neutral Gray, a medium gray acrylic paint, preparing the surface for my painting.

STEP 2

Here, I utilize Phthalo Blue (Green Shade), and Titanium White, along with a flow improver such as GOLDEN Wetting Aid to achieve an inky texture, using these to mark outlines and map out forms and intersections of objects. Think of this as constructing scaffolding for subsequent steps. Rather than employing numerous curvilinear lines, I favor straight lines to delineate the form, focusing on creating a framework rather than a precise contour drawing. I find this approach minimizes mistakes as it involves marking out edges, such as the topmost and bottommost points of the cup, and the points where the napkin intersects with the canvas edges, which often results in straight lines.

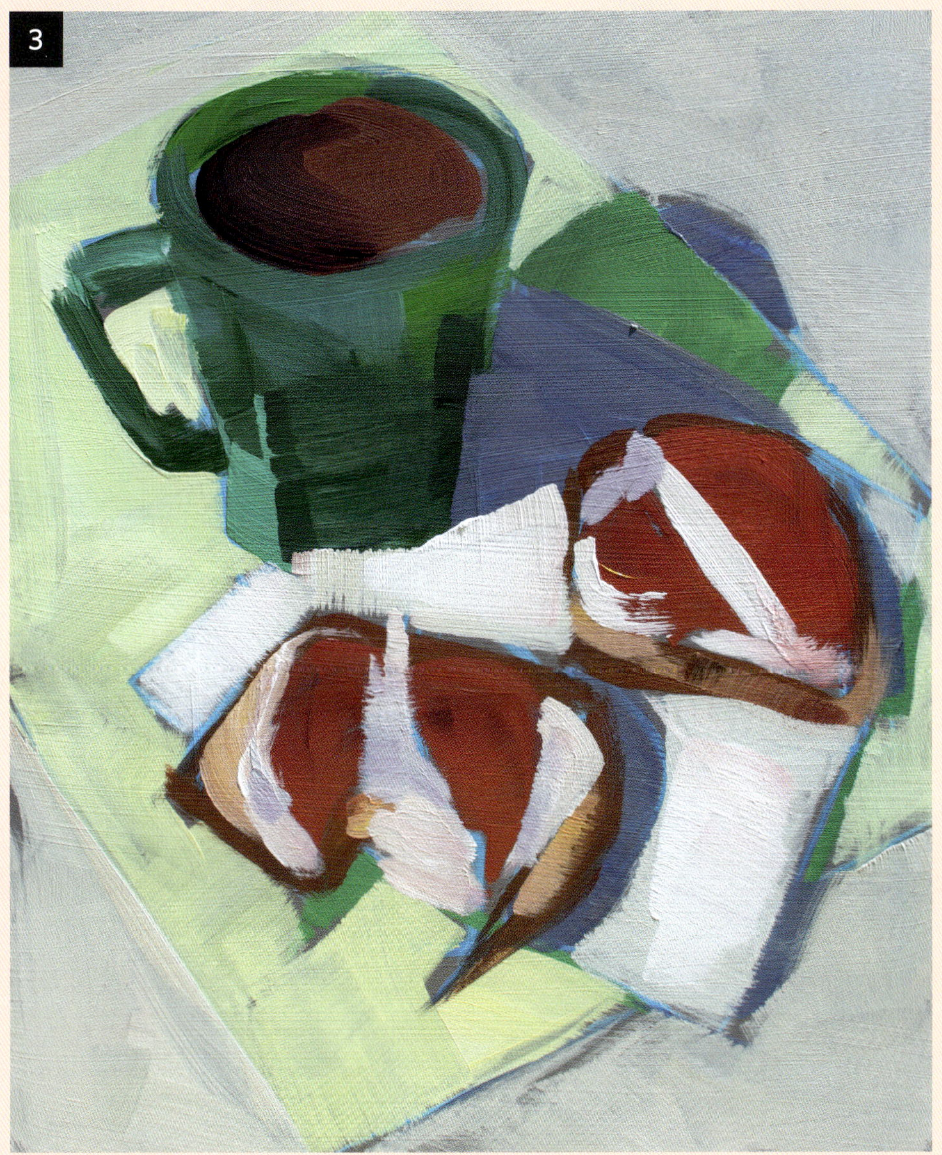

STEP 3

I employ a large brush, sized proportionately to the canvas, to block in the general forms within the composition. The aim here is to cover the canvas with broad shapes and forms, using markings from the previous step as guidelines for placing these larger elements. The size of the brush discourages detailed rendering, often reducing my application technique to dabbing and blocking. However, even with this straightforward approach, significant descriptive work can be achieved when adhering to accurate value and color choices. Sometimes, this step is my favorite, even though it doesn't always yield results I'm proud of. Its ability to communicate so much with so little is inherently valuable.

(continued)

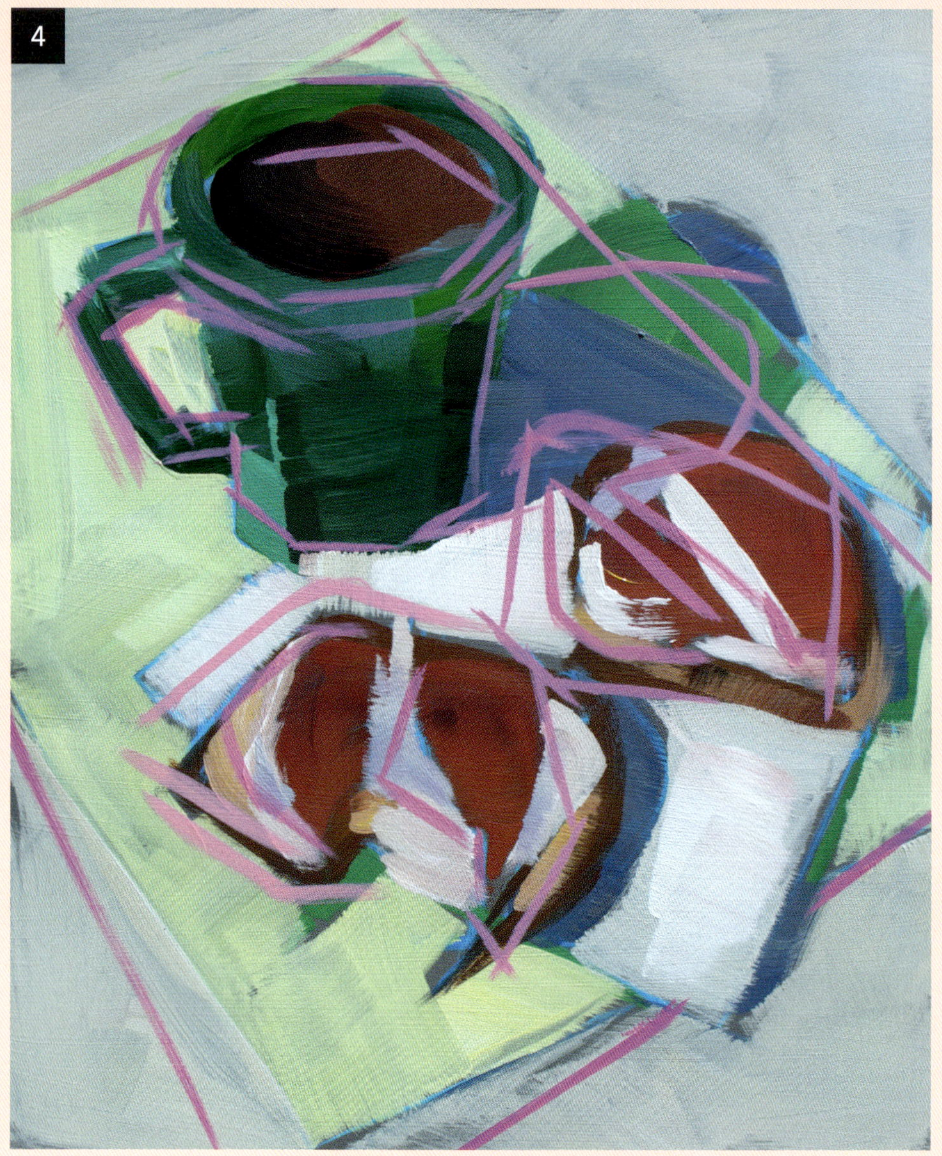

STEP 4

I use Quinacridone Magenta and Titanium White for my redraw line. Noticing that both pieces of toast were positioned slightly to the right, I correct them by shifting them a bit over and also adjusting the edge of the cup and the shadow.

MODERN STILL LIFE

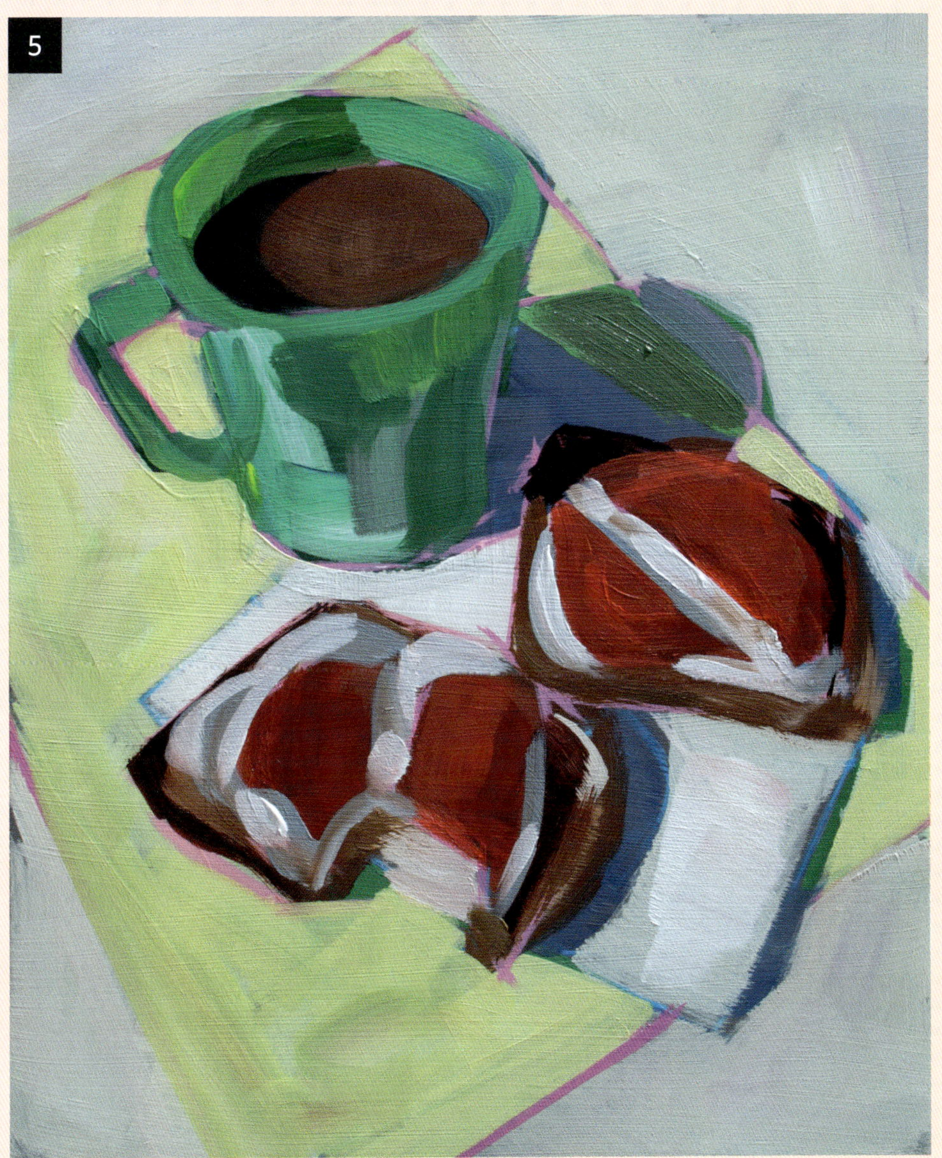

STEP 5

I undertake a more refined version of step 3 due to a noticeable amount of my drawing being off, necessitating the remixing of a significant portion of the painting. While the process of painting and repainting opaque layers might seem redundant, I view it as a generous painting approach that constructively leverages our inevitable mistakes. Despite the drawing inaccuracies, I am able to rework much of the painting, and certain elements from step 3 were retained, though many were not. With my redraw and the values mapped from the previous step, I enhance my color choices this time. The composition initially caught my eye due to the interplay between the green cup and red tomatoes, which are complementary colors, and the intriguing lighting effect created by the yellow paper and its shadows. Though the primary goal of this step is to address the drawing issues, since step 3 had transformed the gray background into colors much closer to my desired end point, I can focus more on finding the yellows in the cup and emphasizing the vibrant reds in the tomatoes.

(continued)

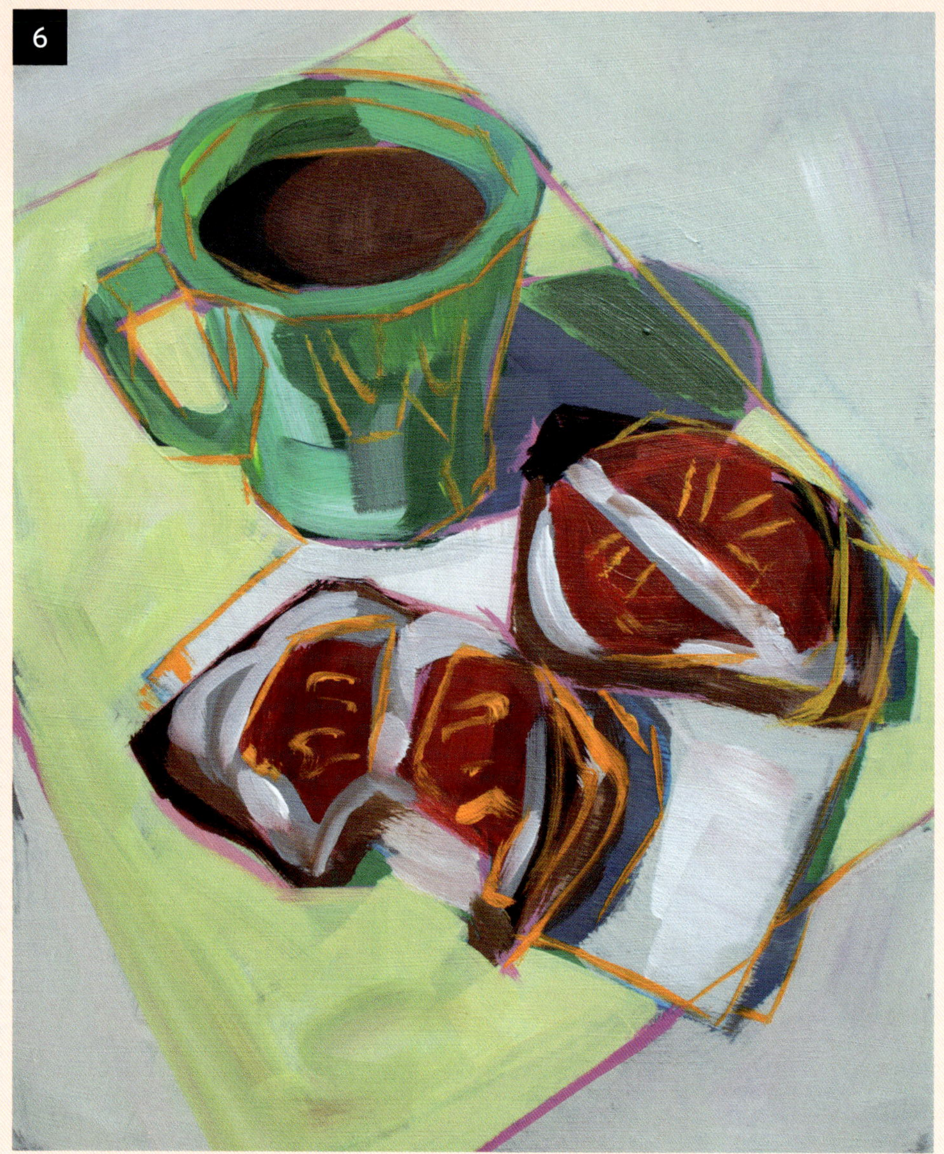

STEP 6

I mix Cadmium Yellow Light with a touch of Cadmium Red Medium to create an orange color for my redraw line.

This step is less about correcting drawing errors and more about identifying and refining some of the smaller and perhaps more subtle details of the painting. Occasionally, details can benefit from utilizing another redraw to discern additional nuances. In this instance, I focus on the segments in the tomatoes from the lighter parts of the flesh to the deeper, as well as the shadows being reflected off of the green mug. While there were a few slight drawing errors, nothing substantial needs to be fixed in this step.

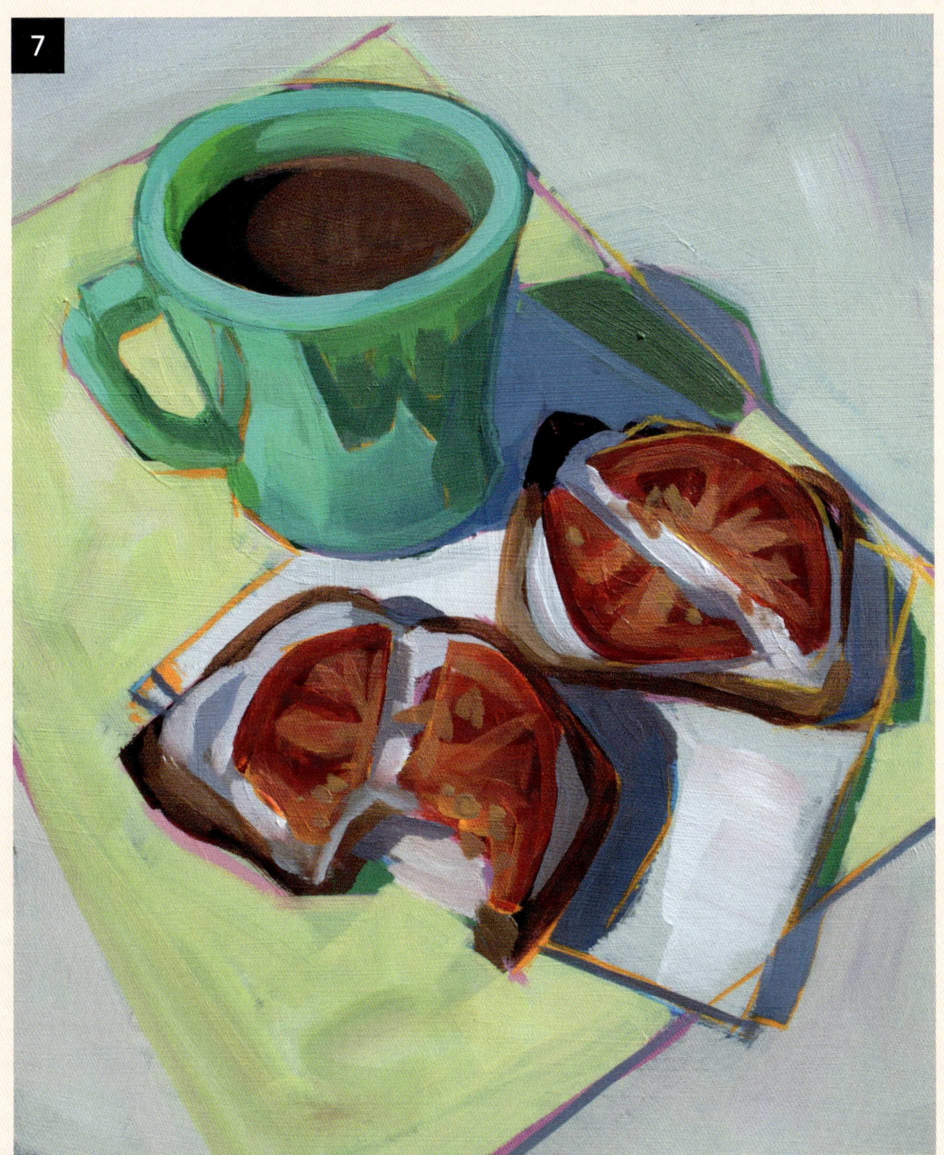

STEP 7

Now, I explore and refine higher-level details, particularly those that I aimed to indicate in the previous step. I focus on the nuances within the tomatoes and fine-tune the shadows and reflections on the mug. It's crucial to articulate these reflections and shadows in a way that doesn't diverge significantly in color and value from the mug's surface, ensuring it won't read as an entirely different object. Often, when dealing with pronounced reflections or shadows on an object, I find it beneficial to err toward making them more homogeneous with the object's surface color. If a reflection seems too bright, consider blending it more with the surface color.

Additionally, I am able to further refine the shadows cast by the toast in this step.

(continued)

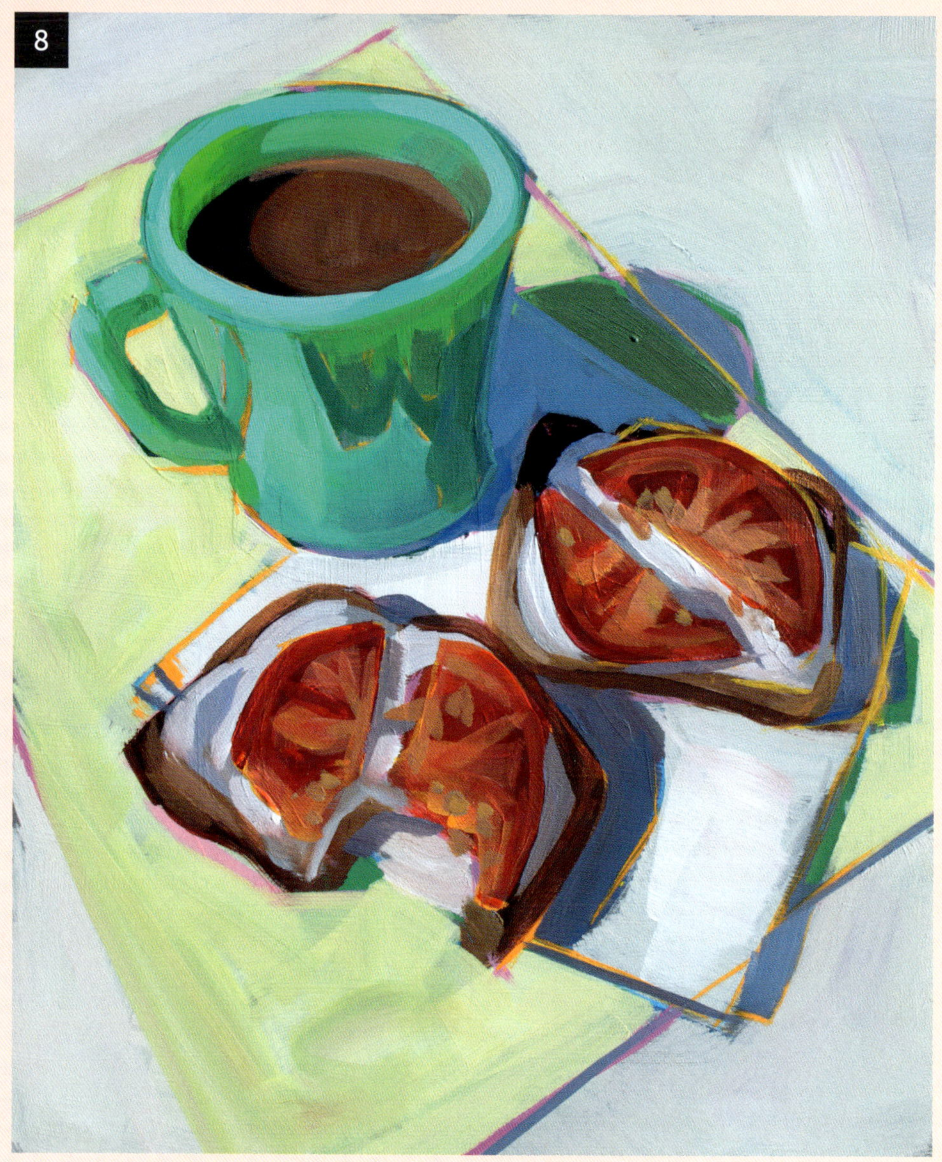

STEP 8

This step is primarily dedicated to refining the yellow paper, napkin, and background, emphasizing the necessity to not solely focus on the main subject but also the negative space throughout all phases of painting—a step I sometimes inadvertently neglect and thus strive to keep forefront in my mind.

I select a lighter, somewhat muted yellow for the distant part of the yellow paper, while opting for a bolder, more saturated yellow at the forefront. Despite knowing that the paper is one consistent yellow color, I employ the concept of color constancy in both the paper and shadows to convey lighting and atmosphere, exaggerating atmospheric perspective by having a muted background and an intense foreground to inject depth into the painting, avoiding flatness. I also utilize color constancy in the discernible shadows, not to describe light quality, as will be discussed in chapter 6, but to indicate to viewers that the apparent blue in sections of the paper and napkin isn't an actual color change, but a shadow—likely from the toast or mug—imparting a slightly cooler and darker hue to those areas.

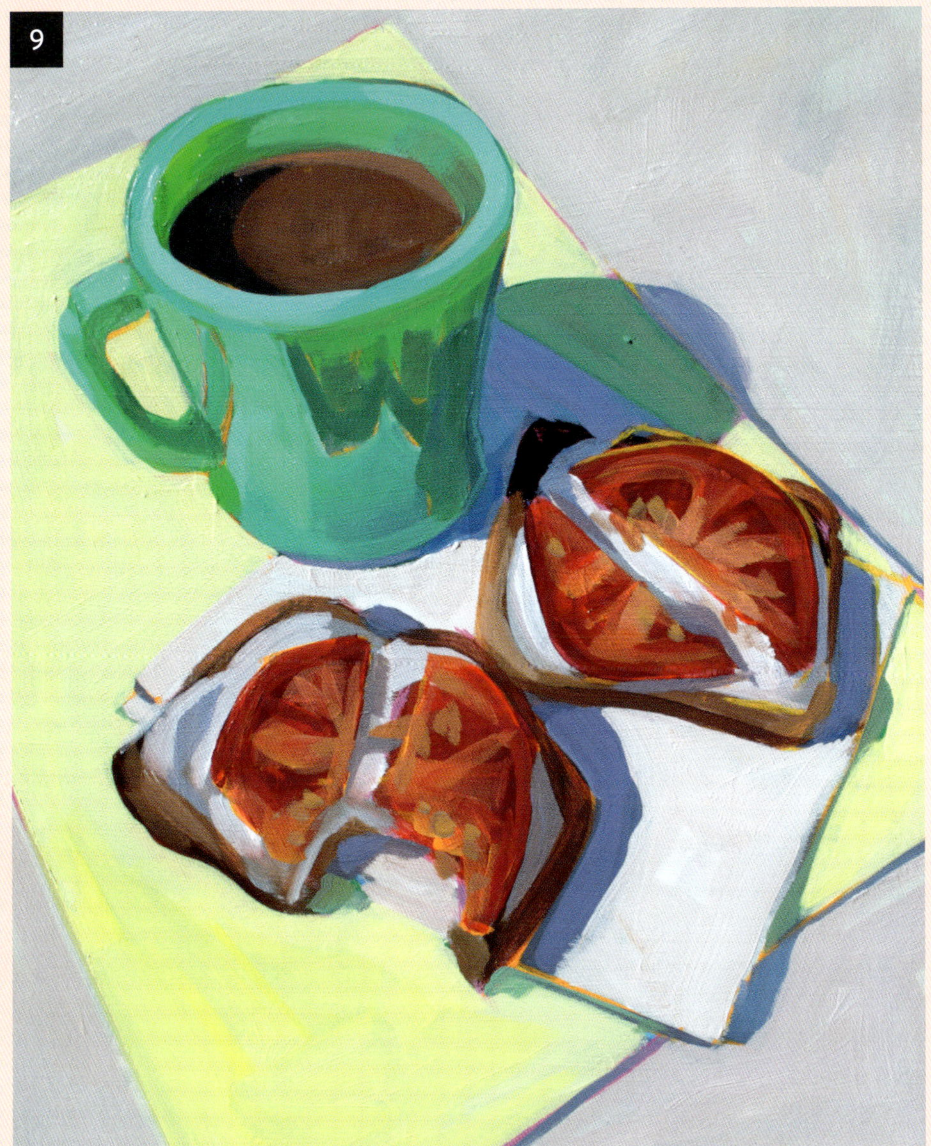

STEP 9

In this final step, I insert the final details, including highlights, and make slight refinements to the reflections on the cup and coffee surface. Sometimes, an element in a painting, such as the coffee here, might appear complete until other parts of the artwork evolve, necessitating further development to maintain harmony across the piece. I very much enjoyed painting the tomatoes and mayonnaise on the toast, which led me to further refine the cup and coffee. Such unexpected enhancements can challenge and develop your abilities as a painter. I also integrate highlights in this step, keeping in mind that they should not define form and therefore saving them for last.

Highlights convey information about texture. For example, paper does not require highlights as it is matte, whereas tomatoes, with their juicy and glossy nature, exhibit a more specular quality and therefore reflect highlights, which I added. The mayonnaise, while slightly wet and shiny, does not possess the same specular (mirror-like) quality as the tomatoes, so its highlights are not as starkly white. The highlights on the mug, being a light green instead of a paler white, assist in accurately communicating its texture and quality. Highlights deserve close attention due to their importance in conveying an object's characteristics.

COLOR RELATIONSHIPS

Color relationships in painting are a fascinating yet challenging aspect of the art form. While it's essential to enjoy the act of painting and its ability to express our inner thoughts and ideas, we can't overlook the critical role that color and value analysis plays, especially when mixed with drawing. Painting often involves straddling the line between actual color and perceptual color, which can be quite tricky.

To illustrate this complexity, consider the blue and black vs. white and gold "The Dress" illusion that sent the Internet into an uproar several years ago. If you recall, there was an image of a dress with horizontal lines of two different colors, and an intense debate developed over what two colors were present on the dress. Some people saw white and gold, while others clearly saw blue and black. How could a stark divide like this transpire over color, something we're used to being so clearly evident?

This is actually a great example of how color perception can vary significantly from one person to another. At its core, this phenomenon highlights something known as *color constancy*. Color constancy is the tendency of our brains to interpret colors based on how light affects them in the environment.

Take a large tree casting a shadow on a bright, sunny day. The grass in the sunlit areas appears as a vibrant, yellowish green, while the grass under the tree's shadow takes on a darker, more muted green, perhaps even a slightly bluish tint in comparison to the sunlit grass. What's fascinating is that we don't perceive the grass as having changed colors within the shadow.

Instead, we understand that the grass likely maintains the same shade of green, and it's the tree's shadow that alters our perception of its color. This color difference can be quite stark. If you were to isolate swatches of the bright yellowish green and the dark, cool green and place them side by side without the context of the tree and the daylight, you'd likely assume they belong to different objects. However, our perception and the way we interpret the world around us through our eyes make this phenomenon seem perfectly logical. This is where the magic of color constancy comes into play.

Now, when some people saw the dress as blue and black, they were perceiving the dress colors as presented on their screens accurately. However, those who saw it as white and gold were viewing a dress that had been exposed to high levels of light. In fact, if you experiment with the exposure settings on the dress photo, you'll notice that, for many, it becomes possible to see both white and gold or blue and black, depending on the exposure level. In painting, we often find ourselves working with and sometimes challenging this inherent tendency for color constancy. It's a dance between embracing the logic of perception and pushing the boundaries of what we can create on canvas.

Colors don't exist in isolation. They're affected by light, surface texture, and most crucially, the surrounding colors.

> Colors don't exist in isolation. They're affected by light, surface texture, and most crucially, the surrounding colors.

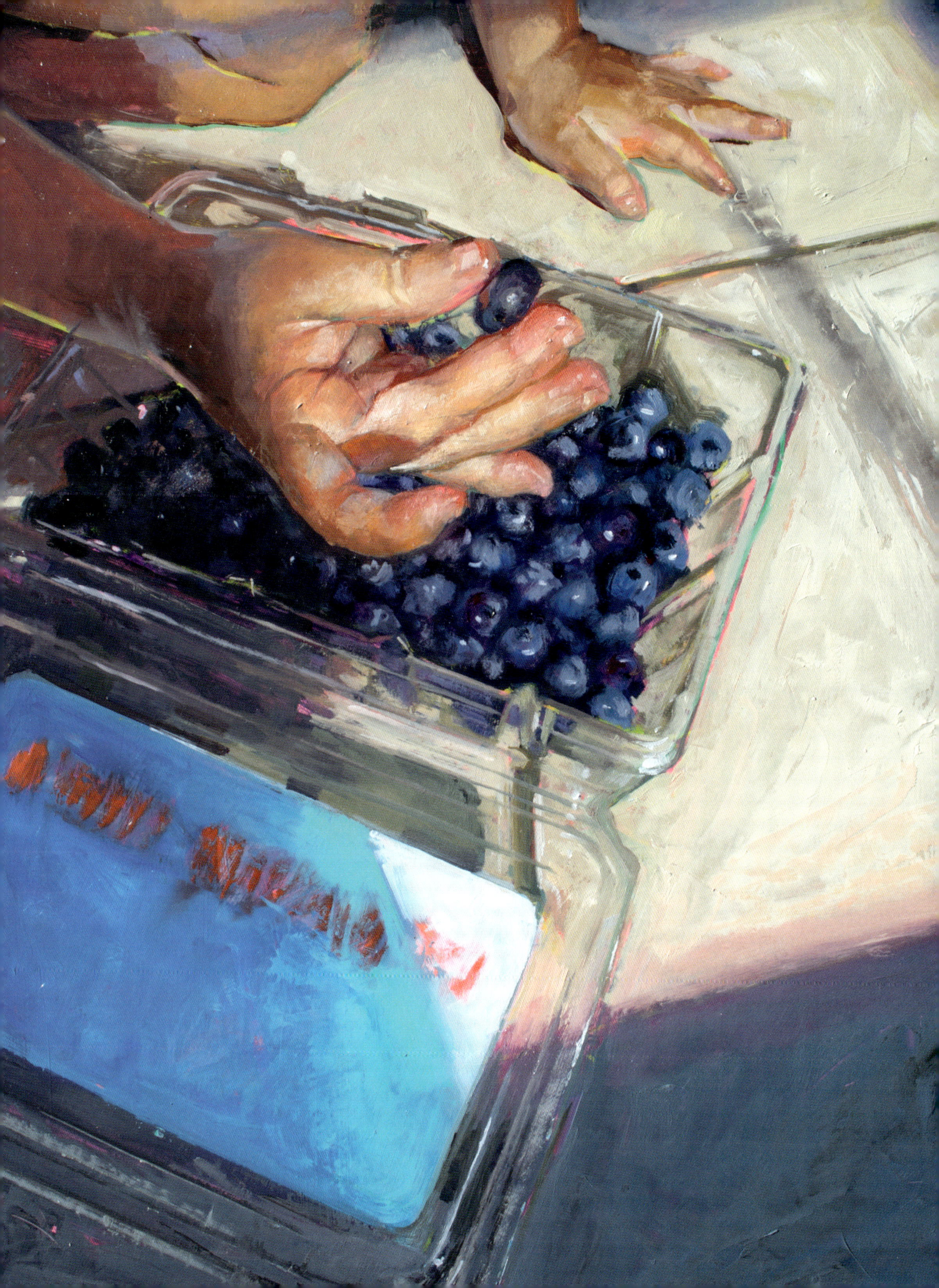

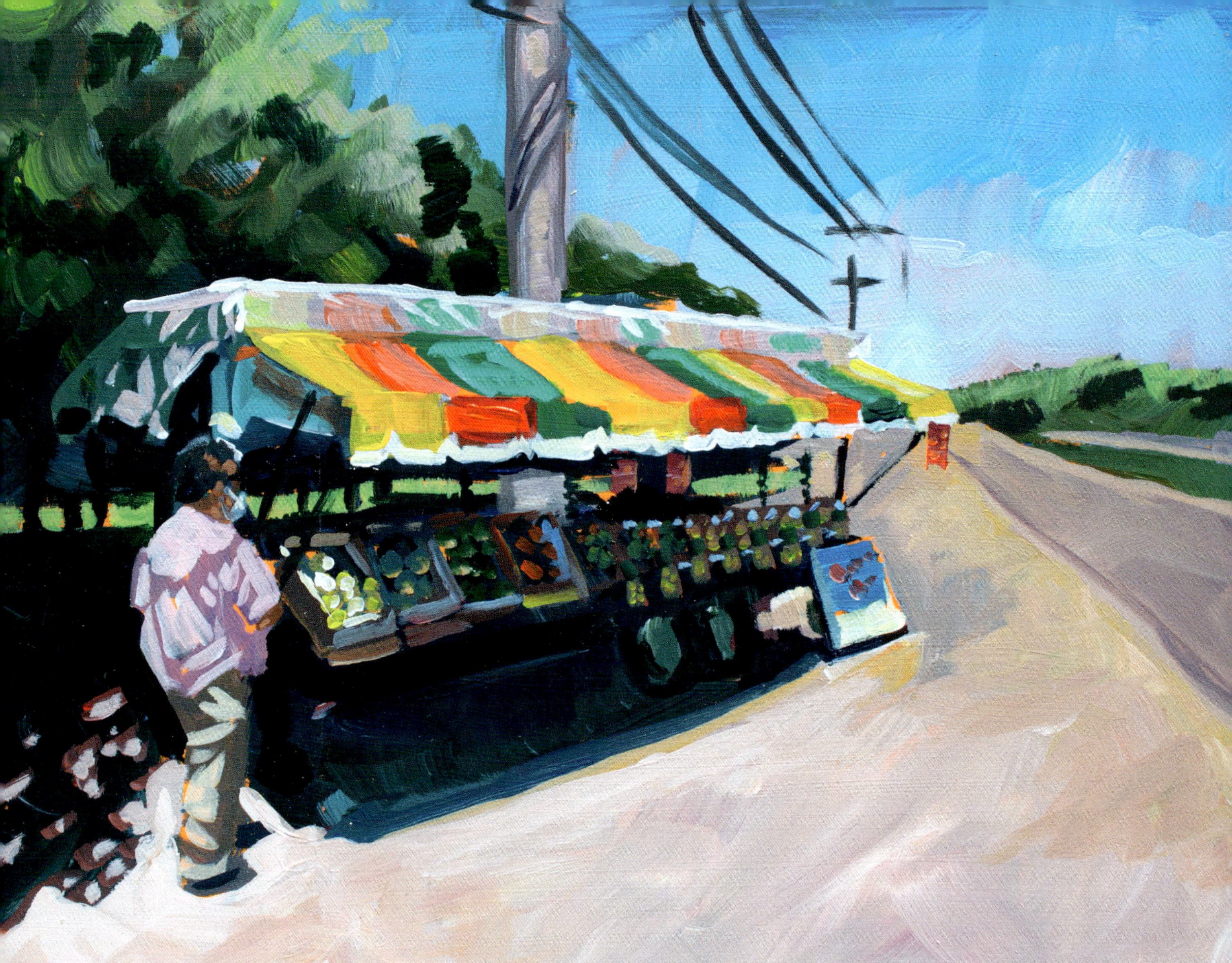

Key Terms

Perceptual color is how we perceive color considering influencing factors like light, surrounding colors, and surface texture.

Actual color is the exact, objective shade of a color, akin to a specific Pantone number.

Typically, individuals inexperienced with color might assume they always encounter actual color. In reality, our encounters are primarily with perceptual color. In painting, this dynamic interplay between perceptual and actual color presents challenges. Painters interpret the color of a reference or subject (perceptual) and re-create it on their canvas (actual). They then gauge its contextual sense against other colors, returning to the realm of perceptual color.

The Act of Painting

Translating colors onto a canvas is intricate. It involves adjustments, mixings, and understanding the transformative nature of colors upon each other, as defined by the following color terminology:

- **Color relationships** Understanding how colors interact with each other can be a linchpin for painting success.

- **Complementary colors** Recognizing a color's complement aids in both actual and perceptual color. For instance, knowing blue complements orange helps in muting the saturation of orange. In a predominantly yellow painting, a true gray may appear violet due to color constancy.

- **Color constancy** Our eyes adjust to understand light nuances in a scene. A shadow doesn't register as a different object. Instead, our eyes perceive it as the same object under different lighting.

- **Simultaneous contrast** Placing complementary colors adjacent to each other exaggerates their differences.

- **Color harmonies** These can include analogous colors (groups of three colors next to each other on the color wheel), triadic colors (sets of three colors that are equally spaced from each other on the color wheel), and neutral colors, among others. Understanding such harmonies aids in creating a cohesive and appealing painting. In essence, to navigate the labyrinth of color in painting, you must grasp these principles, practice continually, and develop an intuitive understanding of colors' intricate relationships.

COLOR STUDY

Now, you're prepared to dive into a color study. In the preceding chapter, we covered the art of creating a map—a foundational drawing that employs mapping techniques for accurate proportions. We also delved into the significance of valuing not just chroma but also value. As we progress, we're essentially adding another layer to our painting juggling act.

If we do imagine painting as juggling, we're now managing drawing, value, and color simultaneously. It's vital to underscore a key practice: just as I advised you not to dive too deeply into the extremes of light or dark values immediately—providing room for evolution in the painting's development—I urge you to adopt the same approach with chroma and saturation.

Particularly with acrylics, it's easy to quickly amplify the saturation, which can lead to a flat appearance. With limited palettes, this oversaturation is harder to achieve, given that you're working with only three colors at their chromatic zenith. However, my recommendation is this: especially in the initial stages, as you begin defining the broad strokes and foundational forms, lean towards muted, low-saturation colors. As the painting unfolds, gradually elevate the chroma to your desired intensity. In essence, exercise restraint in the early saturation levels, granting you more freedom to intensify color later in the process.

The final and perhaps most crucial lesson when it comes to mixing within a limited palette—beyond the foundational knowledge gained from learning to blend your own hues—is realizing how contextual color is within a painting.

Consider my example of the Zorn limited palette. Essentially, this palette doesn't possess a genuine blue. There's a cool-leaning black (Ivory Black) and the Titanium White that tilts slightly towards cool, but you're only going to get a cool gray at its bluest. Yet, despite this, one can easily grasp the essence of the painting because the colors function relative to each other. I suggest beginning with a primary color limited palette. Then, challenge yourself to fully comprehend the context of color. This not only sharpens a crucial skill, but also prevents the pitfall of becoming overly focused on local color—a common inclination among beginners.

While ensuring color accuracy is undoubtedly essential and something you'll naturally focus on as you blend hues, it's enlightening to recognize just how much you can deviate from local color and yet maintain clarity. In fact, many iconic painters have crafted moody, captivating visuals by veering significantly from local color, ensuring the rest of their palette complements this diversion.

This exploration will materialize differently for every artist, which is why I recommend delving into it individually. Experiment with limited color palettes throughout your practice, introducing a spectrum of shades.

Zorn Palette Step-by-Step

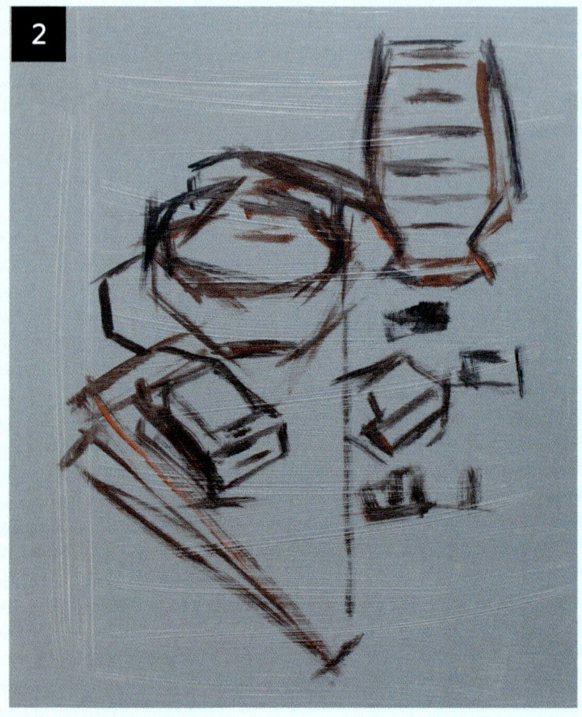

STEP 1

Begin by selecting a neutral mid-value color to prime your canvas. In this case, I have chosen a chromatic gray as the ideal priming color.

STEP 2

Within this step, carefully select a drawing color that has distinct value and color characteristics, differing from your chosen background color. The purpose of this step is to concentrate on the proportions and measurements of the boundaries of your objects, ensuring that your composition maintains accurate proportions. Pay particular attention to the placement of outermost objects and their proximity to the perimeter of your painting. In my own drawing, I discovered several errors during the initial evaluation, prompting me to utilize a reddish color to fix those mistakes.

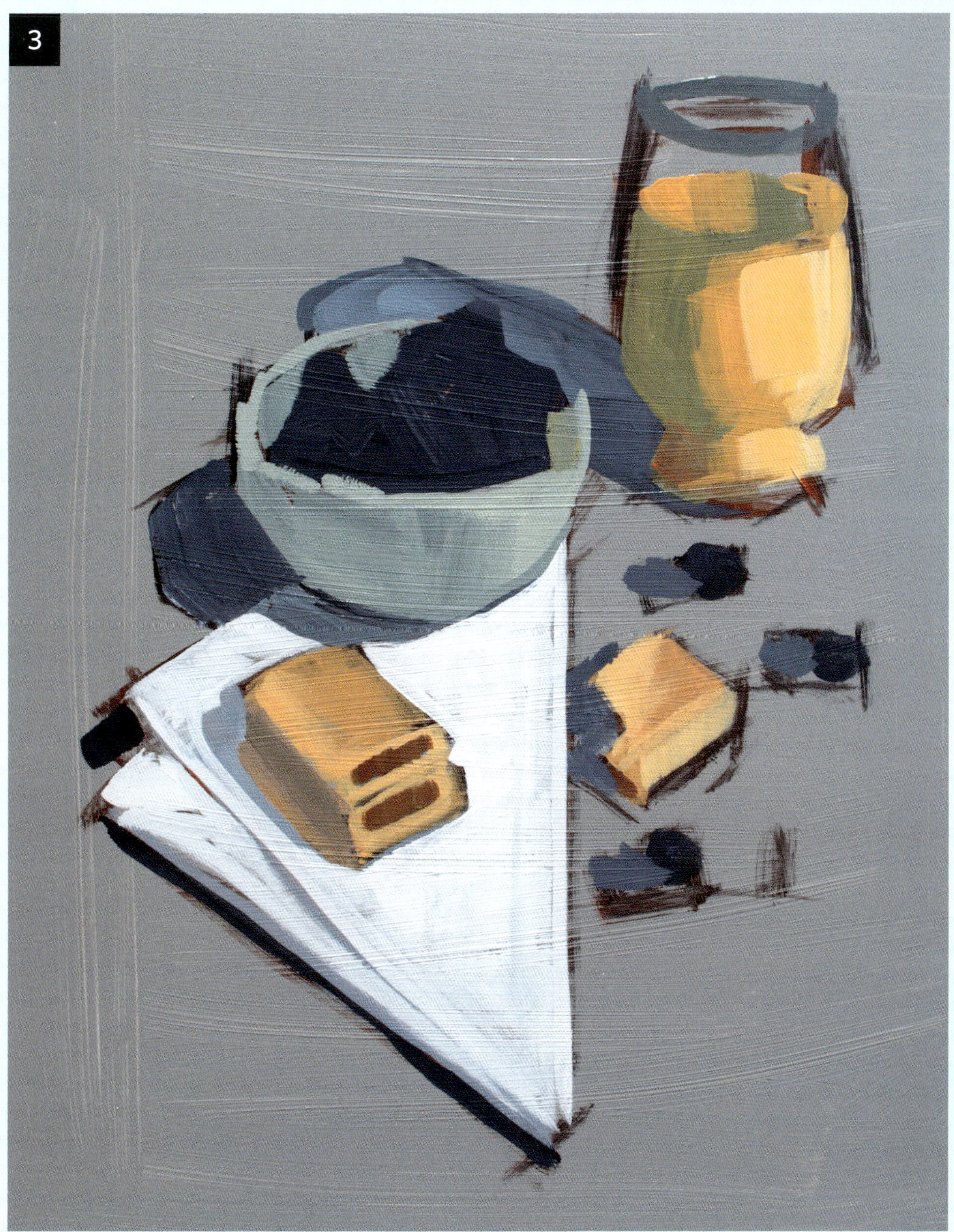

STEP 3

Utilize the limited colors on your palette and strive to accurately match the local color of your reference photo or the objects you are painting from. In this step, focus on painting the majority of your objects, excluding the background, while omitting intricate details. Instead, prioritize capturing larger areas of value and color. Keep in mind that in subsequent steps, you will have the opportunity to refine the painting.

(continued)

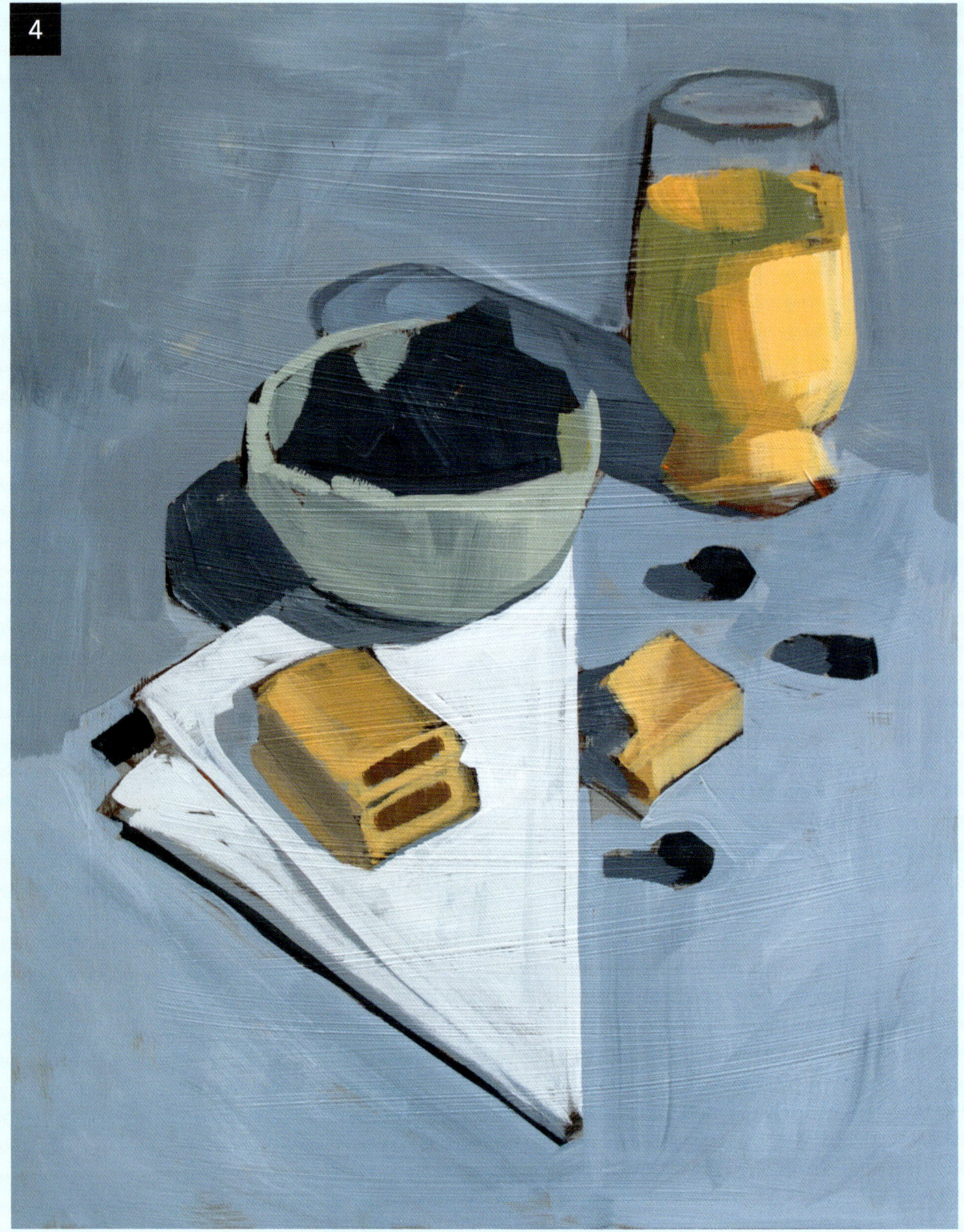

STEP 4

During this step, I focused on blocking in the background values. It's important to note that even though the background is made of a single piece of construction paper, its value subtly changes as it recedes in space. Additionally, I observed subtle variations in the intensity of the blue color used for the background. It's crucial to avoid treating the background color as a flat, single value if it does not accurately reflect what you are observing. Take into account the nuanced changes in value and color intensity when painting the background.

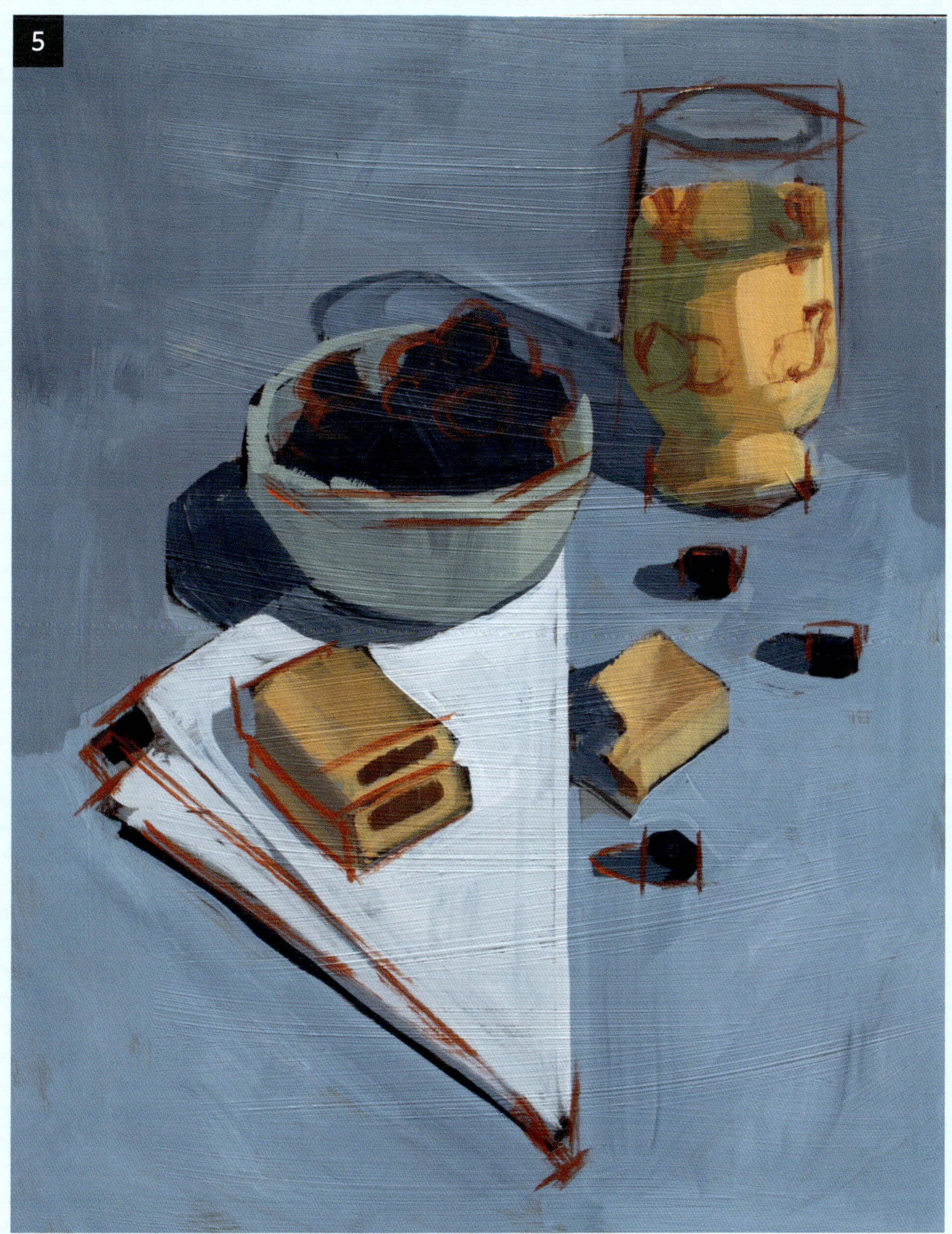

STEP 5

During this step, I employed the use of red as a redraw line to identify and rectify any drawing errors that had accumulated in the previous steps. Since my focus was on capturing larger value areas rather than intricate details, the overall drawing could have become slightly distorted. Additionally, as I became more acquainted with my reference photo, I started noticing drawing errors that were previously unnoticed. To differentiate the redraw lines from the colors of objects in my still life, I intentionally chose a color, such as red, that is not typically present in my composition. This allows the redraw lines to stand out and serve as clear indicators of the drawing rather than blending in with the objects themselves.

(continued)

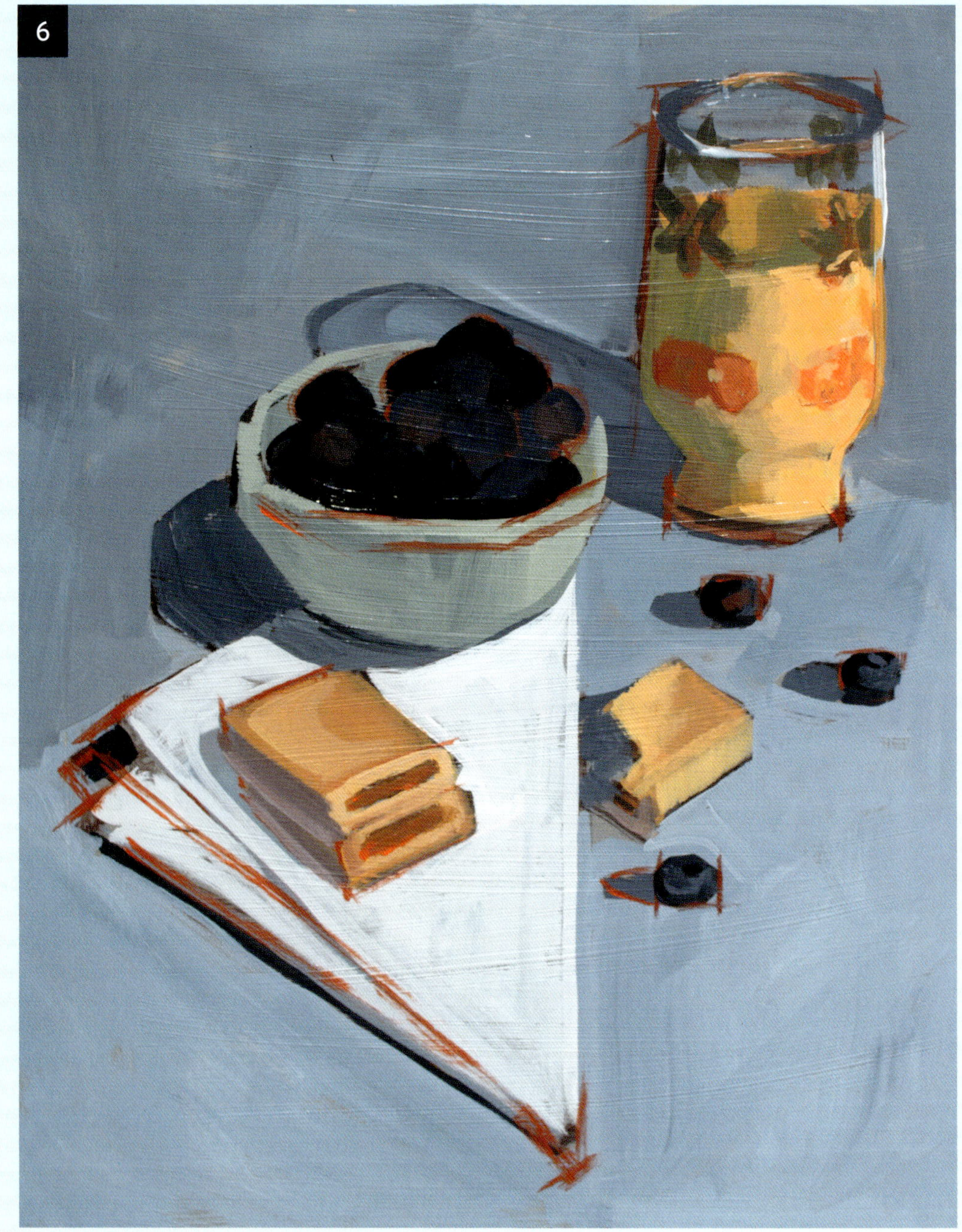

STEP 6

At this stage, I have both redefined drawing lines and a value map, which was created during the rough paint-in executed in steps 3 and 4. With these additional references, my painting decisions can now be fine-tuned and more precise, as I have gained more information to work with. It's crucial to shift to smaller brushes at this point, enabling me to add greater detail and refine the composition further. In this particular instance, I focused on adding details to the orange juice cup and defining the appearance of the blueberries. I dedicated time to rendering the blueberries until they achieved a more distinct and defined look.

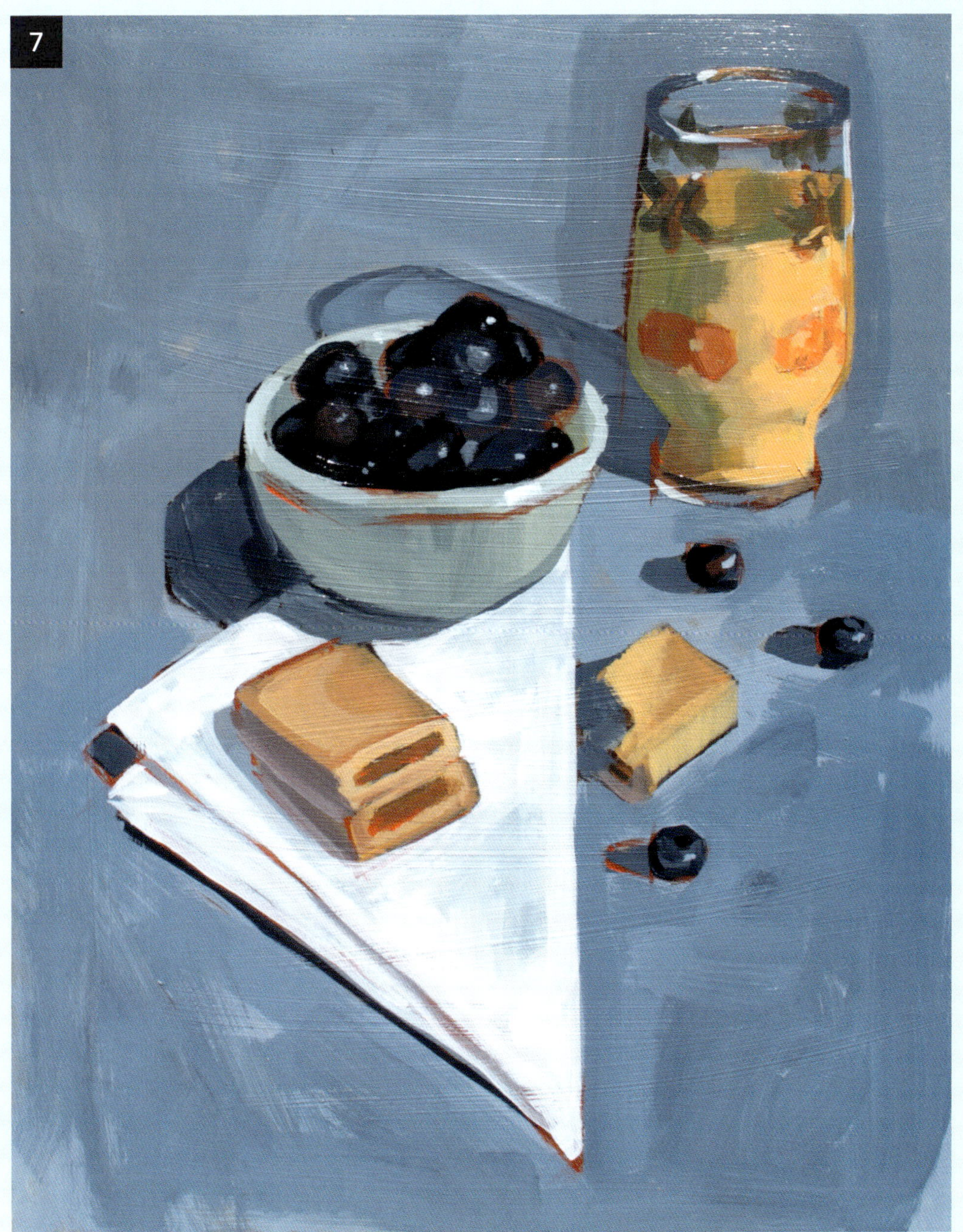

STEP 7

I focused on adding the final highlights and refining details to bring the objects, such as the blueberries, to their full realization. Additionally, I conducted a final analysis of the values to ensure that they harmonize effectively with the overall composition. Notably, I took the opportunity in this step to darken the value of the background color, represented by the blue construction paper, as I perceived it to be too light in the previous step.

This final step primarily involves fine-tuning, which includes a combination of highlighting, subtle value adjustments, and adding more information to transform the previously indistinct color and value blobs into fully rendered objects. Although relatively less paint is applied during this stage compared to previous steps, it is in this last part that the most important details emerge, bringing the artwork to life.

(continued)

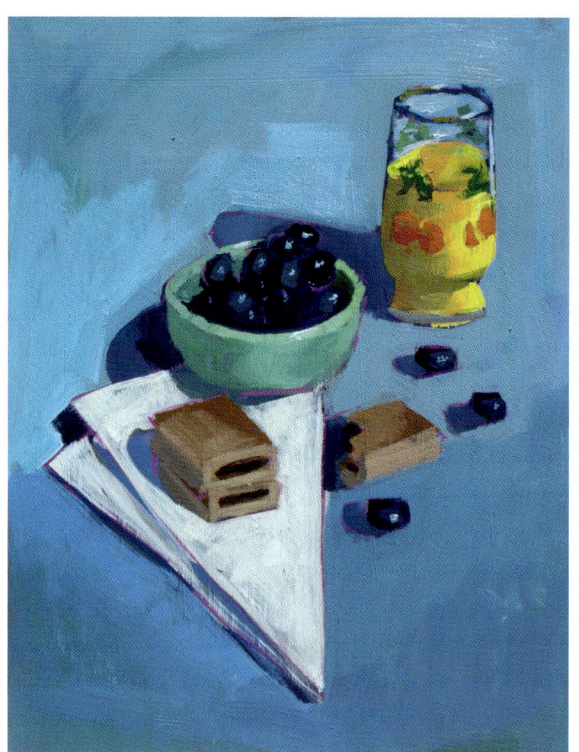

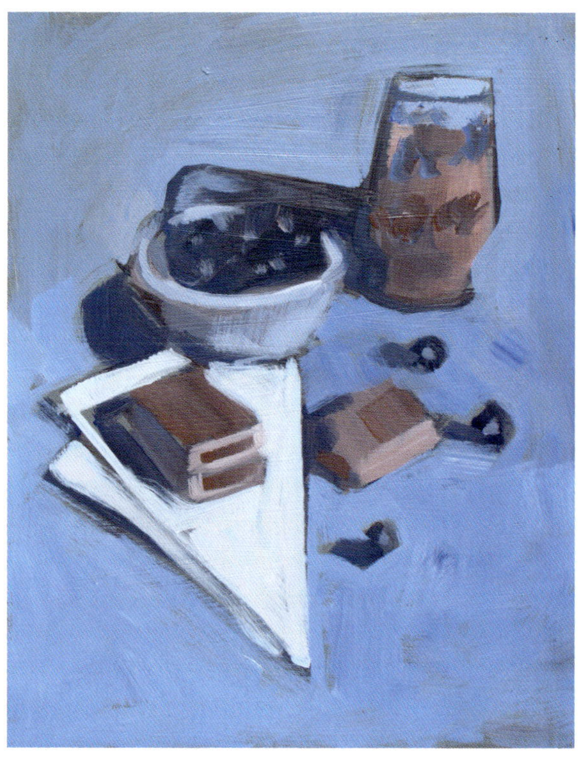

CMY (Cyan, Magenta, and Yellow) Limited Color Palette

For the CMY plus white limited color study, I utilized Quinacridone Magenta, Phthalo Blue (Green Shade), Cadmium Yellow Light, and Titanium White. This particular limited color palette is far from restrictive. In fact, it happens to be one of my personal favorites. The palette consists of cyan, magenta, and primary yellow, akin to the color palette used in printing and photographic reproduction. This palette allows for a remarkably extensive range of colors due to its broad color spectrum. Despite being considered "limited," this palette grants the ability to achieve highly saturated colors in virtually any direction on the color wheel. It serves as my artistic home base, and as evident in this study, I pushed the limits of chroma while maintaining a sense of visual harmony.

Warm/Cool Split Color Palette

For the warm/cool split limited color palette, I utilized Burnt Sienna, Ultramarine Blue, and Titanium White. This study focuses on the interplay between warm and cool colors, with the addition of white to expand the color range. Despite the limited palette, I was able to explore almost the entire value spectrum, achieving a rich, low-intensity blue for elements like the blueberry bowl. However, I encountered some limitations in terms of pushing the yellow hues in high-chroma areas of my reference, such as the orange juice and the green of the bowl.

Nevertheless, I am continually amazed by the breadth of colors that can be achieved with just two colors plus white. Engaging in a split color limited color study always provides valuable insights and learning opportunities.

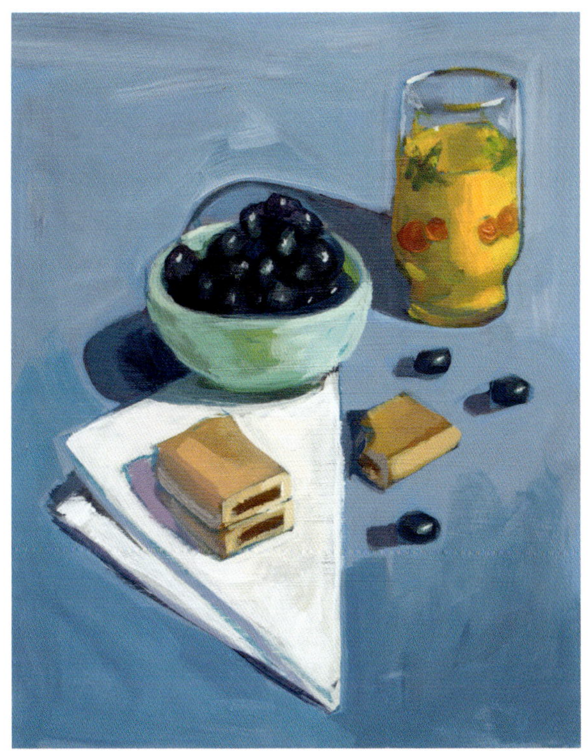

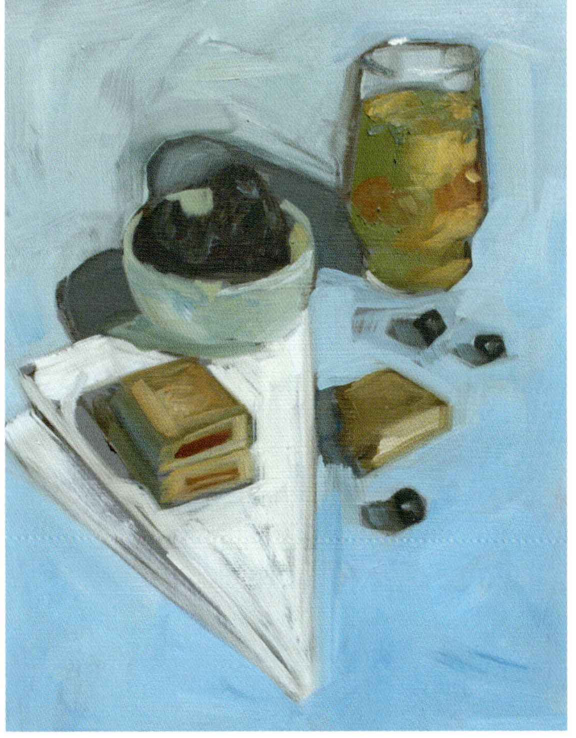

Variation of Primary Color Palette

In this variation of a primary colors limited palette, I used Alizarin Crimson Hue; Cerulean Blue, Chromium; Benzimidazolone Yellow Medium; and Titanium White. This palette is a straightforward representation of the primary colors—red, blue, and yellow. Although the final result may bear some resemblance to the CMY color palette, I found my ability to achieve certain yellows and pinks slightly limited.

Nevertheless, this palette still offers a comprehensive range of colors as it incorporates all three primary hues. I wanted to showcase this study to demonstrate that with relatively good primaries that possess opacity and high intensity, you can still achieve a wide array of colors.

Earthy Primary Color Palette

For the Earthy Primaries limited color palette, I utilized Yellow Ochre; Transparent Red Iron Oxide; Cerulean Blue, Chromium; and Titanium White. In this palette, I opted for earthy alternatives for all the primaries except for Cerulean Blue, Chromium. Despite the lower intensity and darkness of the yellow and the transparency of the red, I discovered that I could still achieve a considerable color range.

However, there were limitations in obtaining vibrant and light yellows and reds due to the nature of the chosen colors. Nevertheless, I was pleasantly surprised by the final image, which highlights the notion that colors only need to make sense within the context of their own world.

Despite the subdued nature of the orangey yellow representing bright orange juice and its contrast to the surrounding objects, along with the context clues provided by the glass and orange-themed imagery, it still successfully conveys the impression of orange juice.

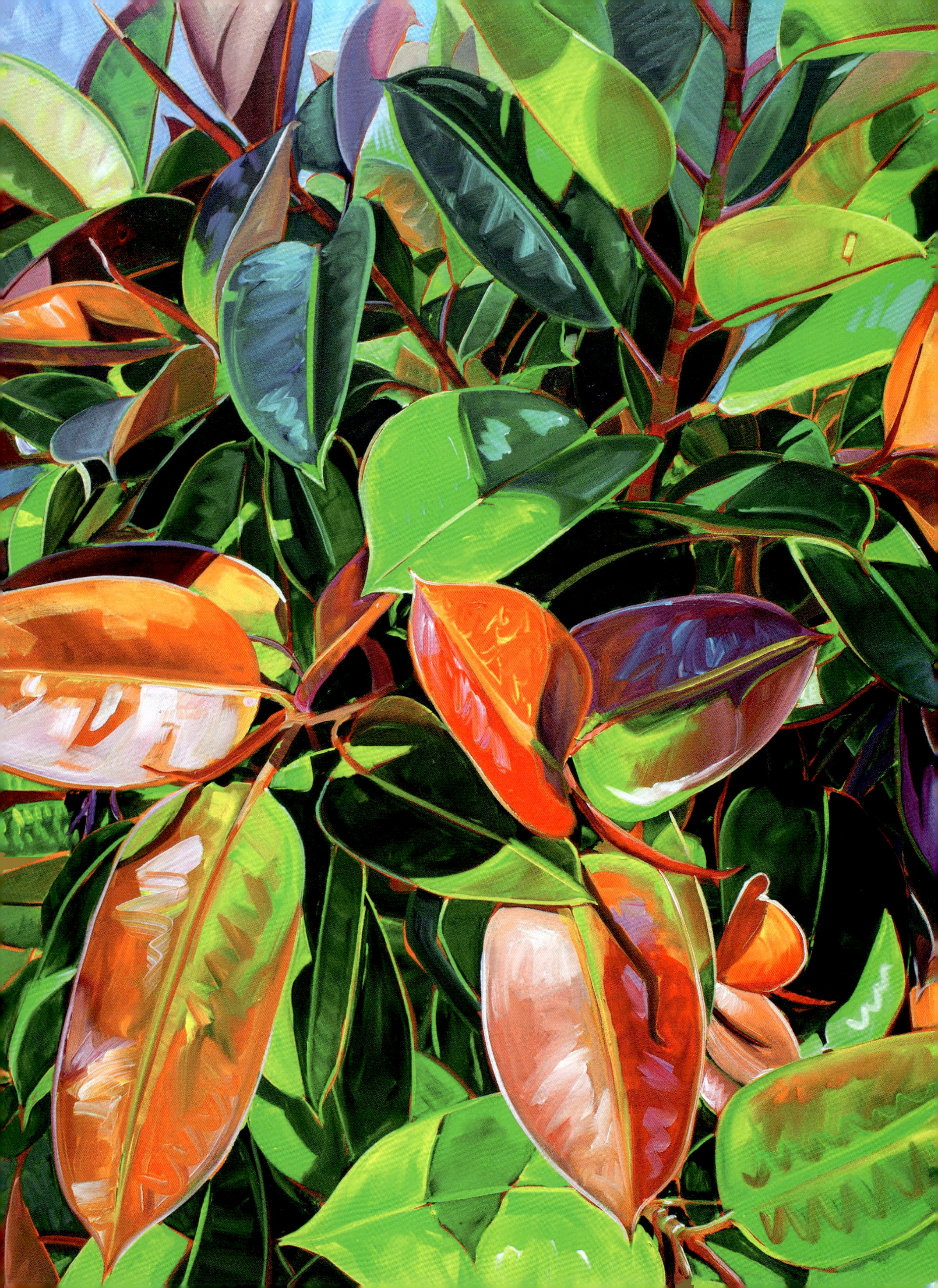

Warming &
Cooling

IN THE LIMITED COLOR PALETTES
section, I touched on the principle of *warming*
and *cooling* colors as a method to navigate
the color coordinates on your color wheel.
Essentially, any hue or color, be it red, green, red
orange, yellow green, blue, or violet, can possess
either a cool or warm tendency.

While the color wheel showcases both warm
and cool sides, it's vital to understand that color's
relationship with our psychology is profound.
Scientific studies have shown that cool colors,
like blues and greens, evoke sensations of feeling
cooler. Conversely, warm colors inspire a sense of
warmth. This psychological-color connection is
deeply embedded in us, as evident in marketing
strategies where colors like yellow and orange
induce hunger, while blue promotes calmness. In
the context of painting, one might aim to elicit a
sensation of lighting in the viewer.

A common question painters ask is, "How do
you capture that sense of lighting?" The answer
lies in adeptly navigating the warming and cooling of colors, in conjunction with maintaining
accurate values. Value imparts a lifelike realism
to your images, preventing them from appearing
cartoonish. By diligently focusing on values and
simultaneously playing the warming and cooling
game, you'll create a compelling sense of lighting
in your paintings.

Another crucial concept in this chapter is
color constancy. Color constancy asserts that
our brain discerns changes in color and value as
alterations in lighting rather than incongruent
colors. For instance, observing a parachute both
in shadow and light, we don't perceive them as
distinct colors or materials. Instead, we interpret
the darker segments as being in the shadow, a
phenomenon rooted in our lived experiences.
Thus, when viewing a painting, we instinctively
apply this understanding, reading changes in
color as effects of light and shadow, even on a
two-dimensional canvas.

To convey a shadow, you must introduce a distinct change in value. Enhancing that shadow to
depict true light involves delving into the warming and cooling dynamics. Essentially, everything

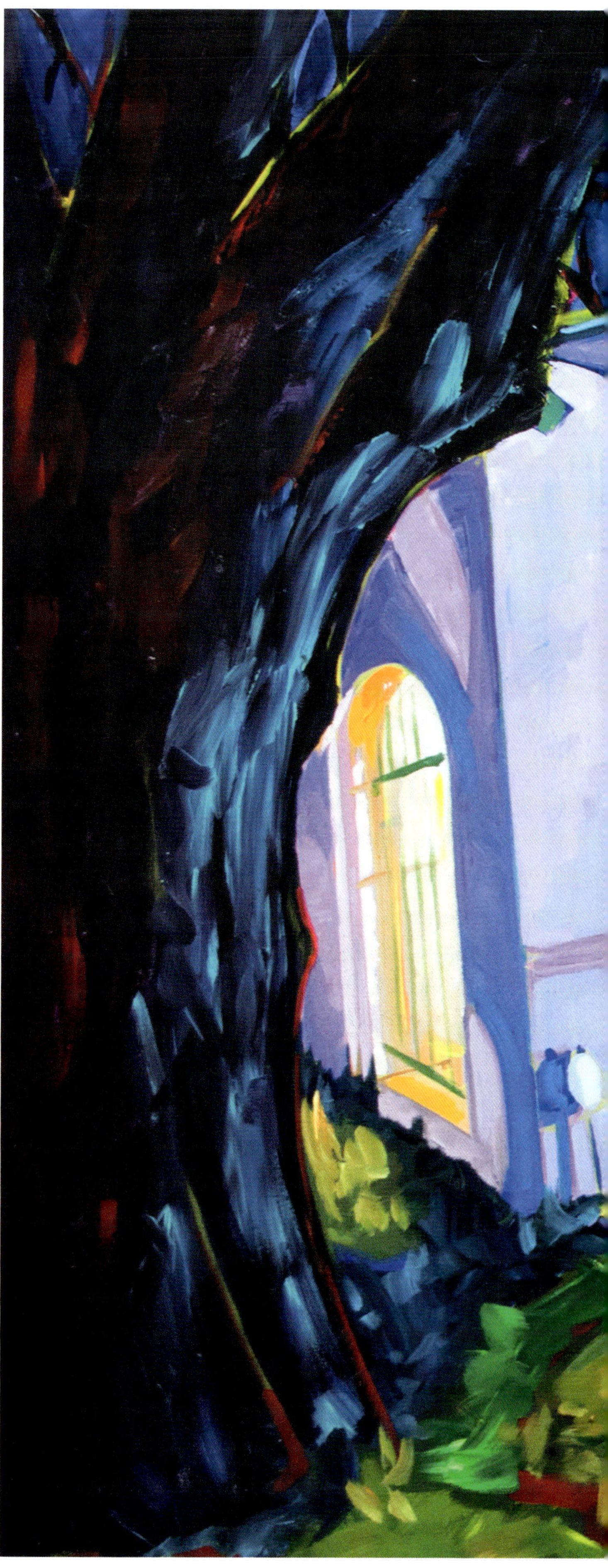

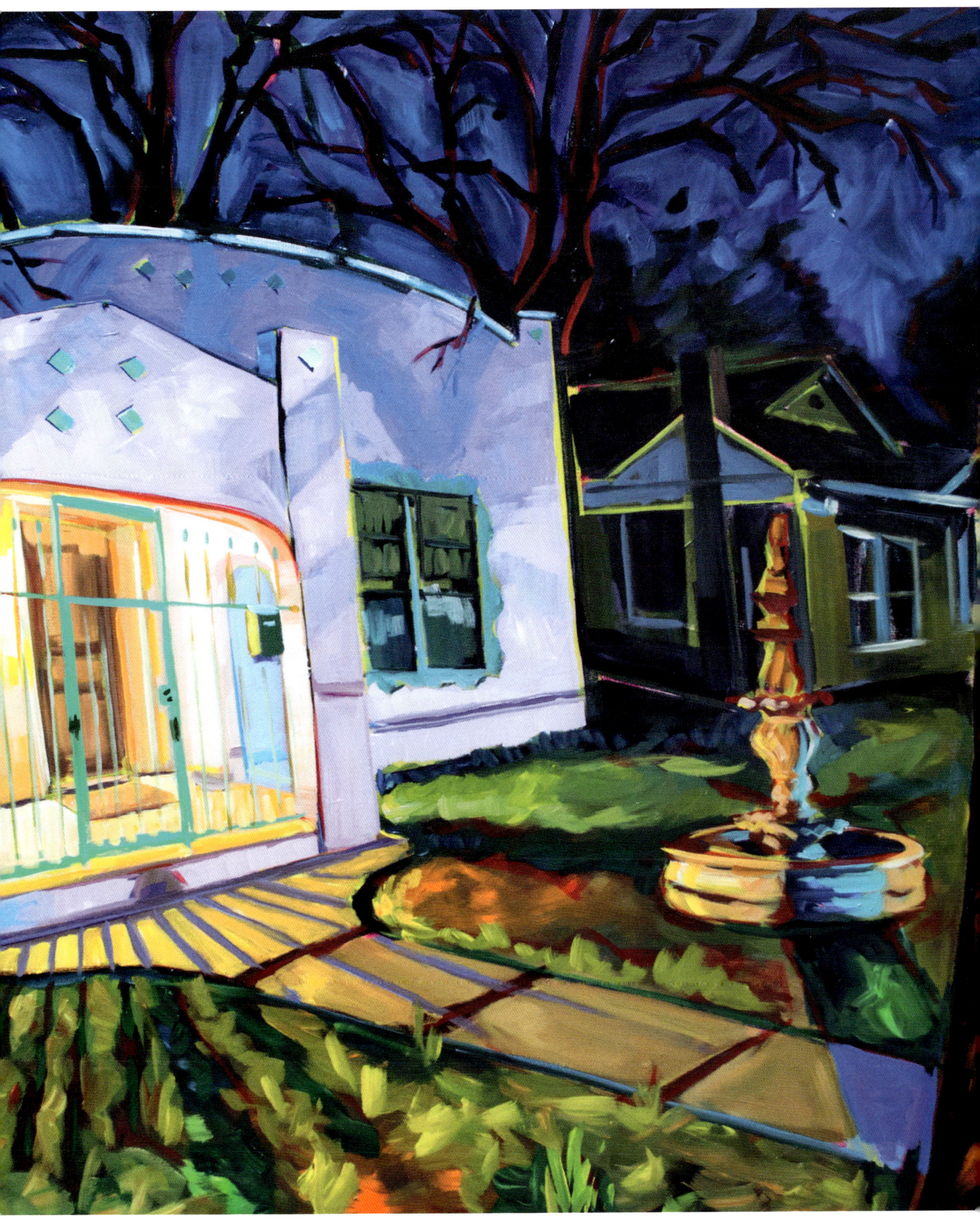

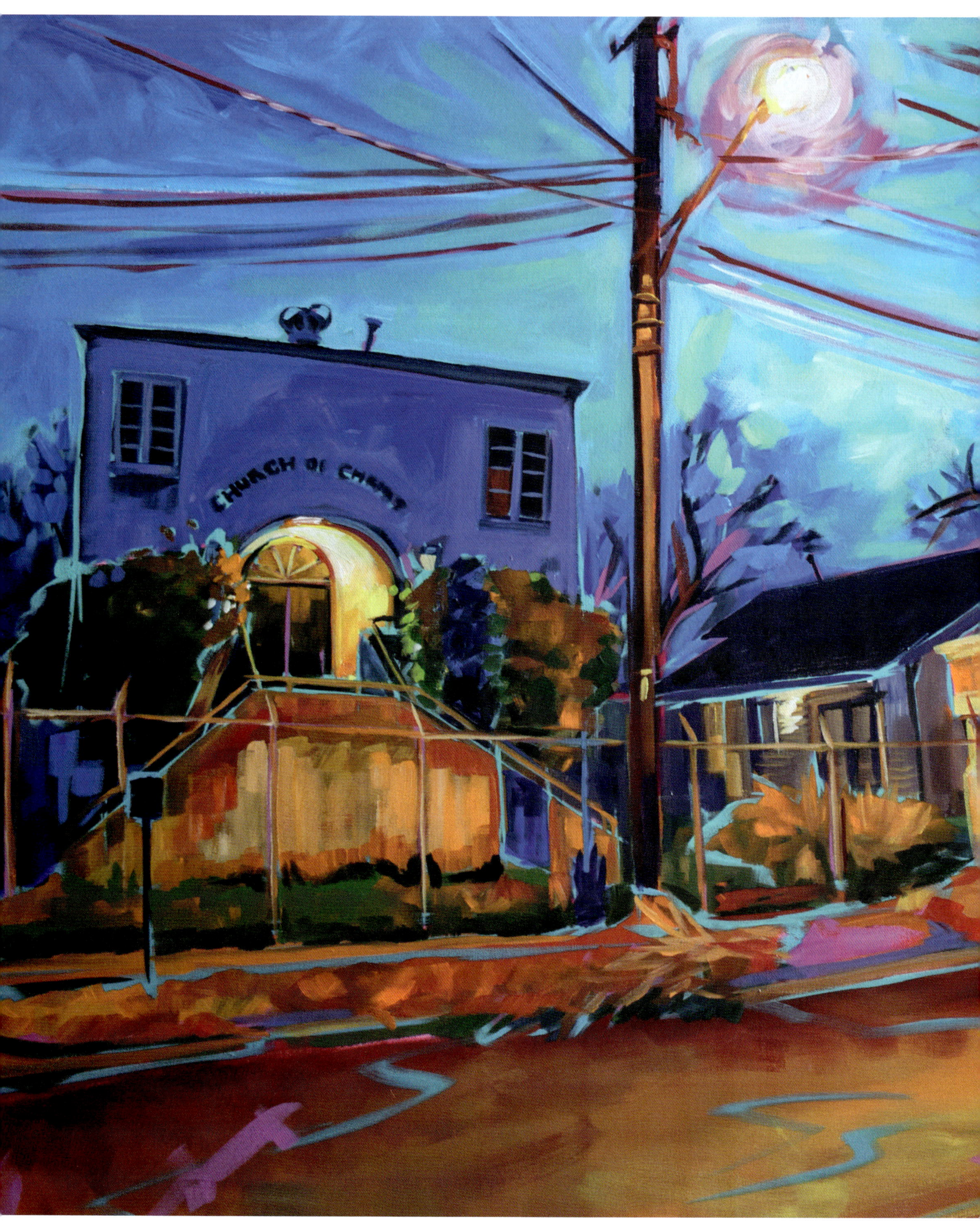

CHURCH OF CHRIST

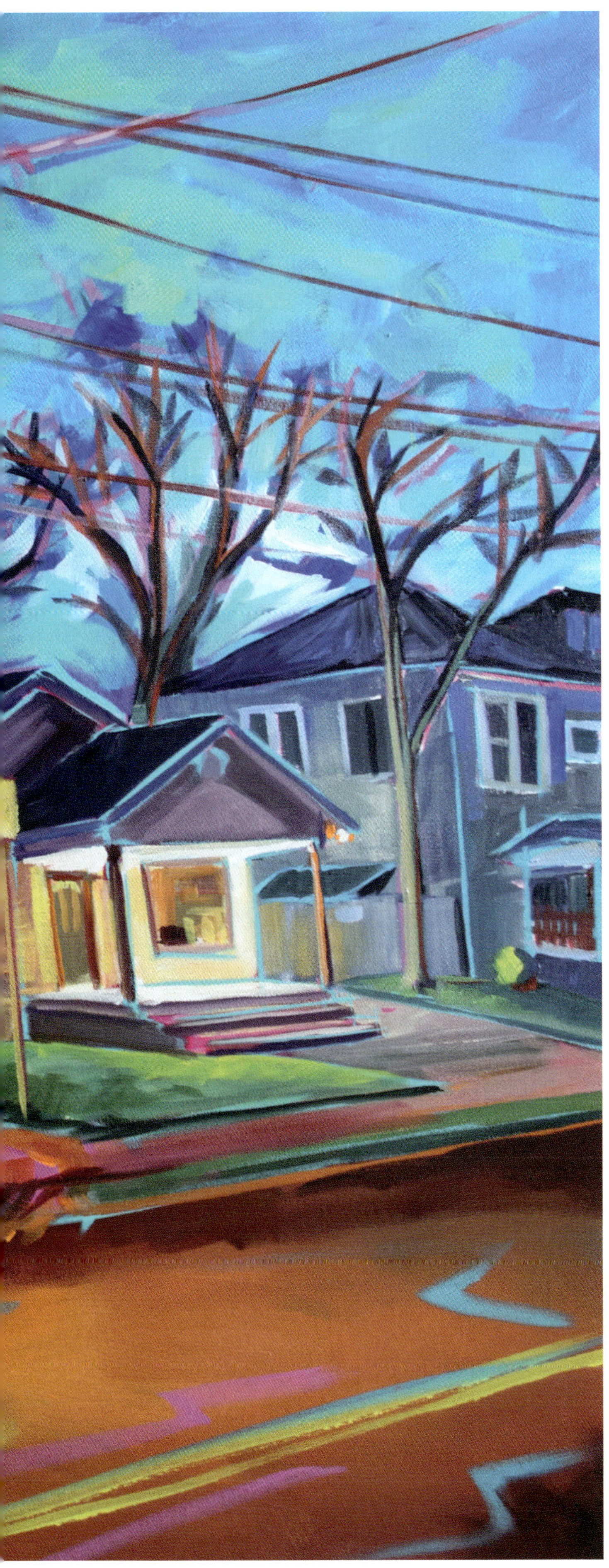

in shadow will appear as a cooler version of its inherent color. Green would lean towards bluish green, while yellow might appear greenish yellow. This is where the color wheel becomes an invaluable tool. For example, take a warm color like orange. To portray it as being in shadow, you'd not only darken its value but also shift it towards a cooler hue, resulting in a reddish violet orange. Similarly, the shadowed side of a lemon might lean more towards green.

It's important to recognize the myriad "games" or techniques available to painters to deviate from local color. These techniques can be as direct as warming and cooling, where colors are subtly altered to resonate with our psychological perceptions, creating desired feelings or effects in the artwork. Alternatively, they might be more understated, using cool muted tones to evoke a sense of melancholy and stillness or employing vibrant high-key colors to inject energy. There's no singular "correct" approach. The canvas is a space for both representation and experimentation.

There's no singular "correct" approach.

Game Room Step-by-Step

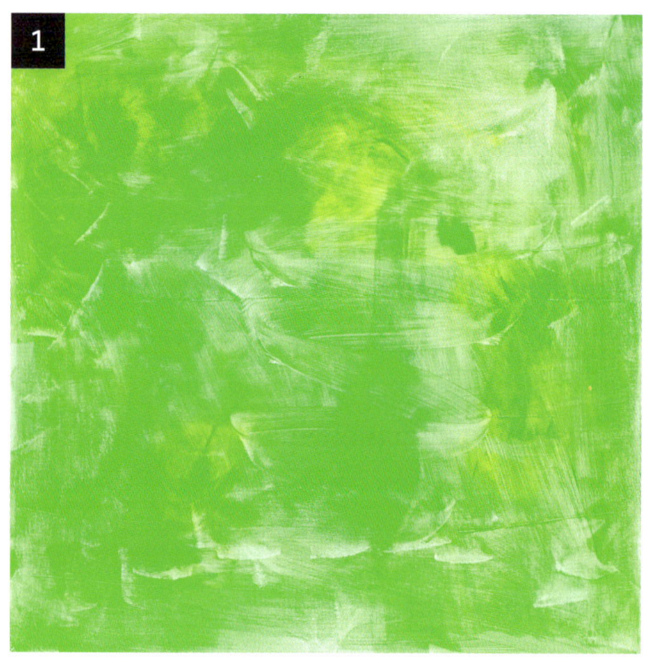

STEP 1

To start, we prime our canvas. I've chosen a bright lime-green color because my reference photo contains a lot of reds in the composition. My hope is that some of this green will peek through at the end, creating a unique composition. I'm also at peace with the possibility that I may paint over all of it—that's fine too.

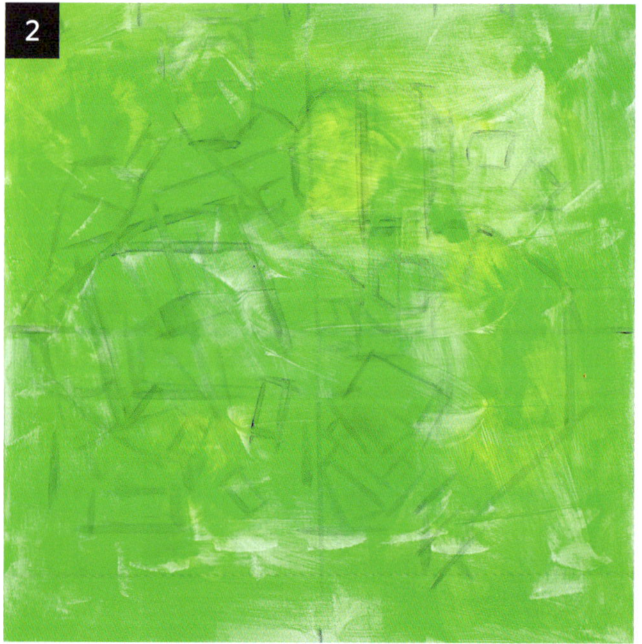

STEP 2

I use a light blue color to lay out a grid and block in my drawings. For additional support, I'm using a loose grid, dividing the painting into quadrants, and adding measuring lines at the top of the composition for extra guidance. This is an attempt to demonstrate versatility in the various ways you can approach the gridding and measuring process in this painting style.

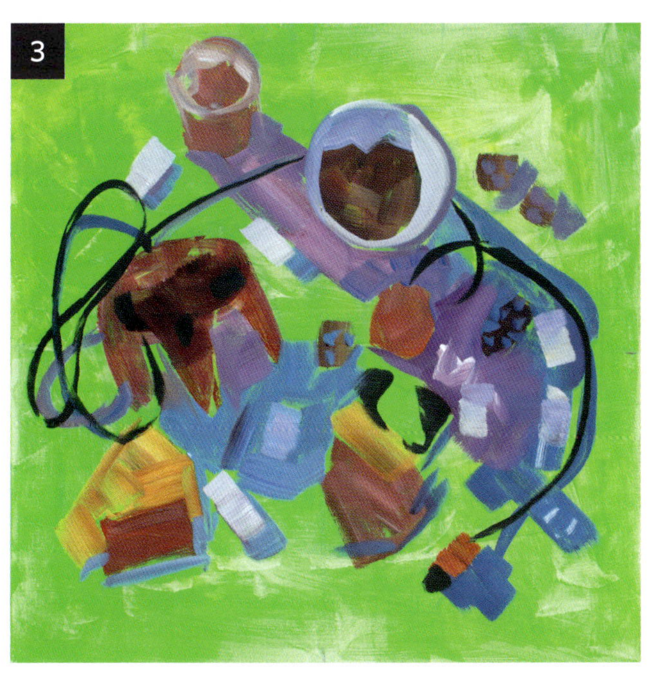

STEP 3

Now, we paint the objects and their shadows using a large brush. Choose a brush that's slightly larger than you're comfortable with. Instead of focusing on specific objects or details, aim to fill in large areas of value. For example, treat the top and bottom of a bowl as two separate colors, particularly when considering the play of warm and cool lighting. Remember that shadows, even on a white ground, should be treated as their own form due to their distinct color and value. The goal in this step is to cover as much ground as possible before moving on to painting the white background.

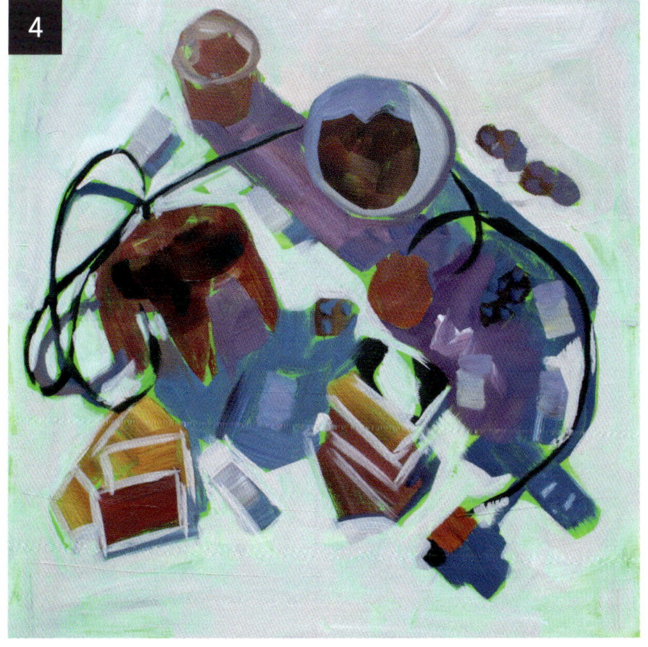

STEP 4

I fill in the background and any other areas that share the same color and value using a large brush. Both this step and the previous one allow for significant progress in a short time. Don't be too precious at this stage. Your drawing may be slightly off, but aim to get about 75% of the way there in terms of value and color. For instance, the cup of Kool-Aid near the center of the composition is currently just a red circle. While it lacks detail now, I know it will make sense once those details are added. At this point, focus on capturing general shapes and large areas of color and value.

(continued)

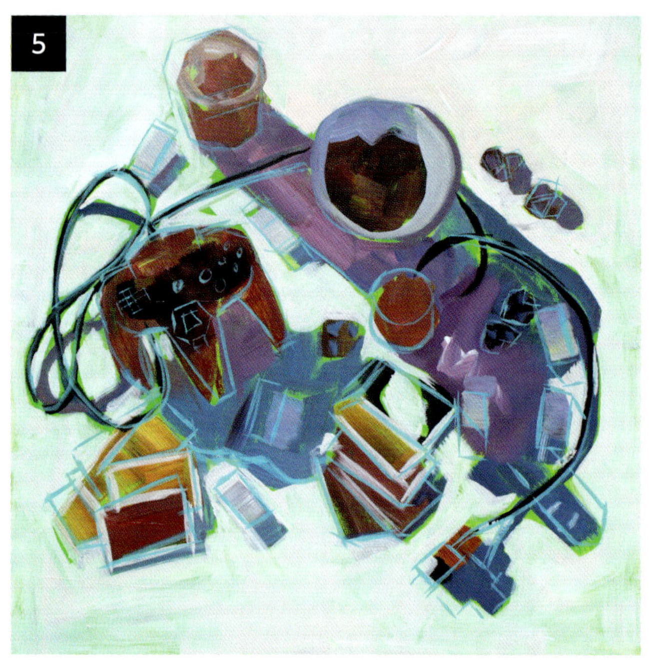

STEP 5

I use a teal color to make necessary corrections to the drawing. Despite my initial diligence, there are some slight to moderate errors, largely due to the large brush I used earlier, which made precise strokes challenging. However, the goal isn't perfect accuracy. It's all about building a good foundation quickly. Moving swiftly in the initial stages helps you get past the overwhelming beginning and sets the stage for adding detail later. At this point, correcting errors becomes relatively effortless. For instance, cords in some areas might be misplaced, or the position of the cup and the plug on the video game controller may be slightly off. As more value and color are laid down, it becomes easier to make more accurate adjustments.

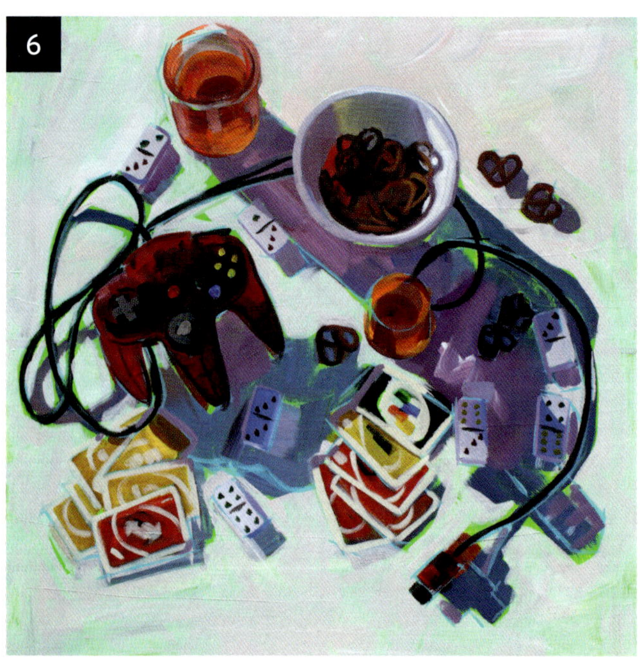

STEP 6

Now, we add a second level of detail or information rendering. Given that the canvas is 24 inches by 24 inches (61 cm by 61 cm), we continue to use a fairly large brush but introduce more detail. By step 4, we had already mapped out general value and color areas. Now, we aim to quickly add the next level of detail. I opt for a slightly smaller brush that's still larger than what's needed for fine details, like highlights or hyper-realistic rendering. At this stage, we focus on elements like buttons on the game controller or dots on the dominoes, without diving into extreme detail.

From a distance, the painting begins to look more complete, even though up close it's still a bit messy. The goal is to move quickly, making broader value choices at a relatively similar scale. By embracing this approach, you'll cover a lot of ground without worrying too much about mistakes. Remember, the layering process with acrylic paints allows you to correct any errors later on.

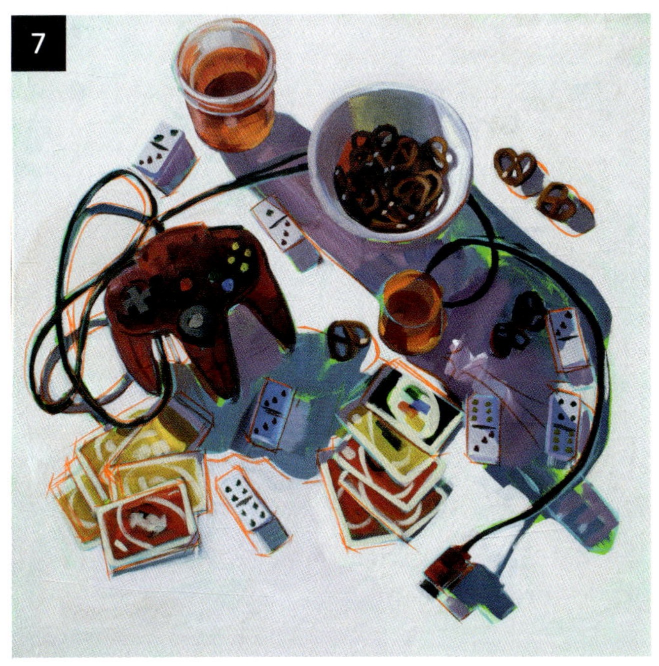

STEP 7

I refine the forms by carving them out with more of the background color. Your drawing is not only shaped in the redraw phase but also through the interplay between the background and foreground to achieve sharp lines. For instance, the goal isn't to draw objects like pretzels or dominoes perfectly the first time; rather, it's to get close enough and then refine their contours using the background color. This approach allows for crisper lines and reduces pressure. Additionally, I use an orange color for another round of redraw. These lines are selective. They're heavier where there were significant drawing errors, like in the shadows and the UNO cards. The redraw lines can also be used to start adding details, such as the light effects from sunlight through the Kool-Aid cups. These details become relevant as the painting gains more focus.

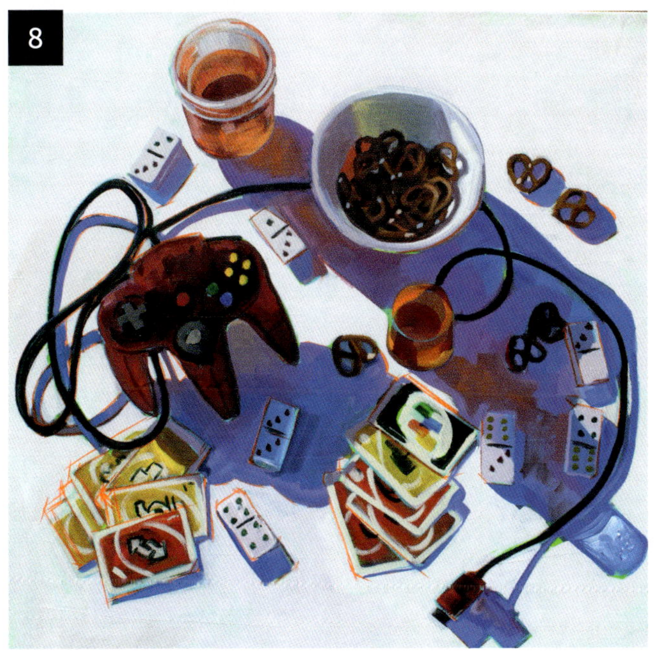

STEP 8

My primary focus is on enriching the details within the shadows. As the objects in the painting, like the pretzel bowls and the video game controller, near their final rendering stage, it's important to give due attention to the shadows. I aim to find subtle variations within them, just as I've done with the objects. Unlike the background, which is primarily white, the shadows contain shades of violet, blue, and even red. I continue the carving and blocking approach, using shadows to refine the painting. The goal is not to dive into the minutiae yet, but to bring the entire painting to the same level of detail simultaneously. This ensures a cohesive style and color palette, as I aim to resolve the painting at a consistent pace.

(continued)

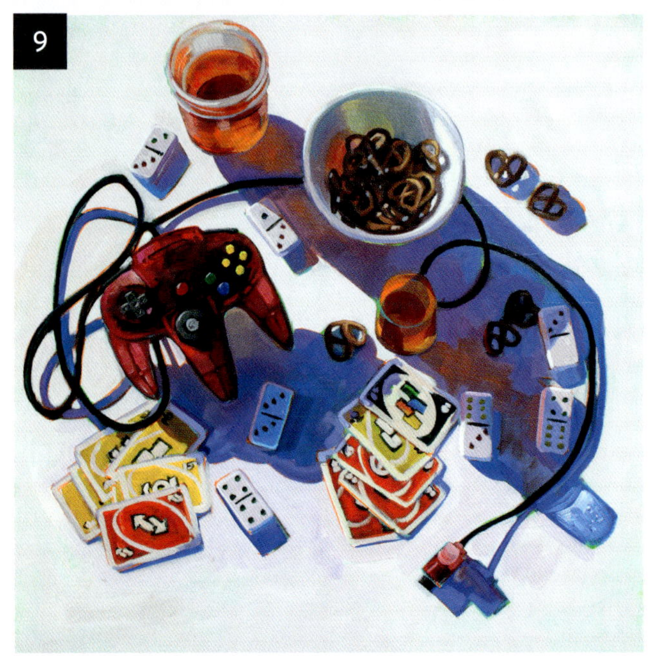

STEP 9

Now, we focus on fine-tuning. While most of the painting is complete, these final touches make a significant difference in how the artwork pops. Just as with earlier stages, the shadows receive equal attention to maintain the warming and cooling effects. Neglecting the shadows at this stage would diminish the overall lighting impact. Details on objects like the game controller, cards, and dominoes are now coming into focus. Pay attention to subtle lighting nuances, such as the warmth in the shadows cast by red objects like the Kool-Aid cups. This warmth is reflected on the edges of the dominoes, enhancing the painting's overall lighting effect. Note that I'm holding off on adding the final highlights. This restraint ensures that the painting reaches a point of near-completion before deciding on those last touches.

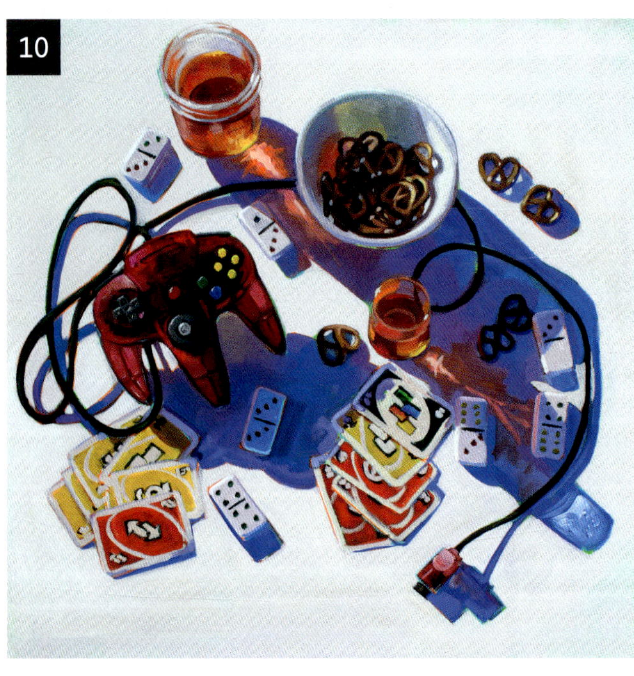

STEP 10

In this last step, I add the final touches. Ideally, the painting should already be able to stand on its own without these flourishes, signifying a solid foundation. One of my goals was to emphasize the importance of exploring shadows to create warming and cooling effects. Having built convincing shadows with accurate values and tones, I can now add striking lighting effects, especially around the two Kool-Aid cups, without them looking unnatural. In addition to these lighting effects, I've added subtle highlights to the shiniest objects, such as the cups and the video game controller. This is also the time to correct any remaining major drawing issues or other elements that have been bothering me. I recommend taking a break between this step and the previous one. Fresh eyes are invaluable for this final phase, which can otherwise become overwhelming. Though it may be tempting to immediately add highlights, patience is crucial to avoid overemphasizing them and detracting from the painting's overall effect.

Fruity Flamingo Step-by-Step

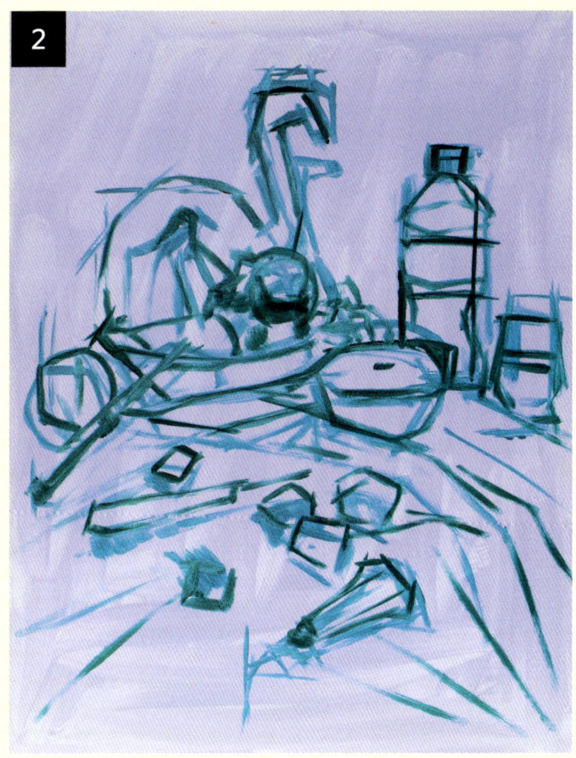

STEP 1

I begin by priming my canvas with a pale purple hue. While this choice may seem too light for those aiming for a middle gray base, it suited my goal of creating a bright, high-key composition. The underpainting color is more flexible than you might think. The key is to avoid colors that will be diffi-cult to work with later. For instance, if my painting primarily consisted of pale purples, this base color might not be the best choice. Since it doesn't, though, this color works well.

STEP 2

I use a teal color to establish the proportions and placement of my painting using my dowel rod. I noticed that some areas, particularly the soda bottle, seemed slightly off. To correct this, I layer a darker greenish teal to clarify the placement. During the initial drawing and redrawing stages, feel free to use a more definitive or darker shade of the same color if your lines become confusing. The purpose of these guidelines is to provide a frame-work for your painting, not to be part of the final composition. Most likely, they will be completely covered, so they only need to serve as a functional guide for you moving forward.

(continued)

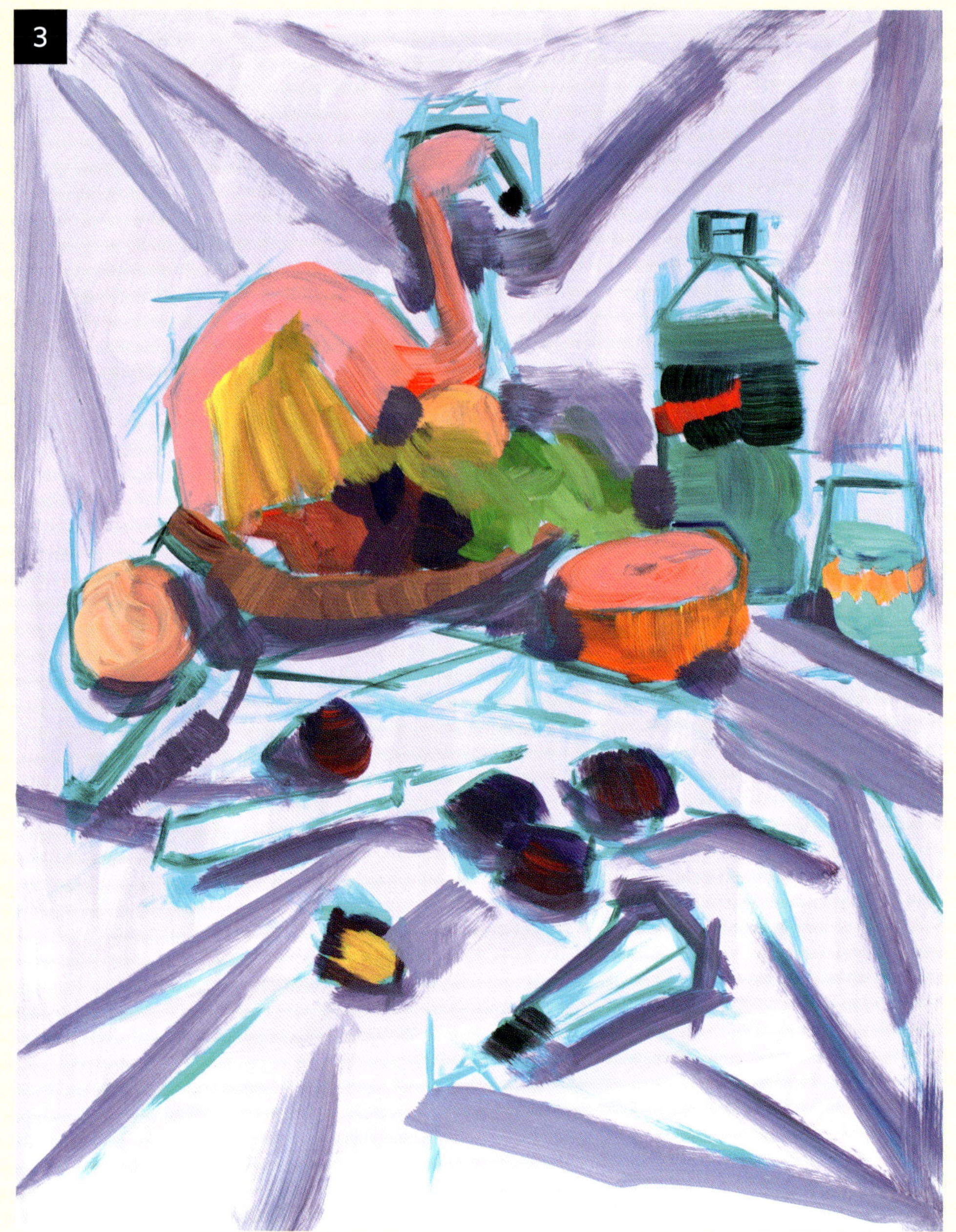

STEP 3

Here, I chose a brush slightly larger than what I'm usually comfortable with. The aim here is not to paint details, but to map out large blocks of value and color. Since the drawing is already done, I can focus solely on making good general choices regarding value. In these initial stages, it's crucial to concentrate on the prominent blocks of value and color rather than details.

This could range from the striking red hue on the Mountain Dew bottle to the bold shadows created by direct lighting. Challenge yourself to see your composition not as objects, but as blocks of value, color, and form. While this might be difficult at first, with practice, it eventually becomes a natural way to view the world and your art.

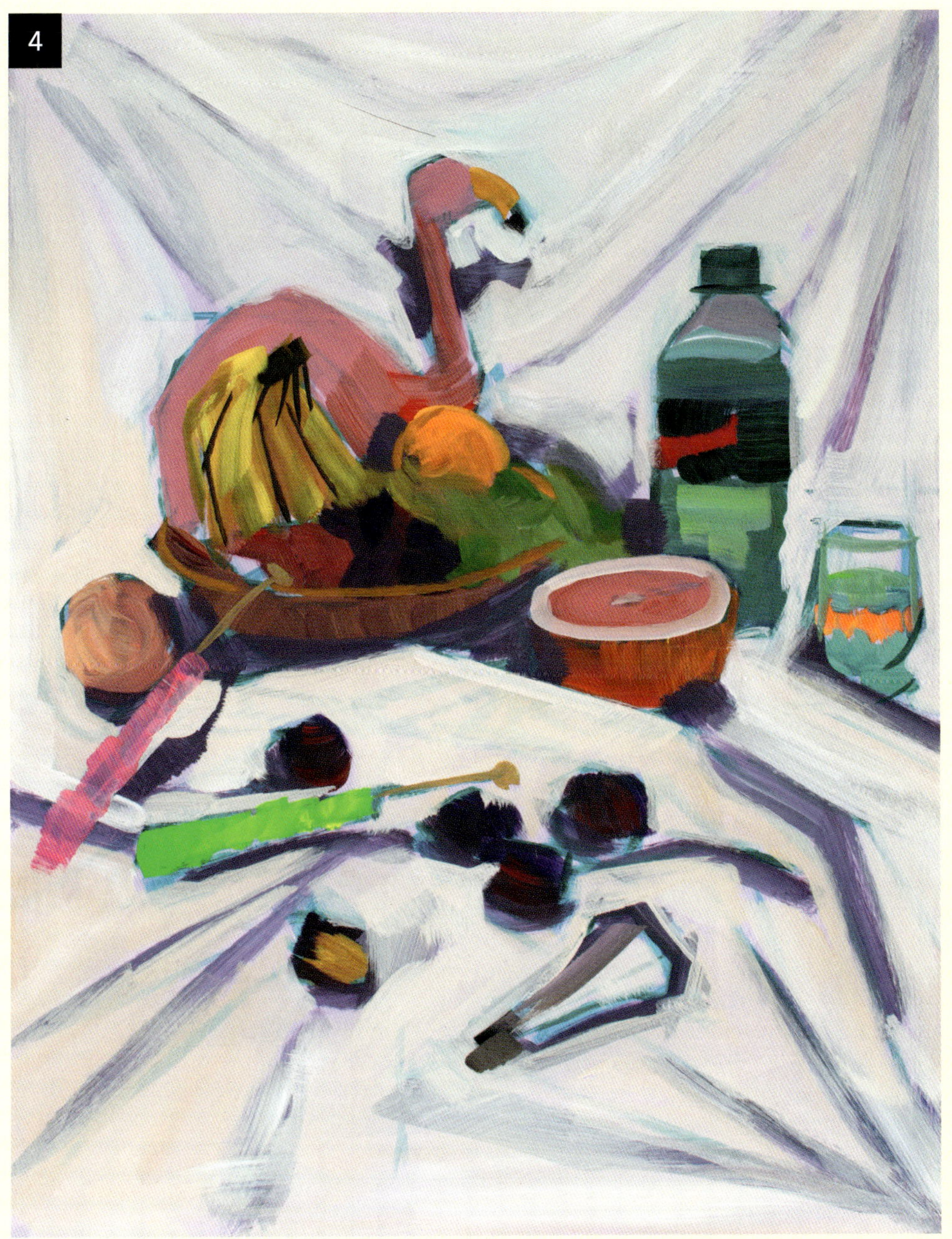

STEP 4

I start to block in the background color along with the other major colors and values. The goal here is to quickly cover the composition with the most general forms possible. I like to think of this step as the prelude to the "real" painting process. While this stage is important and significant progress is made, the focus is not on detailing but rather on capturing the largest and most crucial blocks of value and color. Think of it like fine-tuning a microscope: you start with a blurry image and gradually refine it. In the early stages of my paintings, things often feel "blurry" in a sense. For example, if you view the painting as a thumbnail or from a distance, it appears more complete than it actually is. On closer inspection, you'll see that the details are still rudimentary. Since we're using acrylics, which are fast-drying and opaque, you can freely and instinctively block in forms and values. If you make mistakes, they can be easily corrected in later stages. This approach encourages speed, trust in your instincts, and a willingness to make adjustments.

(continued)

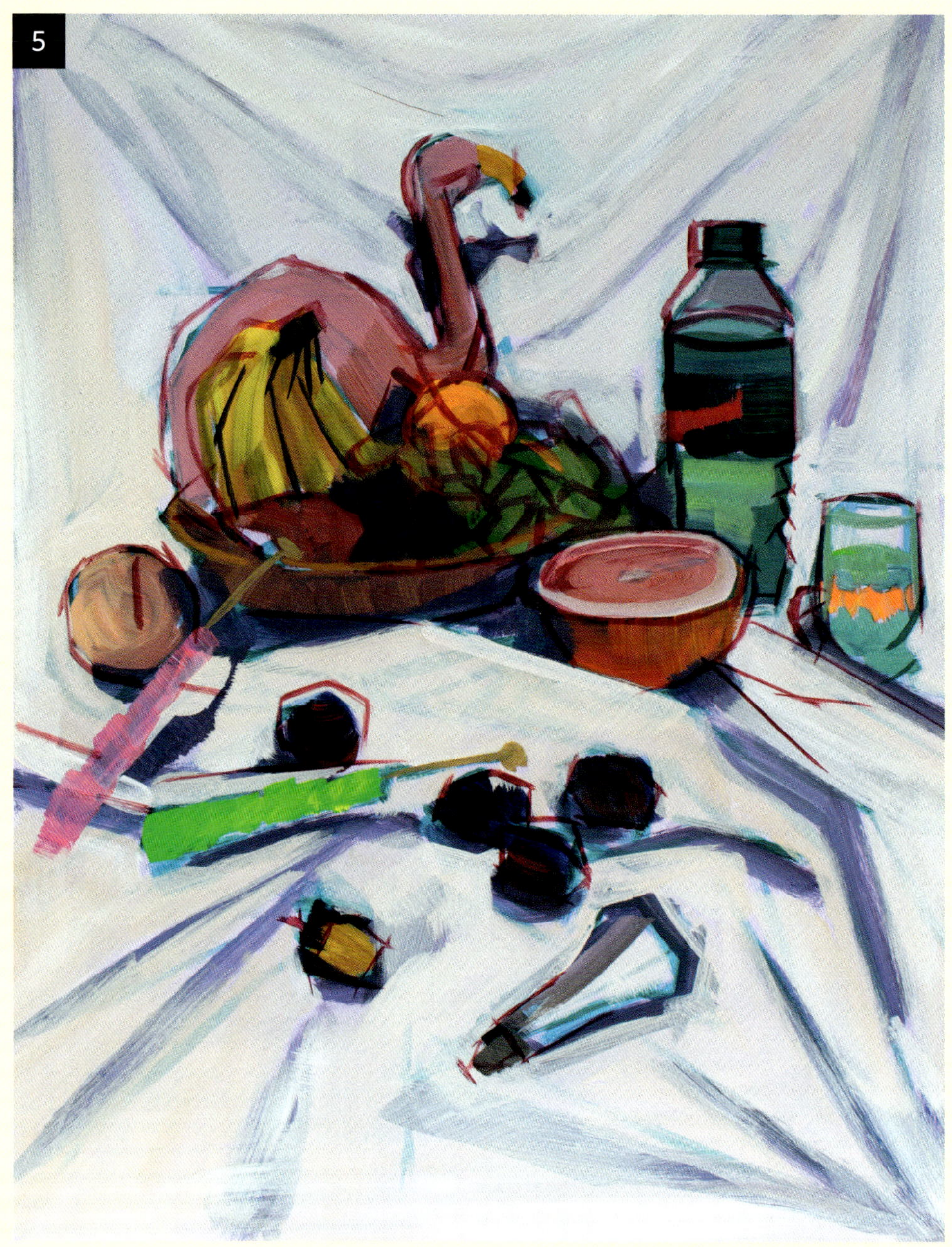

STEP 5

I use Alizarin Crimson Hue for a redraw, aiming to refine the shapes, particularly of the grapes, that may have lost some accuracy due to the use of a larger brush in previous steps. In this redraw, I'm not focusing on intricate details but rather on correcting placements. As I continue to fine-tune the painting, more opportunities will arise to add details, like the soda bottle's label or the flamingo's face. At this point, my aim is to further develop mid-level information—for example, defining the individual grapes and bananas and solidifying the shapes and forms of the plums.

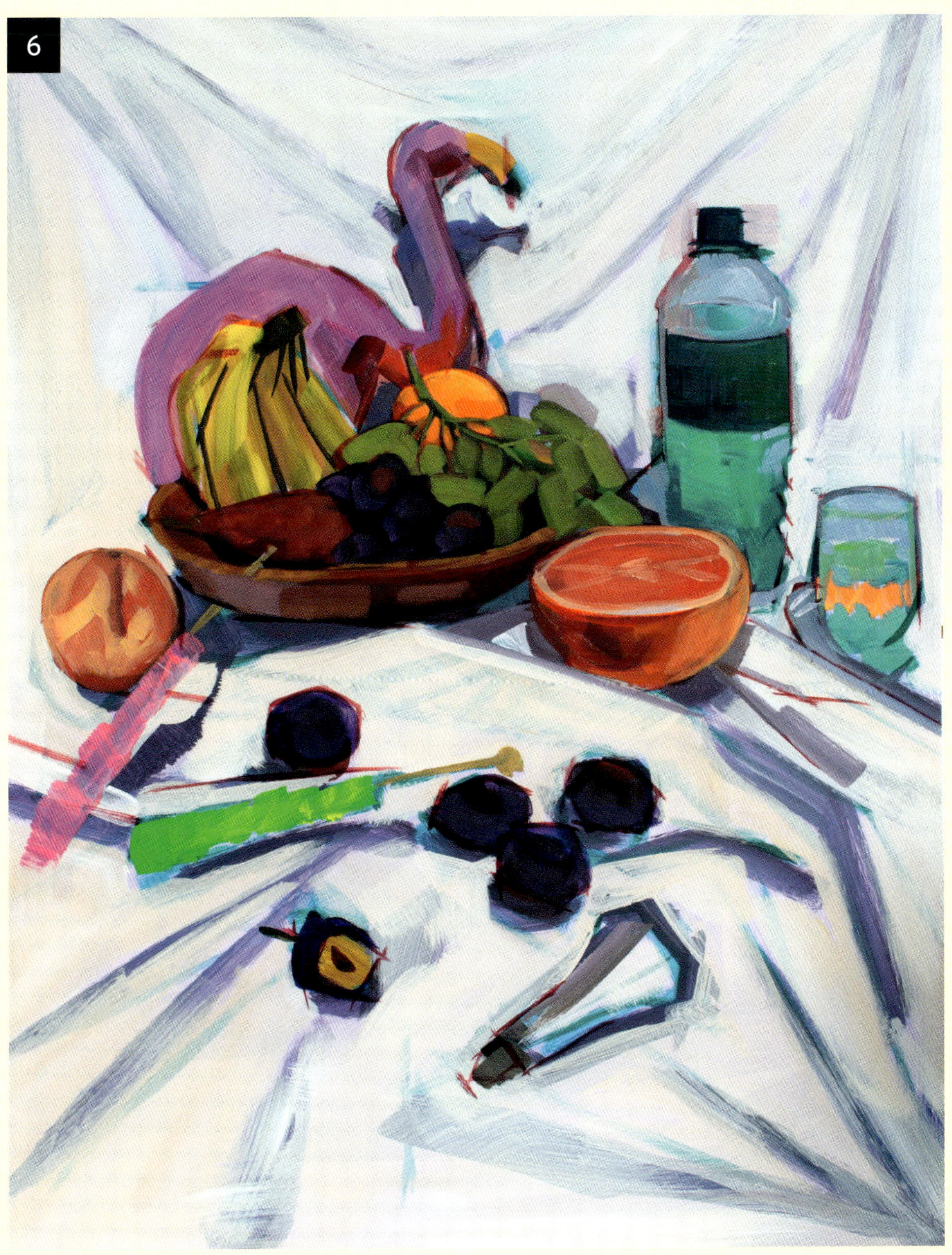

STEP 6

I switch to a smaller brush to capture more details, particularly in areas I redrew earlier, such as the fruit bowl, the flamingo, and the color variations in the soda bottle, glass, and plums. In some spots, I manage to include a significant amount of detail. For instance, even though my initial goal wasn't to fully finish the peach on the left side, sometimes the block-in stage can produce surprisingly accurate results. So in this step, I'm focusing on refining and adding more detailed information to the painting.

(continued)

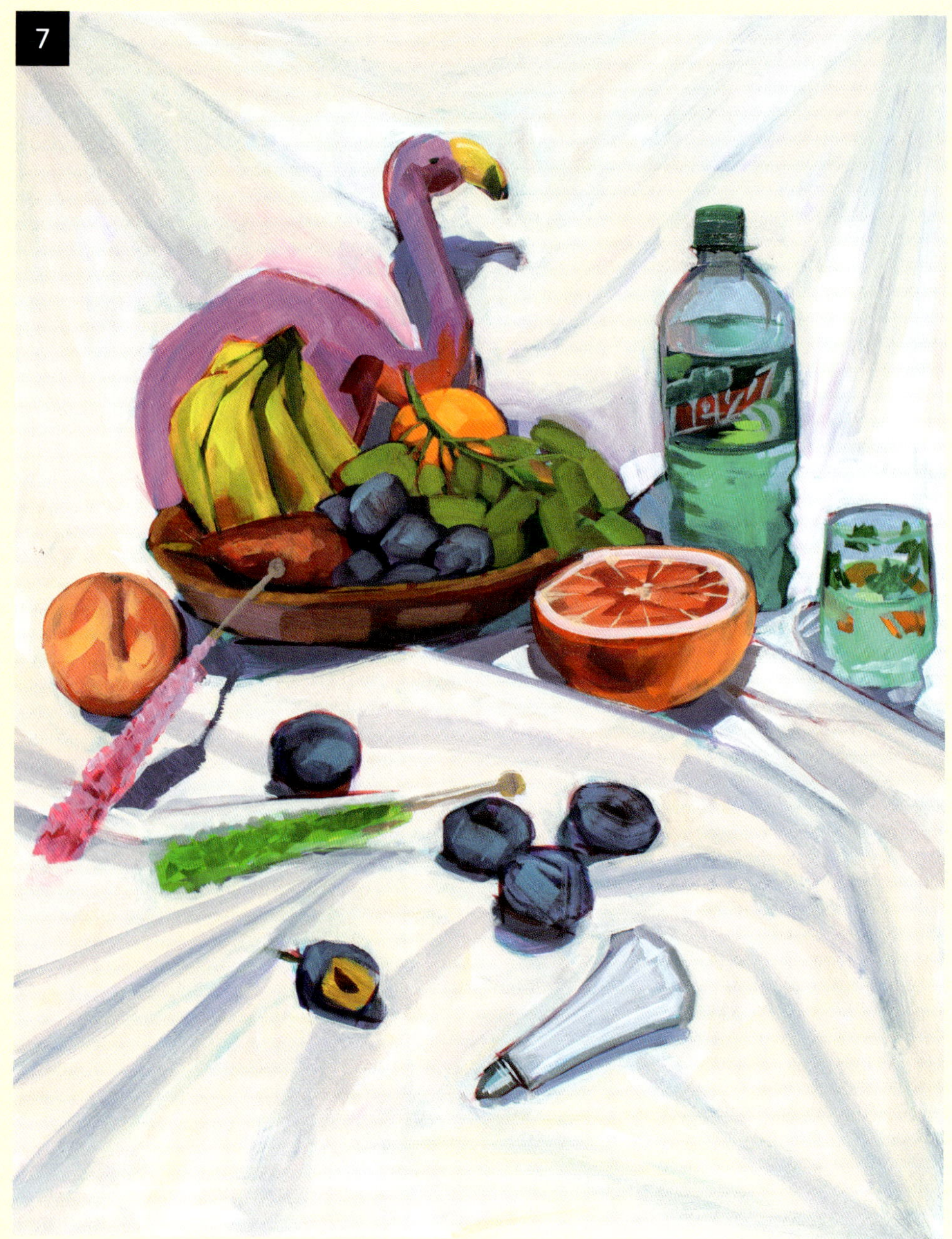

STEP 7

I use the white background to further define the forms of my objects, focusing particularly on the tablecloth's wrinkles to enhance the lighting effects in the painting. This includes both direct lighting, which casts pronounced shadows like those from the flamingo head and the base of the soda bottle, and subtler light play creating softer shadows from the fabric folds. I mixed softer purples and blues for these subtle shadows, reserving the lightest highlights for later stages.

I also started to add details to the soda label, the cup, and various fruits like the plums and grape-fruit. As the painting progresses, these objects and details are becoming more defined. For complex elements like labels, I expect to revisit and redraw them multiple times to get closer to the final product. The process is repetitive: block in, redraw, add details, and repeat. Whether you choose to finely detail elements like patterns or leave them looser depends on your artistic style.

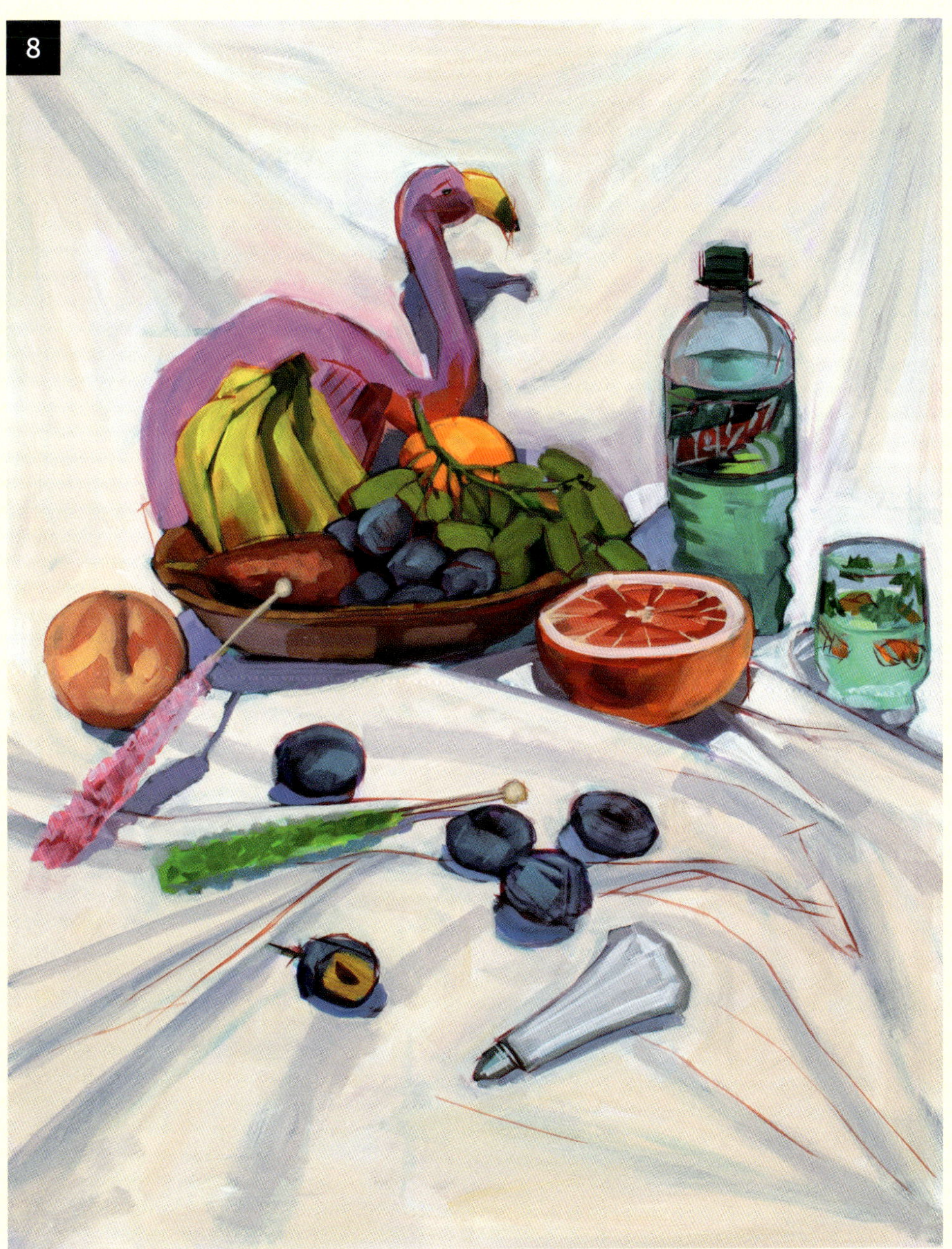

STEP 8

I use a thin line of Alizarin Crimson Hue to make minor adjustments to the bottle and the fabric folds. I wanted to treat these details with the same attention as other elements in the painting. It's crucial to approach shadows with the same intensity as the rest of the painting to convincingly portray lighting effects. By focusing on these aspects, I was able to identify the most distinct shifts in value, treating them as specifically as any other object in the composition. I also corrected minor drawing errors and added some shadow behind the flamingo.

(continued)

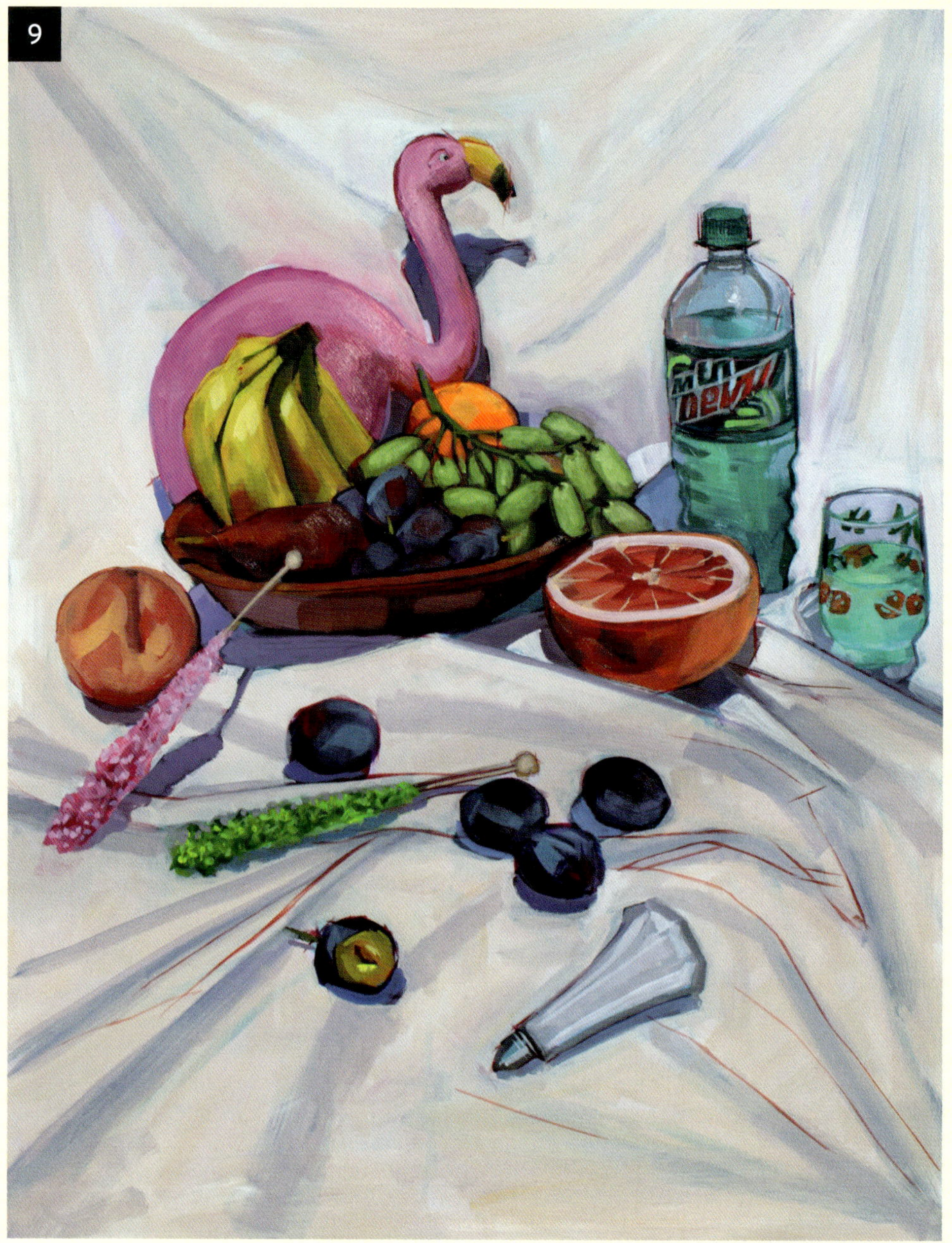

STEP 9

I am focused on refining the painting based on my redraw lines in the bottle and shadow, among other areas. Specifically, the label on the Mountain Dew bottle and the pattern on the glass are now more aligned with my intended final appearance. I also worked on capturing subtle shifts in color and value on the flamingo, its face, and some of the fruits in the bowl, as well as key details on the rock candy. The goal is to bring these objects into focus to a point where they can stand alone, even if I haven't yet added the final details and highlights. In essence, if I stopped working on the painting now, would I be satisfied with how these elements are rendered?

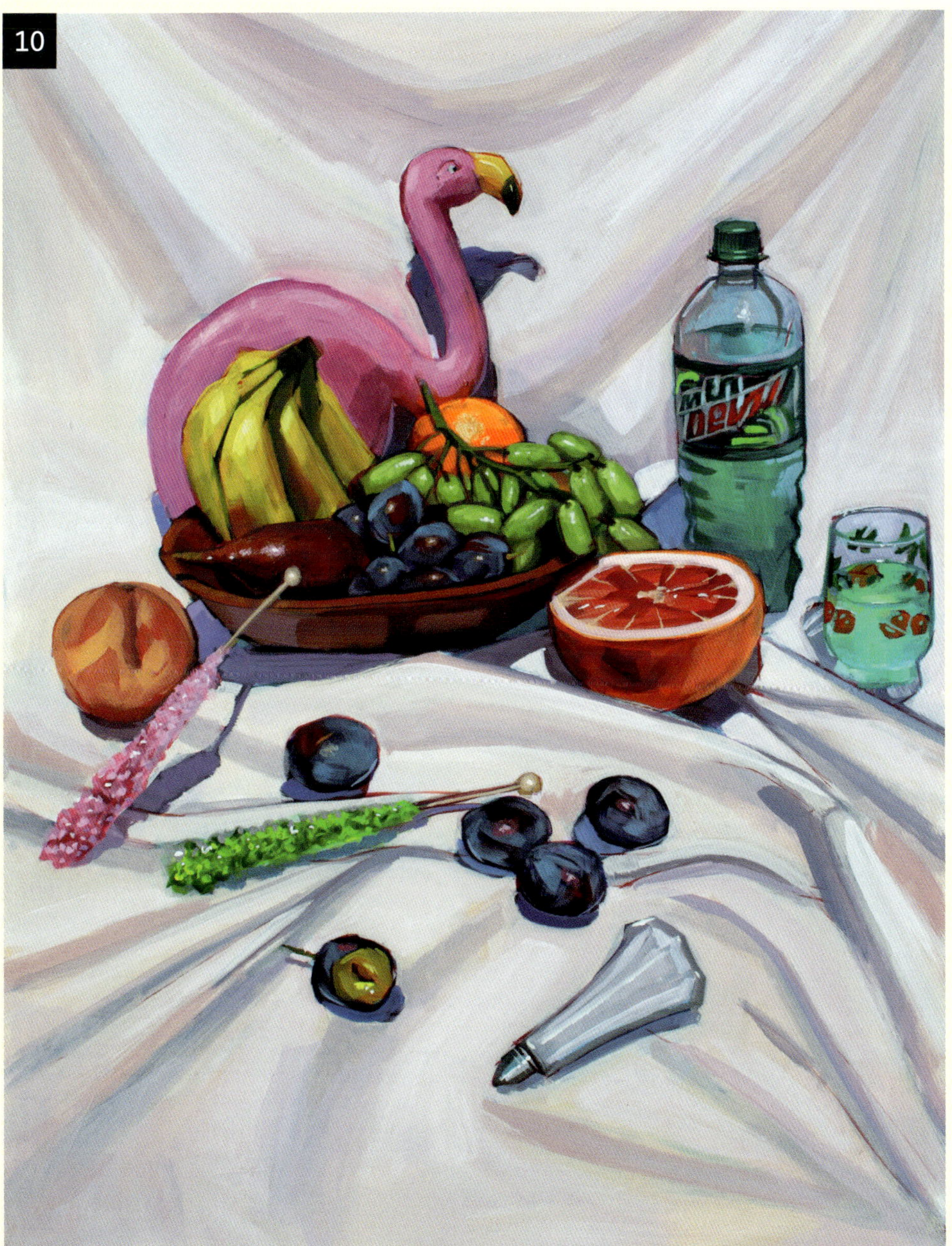

STEP 10

Now, I add the final contours to the fabric. Although the background features a white tablecloth, its folds display both cool, purple hues and warmer tones depending on the lighting conditions. By adhering to the principles of warming and cooling, even in subtle shadows, I was able to create a convincing sense of lighting throughout the composition. This is evident not just in stark contrasts from direct light, like the shadows cast by the fruit bowl, grapefruit, and rock candy, but also in the nuanced lighting across the fabric.

Additionally, I added the finishing touches, including final highlights and minor details to enhance the painting's overall polished look. By the time I reach this step, I make sure I'm pleased with the foundational work done in earlier stages. It's important to exercise restraint when adding highlights, as they can easily be overdone. From refining the fabric to adding the last bits of highlight that emphasize textures in the fruits and plastic surfaces, I consider this painting complete.

Optimist at Heart Step-by-Step

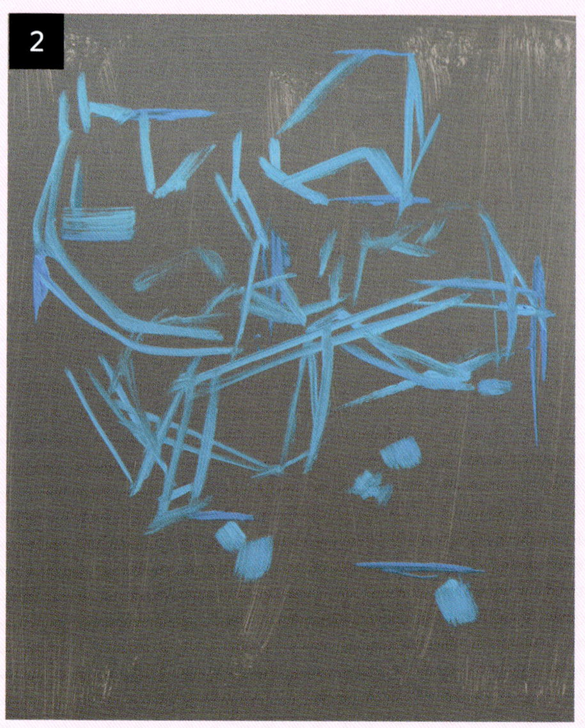

STEP 1

I've primed my surface with a medium gray value to best prepare myself for making value choices in the upcoming steps.

STEP 2

Here, I use mapping and gridding to establish the proportions and create a scaffolding, focusing on the general shape and the relationships between object edges. This will prepare us to apply our first round of color in the following step. I chose a combination of Phthalo Blue (Green Shade) and Titanium White, as I felt it contrasted well enough with the background.

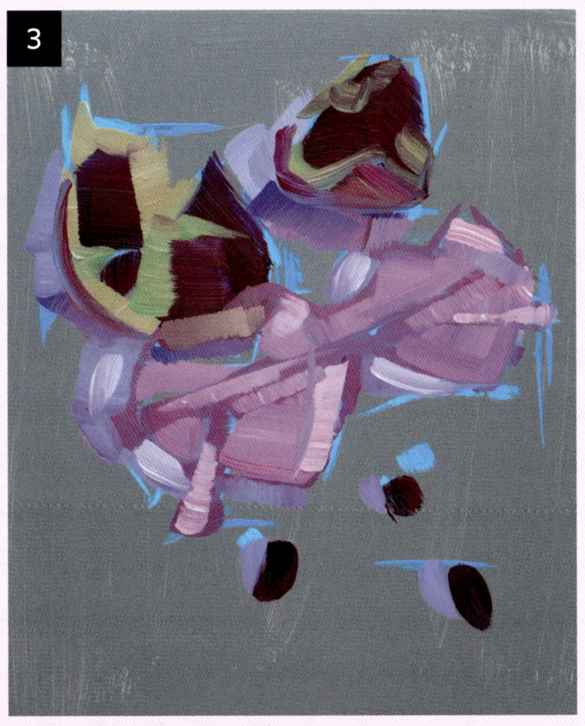

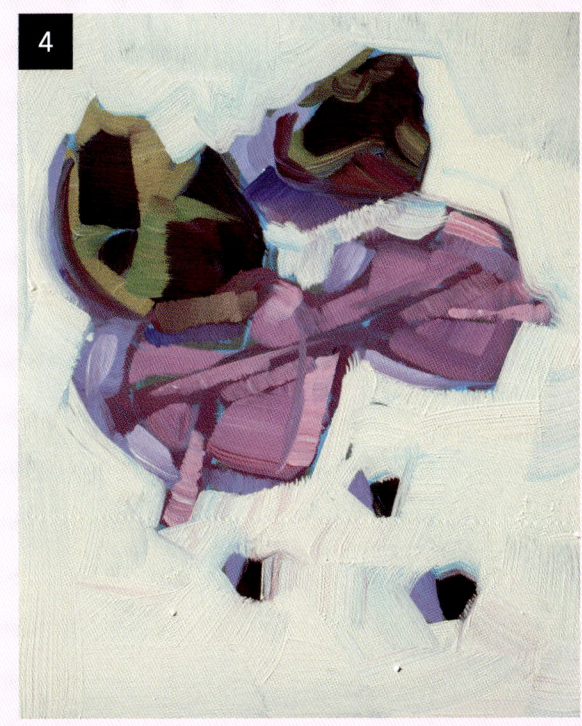

STEP 3

I focus on laying down the largest value chunks and shapes in the painting, using approximately a dozen large brush strokes to create the pomegranates. A brush of significant proportion to the canvas size allows me to efficiently cover a lot of form without becoming mired in detail at this early stage. Although details will be added later, my primary aim now is to use my framework from the previous step to mix a color that is both value-accurate and color-appropriate. I also paint in the shadows at this stage, considering them distinct enough to be treated as their own form due to the direct light source. Leaning into the warming and cooling to depict direct sunlight, I enhance the chroma and coolness of the shadows.

STEP 4

I painted the background using largely one solid color, stemming from a reference photo taken on a whiteboard to simplify the composition. As the whiteboard is lit, I took two main actions: First, I shifted the chroma or hue slightly towards a warm, creamy off-white by incorporating Yellow Ochre. Secondly, to reduce the value of a mixture of Titanium White and Yellow Ochre, I introduced a small amount of Dioxazine Purple, complementing the yellow.

Though more Yellow Ochre than Dioxazine Purple is used to maintain a creamy warm white, the addition of these complementary colors neutralizes into a warm beige brown, providing the desired creamy shade. This warm color aids in emphasizing the warming and cooling effect in the painting, while the marginally lower chroma provides flexibility to enhance the value in subsequent steps.

(continued)

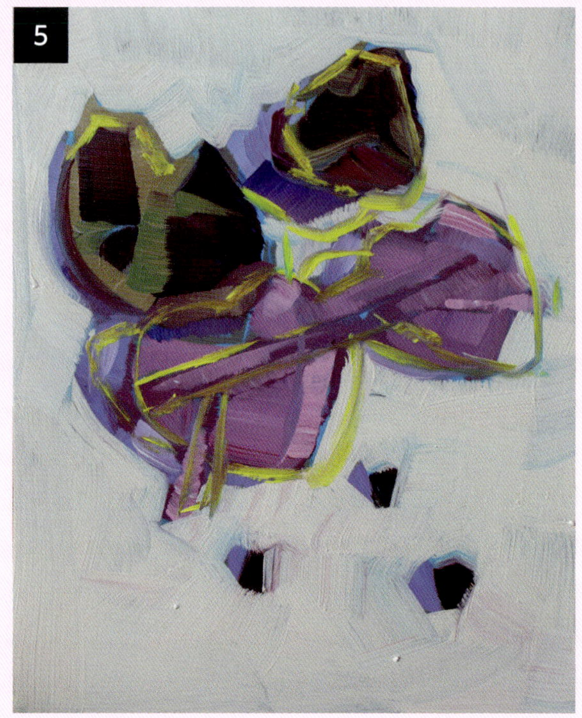

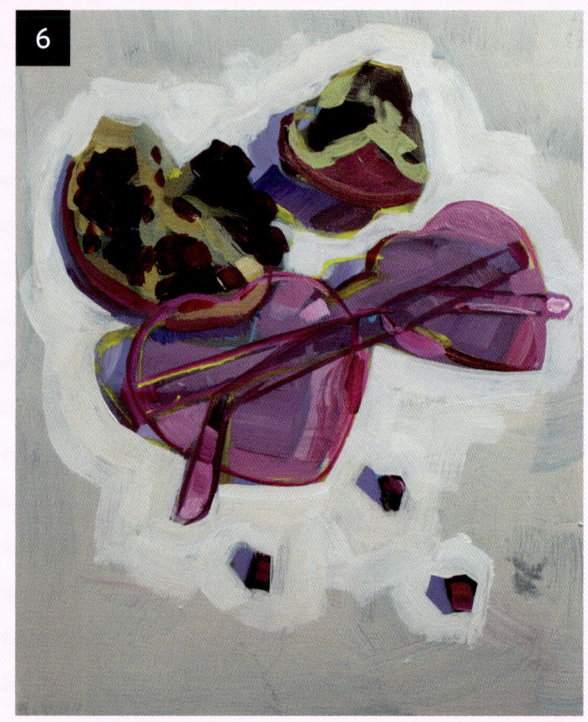

STEP 5

I utilized Cadmium Yellow Light for my redraw line. During the initial block-in, my drawing, especially of the heart shaped sunglasses, veered slightly off, as did the precise proportions of the pomegranate.

It's important to note that although two pomegranate seeds in the front were slightly mispositioned, I chose not to adjust them. Since they didn't intersect with anything and no other object's proportions were dependent upon them, I exercised creative license and allowed them to remain slightly askew.

STEP 6

I began this step by addressing the darkest values, focusing primarily on the pomegranate seeds and the darker aspects of the sunglasses. It's crucial to note that while many of the darker parts of the sunglasses are at the edge, they don't form a single distinct outline. When painting something translucent, avoid enclosing it with a solid outline and instead, observe closely where the outline vanishes. Often, the edge of the glass is only visible where the light strikes it perfectly. In most other spots, it's invisible. Instead of a clear edge, rely on subtle gradients and value chunks to convey the translucency of the form. Although this can be challenging, building translucency by heeding this specific detail is key. Additionally, in this step, I tidied the form's edges and corrected the redraw error using a slightly lighter background color, often executing my drawing with the outline color, as is the case here.

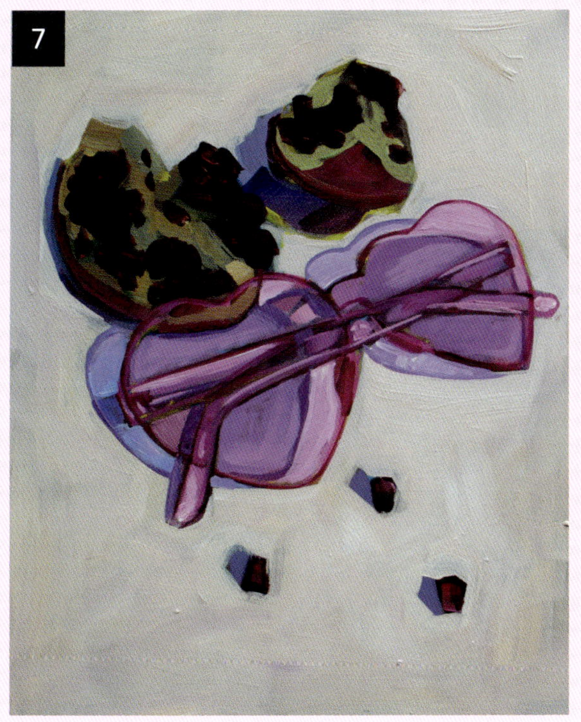

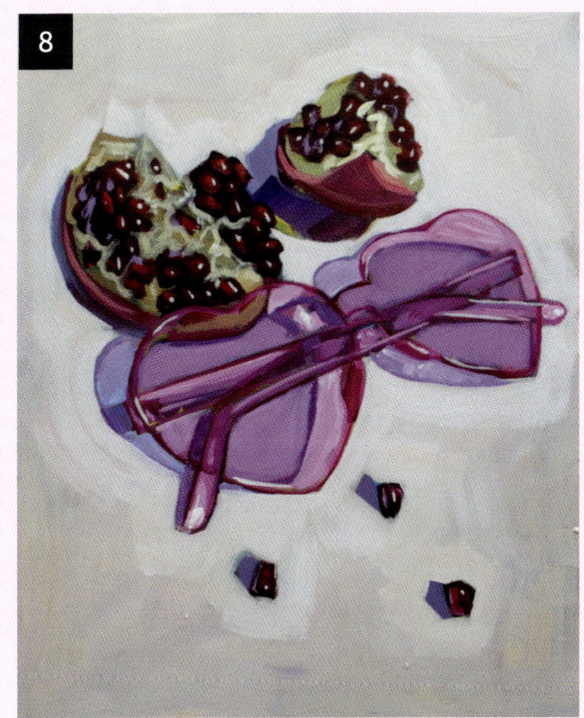

STEP 7

In this phase, my focus shifted to identifying more mid-tone values, steering clear of highlights for now. Particularly in the pomegranates, where I delineated darker values previously, I now introduce a color that sits midway between the lightest and darkest hues within the seeds. I also prioritized painting the shadow forms of the sunglasses, recognizing that their translucency allows more light into the shadow than a solid, opaque object like the pomegranates would. In areas where the translucent plastic of the sunglasses is layered, such as where the arms fold over the lenses, less light can permeate, resulting in a darker shadow.

Paying close attention to these shadow variations enables the effects of translucency and warming and cooling to be fully realized. Often, capturing a light effect involves noticing the subtle, yet straightforward, ways shadows shift in relation to the materials casting them. Additionally, I utilized more of the white from the previous step to complete the remaining background color.

STEP 8

This step zeroes in on the lighter values to round off the form-building executed throughout the painting. In general terms, our journey took us from darker values to mid-tones and in this step, to lighter values.

Attention was given to the brightest areas and highlights in both the pomegranate seeds and sunglasses, which can be distinct and differ from object to object. The highlights on the sunglasses, especially, deliver tangible texture to the painted object. Additionally, I performed a final pass with the light white background color to clean up the outlines. Notably, I employed a purple color, present in the shadows of both the pomegranate and sunglasses, to craft cool, reflected light on the pomegranate sides, executing this with small squiggles rather than detailed shadow rendering to maintain a loose, brushy effect. An essential note on creating lighting effects in painting involves heeding subtle aspects, like the coolness of light reflected from shadows. Attuning to these nuanced shifts, even in the warmth of reflected light, is pivotal for crafting a realistic lighting effect.

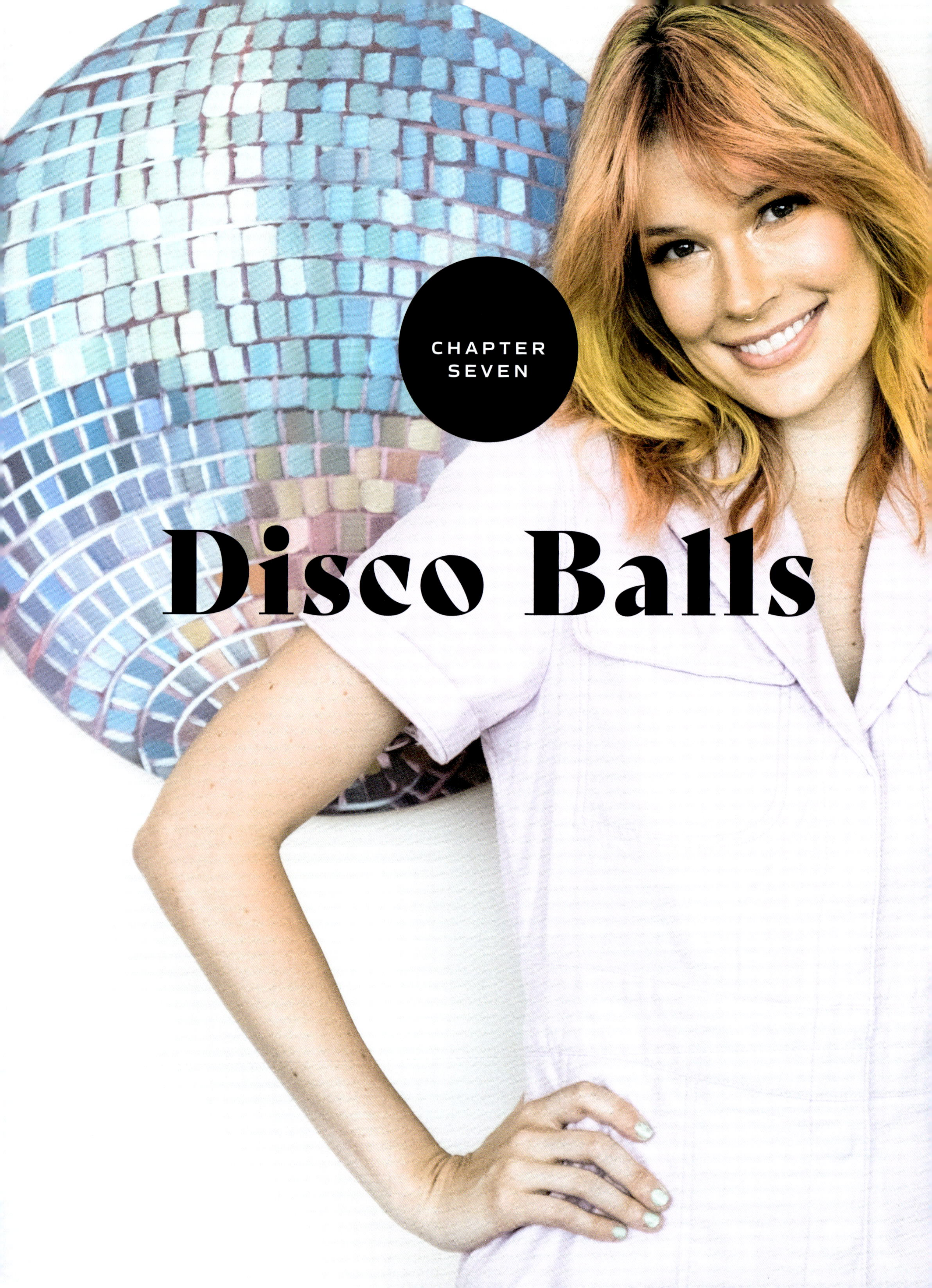

Disco Balls

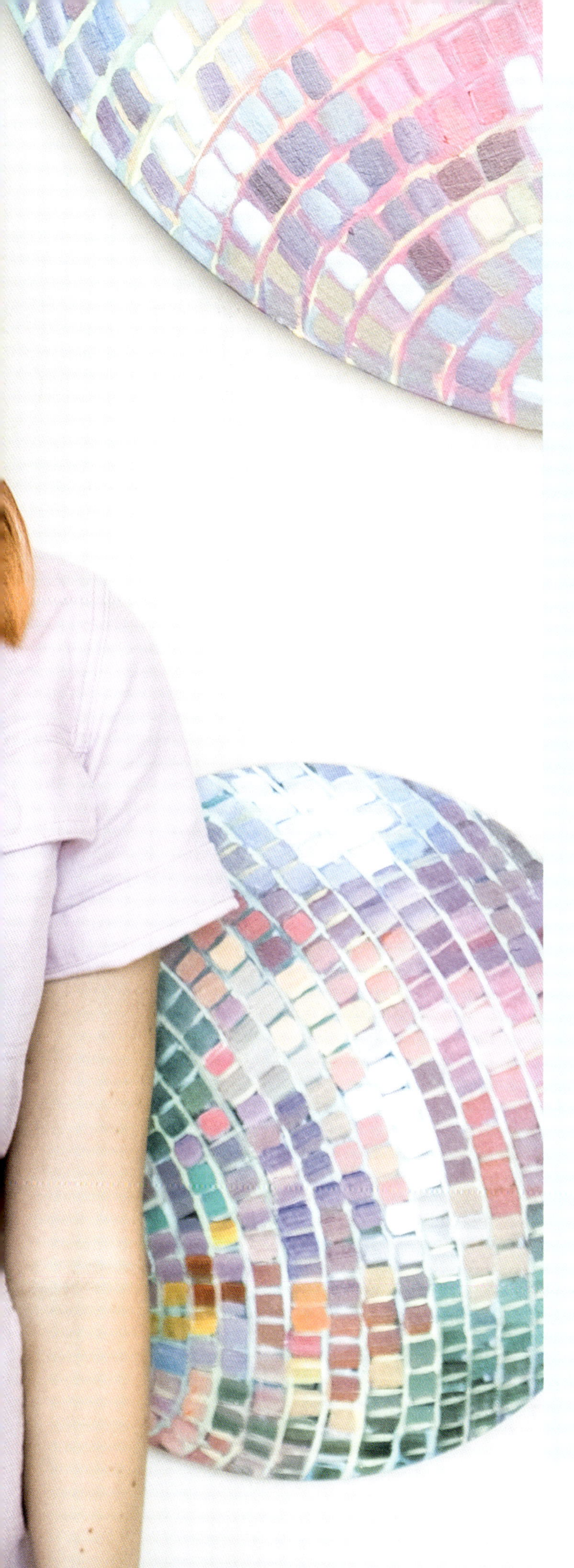

My Story

CREATING MY ORIGINAL disco ball paintings provided me with a crucial lesson in the fact that when you do the work, when you strive to uncover painting subjects and styles that pique your interest, inspiration will find you.

I remember exactly where I was when the inspiration to paint a disco ball on a round canvas struck me. Usually, cultivating an idea for a painting is a strenuous process of trial and error, and I jump from one adjacent idea to the next until I stumble upon a spot that feels comfortable and engaging. The disco balls presented a different scenario entirely.

Despite my college painting professor's warning to be cautious of circle and square canvases—given the challenges in finding suitable compositions—I had nonetheless amassed a handful of circle canvases in the summer of 2019. They sat there collecting dust in my studio for a few months, mocking me, until I suddenly knew exactly what to do with them.

It was on a Saturday, while dancing in the backyard with my then toddler son, that a pivotal moment arrived. We were listening to disco music on the radio as part of *70s Saturday*, a rare tradition from my childhood that I was comfortable sharing with my children. Saturdays were days spent with my mom—who worked exhaustive hours in a warehouse during the week—either exploring thrift stores or sometimes just lounging on our apartment's back patio, dancing to the local radio station's disco tunes. Despite a tumultuous childhood marked by poverty and parents grappling with addiction, *70s Saturday* was a bright spot for me, and happy memories flooded back to me as my son and I grooved to the Bee Gees and Donna Summer.

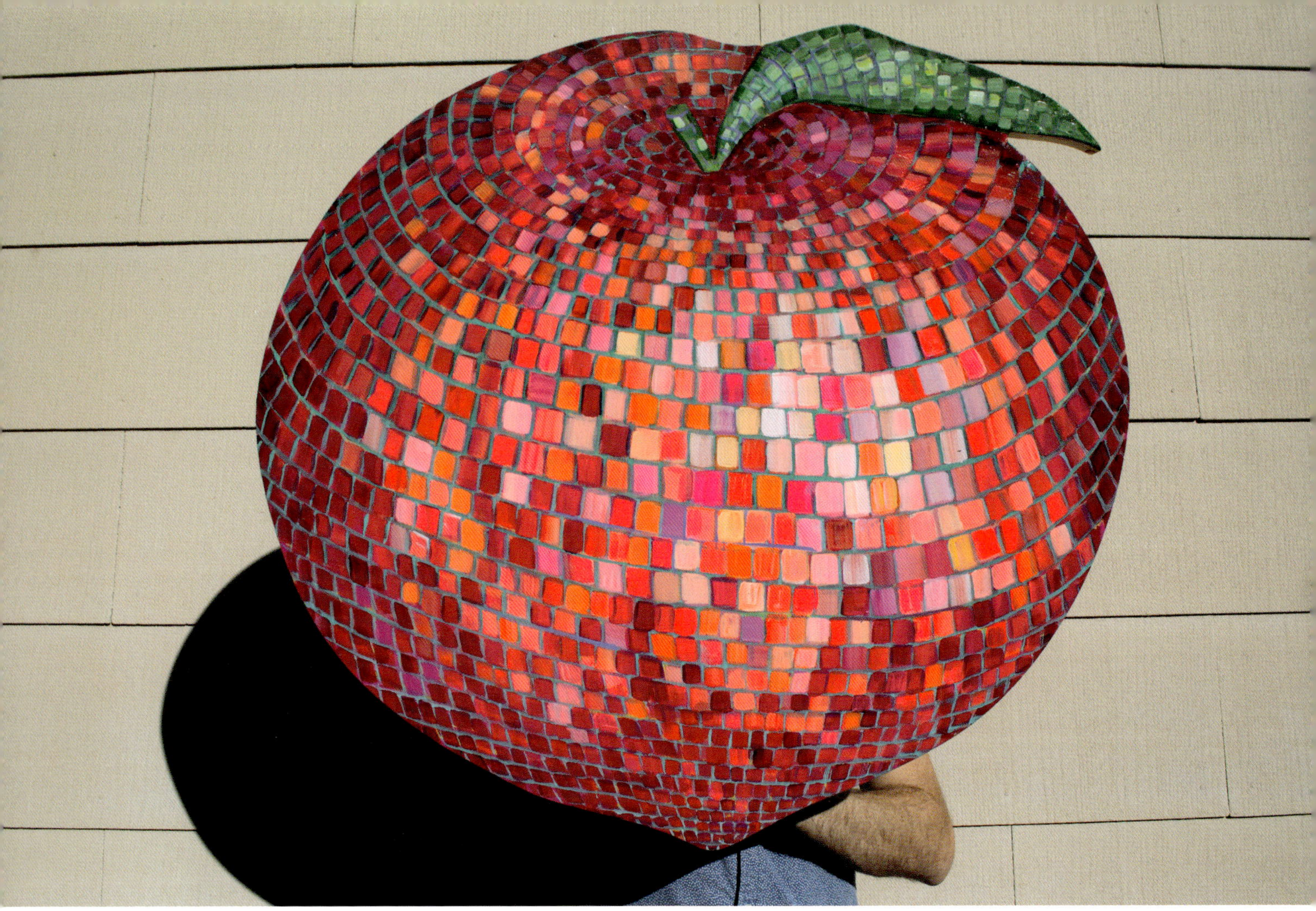

At this moment, it suddenly made perfect sense to turn those pesky circle canvases into shimmering disco balls that I could punctuate with all the bright colors I was already using. They would be representational, but also abstract, in a way that would allow me to tap into my stylized realism while embracing the whims of color inspiration that would come to me at the easel.

The idea to paint disco balls on circle canvases seemed almost too good to be true—I thought surely someone had already done it. But surprisingly, a thorough Internet search produced no such precedent. There were grayscale paintings on square and rectangular canvases, but nothing on a circle frame. I was elated and immediately eager to get to work.

Of course, every artist knows that even a great idea has its challenges when put into practice. Entering the studio with a disco ball reference photo, a tinge of intimidation lingered. My representational painting skills were still, to put it nicely, somewhat impressionistic. Disco balls, with their scores of tiny mirrors reflecting the surrounding room, posed a challenge. Those previous disco ball paintings I found on Google typically showcased black-and-white-looking studies, capturing a perfectly hyper-realistic disco ball. However, I leaned into my color palette, applying my signature flat and bright paint brush strokes and styles to introduce and exaggerate colors while staying true to the values.

What emerged was a colorful disco ball remix, slightly imperfect, especially in the initial attempts due to the canvas shape. But it created an optical illusion that made it appear like a real disco ball when photographed. Many years and hundreds of disco balls later, it has since become one of my most successful bodies of work. The popularity of this series is a big reason why I was able to transition from part-time artist to full-time.

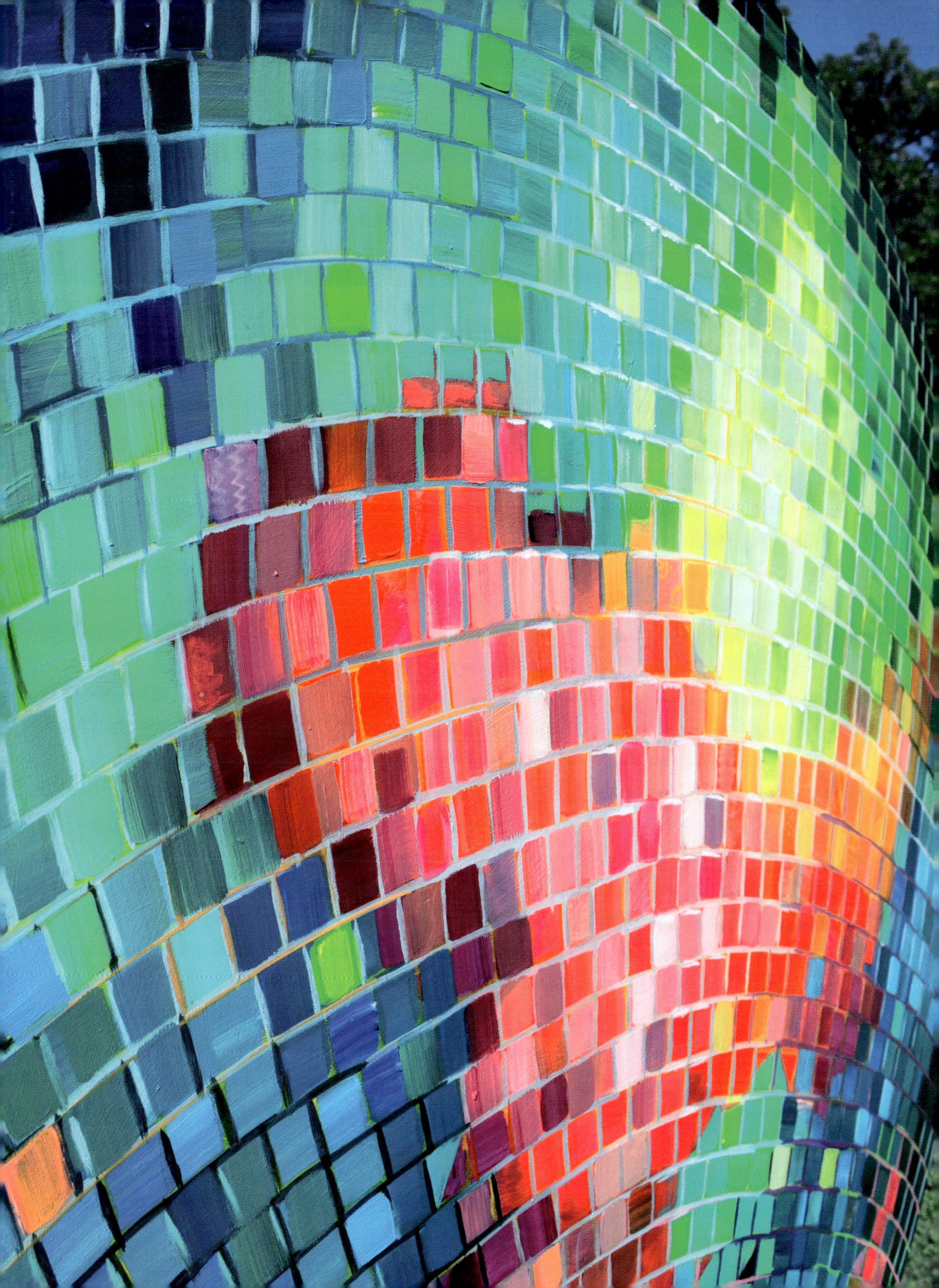

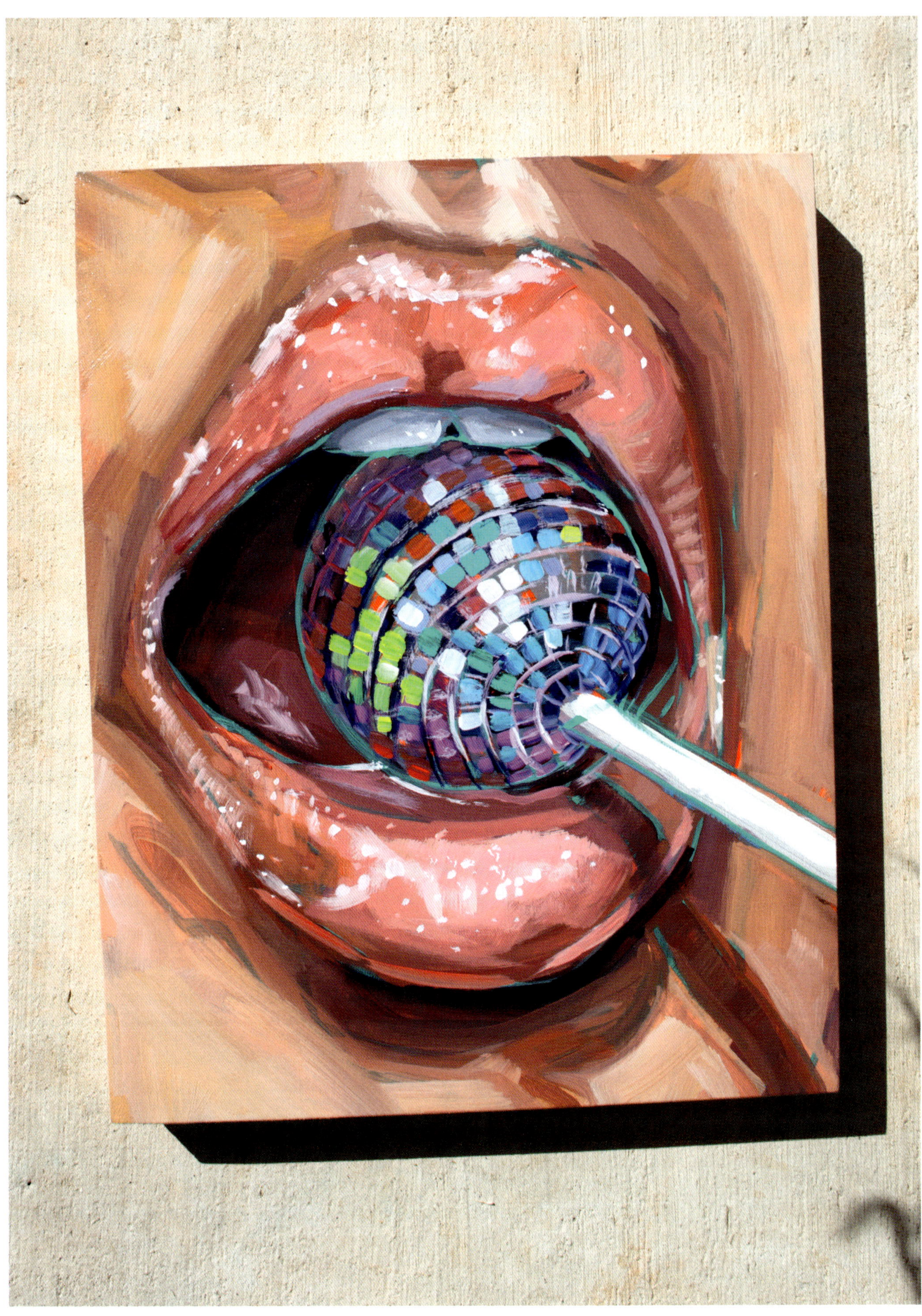

MODERN STILL LIFE

I wouldn't be the artist I am today without my disco ball paintings, and even five years on since I started painting them, I still cherish every opportunity to break out a fresh round wood canvas and turn it into a glittery orb of magic. The fact that collectors, students, teachers, and fans alike have resonated so much with these paintings has given my career much more purpose than I could have previously imagined.

Not everyone will relate to the particulars of my disco ball story, but everyone can relate to the pursuit of joy and building on shared traditions. These paintings started from a place of love for myself and my young son, and my hope in sharing them with you is that you can be inspired to create something similarly impactful in your life.

What can we learn from disco balls? In earlier chapters, I explained how I visualize my painting style: tiling in value and color chunks to develop form. My disco balls exemplify this technique, an idea I expanded upon from college.

What can painting a disco ball teach us in practical terms? Though it might seem like simply a playful exercise at first, the disco ball presents a unique opportunity to explore critical art principles, such as *trompe l'oeil*.

This French term, which translates to "deceive the eye," represents paintings so lifelike they appear real. In college, I learned of a competition between two hyper-realistic painters. One painter's depiction was so convincing that the judges believed a draped cloth over his artwork was real, only to discover it was painted. Hyper-realistic painting isn't the sole marker of talent—consider Marcel Duchamp's *Fountain* and his "readymade" series as proof of art's wide scope.

However, mastering representational painting techniques can captivate audiences more effectively in the visual sense. This is evident in my heart-shaped Valentine box, pearl, and disco ball paintings.

Another lesson from disco balls is understanding values. Correct value alignment is crucial for their appearance—any deviation can make them look distorted. This makes them an excellent study in value application. They also demand a basic grasp of drawing, particularly forced perspective, to ensure the appearance of three-dimensionality on a two-dimensional surface.

Then, there's the main attraction: color. Disco balls offer a chance to revel in pure color experimentation. Ironically, while they're optical illusion paintings, they are also the closest I've come to abstract art. I very much cherish the opportunity to dabble in realism and abstraction within one work.

For underpaintings, I often select color palettes inspired by nature, décor, historical art, or even sunsets. If you love color and appreciate a bit of repetition, the disco ball painting is for you. Even if it's the sole technique you adopt from this book, trust your instincts, persevere, and with a few steps back, a realistic disco ball can emerge before you.

Disco balls offer a chance to revel in pure color experimentation.

Disco Ball Step-by-Step

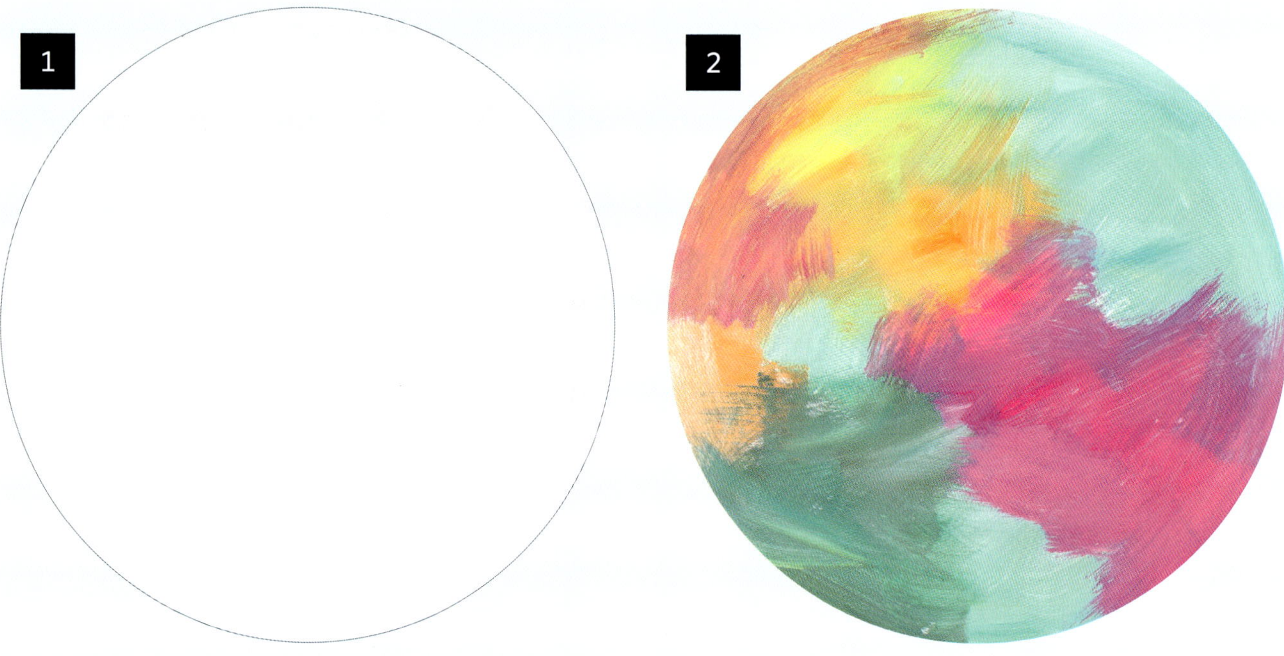

STEP 1

Begin your disco ball by priming and applying gesso to your chosen circular surface. Ensure that the surface you've selected is smooth and suitable for acrylic paint.

STEP 2

Your objective in this step is to cover the entire canvas with a layer of color, serving as your chromatic map for the rest of the piece. Although you may eventually conceal much of this layer in the subsequent steps, it will function as your guide for selecting colors throughout the rest of your painting. Feel free to indulge in some playful experimentation with your color palette beforehand, using a small piece of paper as a study, especially if you're working on a larger surface. This disco ball technique uniquely blends representational and abstract concepts together, as the form is anchored by the tiling, while the endless color possibilities allow for imaginative play.

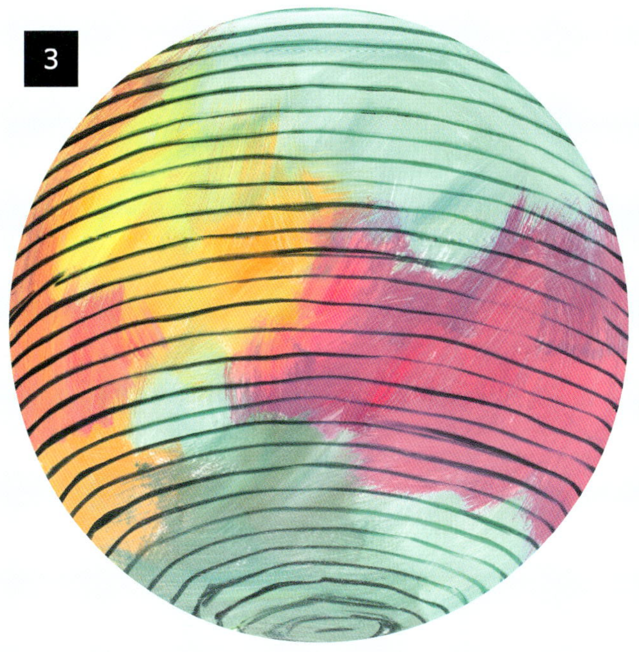

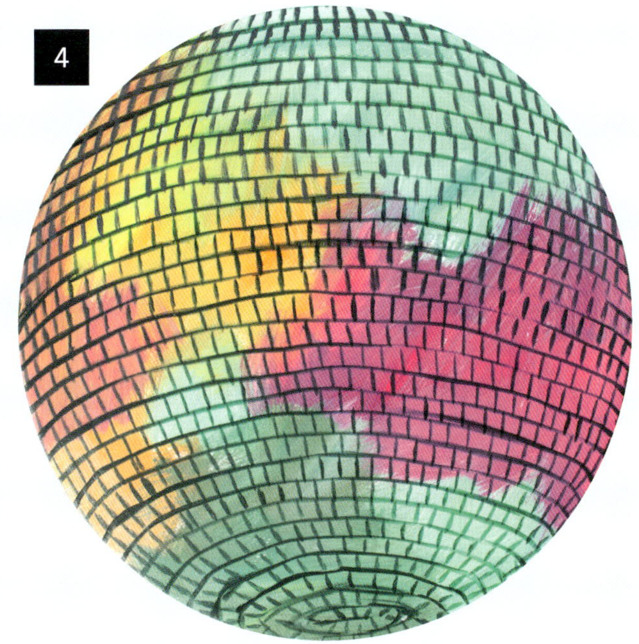

STEP 3

Draw the horizontal lines for your disco ball. Feel free to use practical tools such as a grid or a measuring stick to maintain precision and prevent any unruly lines. However, don't fret if your lines happen to sway off track. As I discovered in my earlier attempts at creating a disco ball, embracing these imperfections can yield shimmering results. Surprisingly, the overall effect of the disco ball remains captivating, even when absolute accuracy is not achieved.

It's crucial to bear in mind that our aim is to depict a spherical object. Consequently, the horizontal lines on the disco ball will appear closer together as they recede towards the top and bottom, compared to their spacing at the center. Moreover, pay close attention to the lines encircling the perimeter of the disco ball, especially on the left and right sides (assuming our shared orientation of the disco ball). These lines will subtly curve to accommodate the rounded shape and the slight perspective.

To ensure accuracy and guidance, I recommend keeping a reference photo handy. If you happen to have an actual disco ball nearby, capture a snapshot and pay particular attention to the grout lines, especially the horizontal ones. Let this visual reference serve as your companion throughout this step.

STEP 4

Apply the vertical lines to your disco ball. Unlike the previous steps, this one primarily consists of valuable tips rather than actual instructions. While proceeding, I advise referencing an actual photo of a disco ball, especially if you are new to painting this subject. This visual aid will greatly assist you in achieving accurate results.

Take note of the perimeter tiles, which may appear more condensed due to the effect of foreshortening. These tiles give the illusion of being narrower compared to the tiles positioned at the center of the disco ball. Remember, as we progress, subsequent layers will be applied over these tiles, so there is no need to overly fixate on them during this particular step.

Additionally, pay attention to the irregularity of the disco ball tiles. They often exhibit a slight staggered arrangement, akin to a brick wall, rather than aligning perfectly. Embrace these nuances and variations as they contribute to the character and authenticity of your disco ball rendering.

(continued)

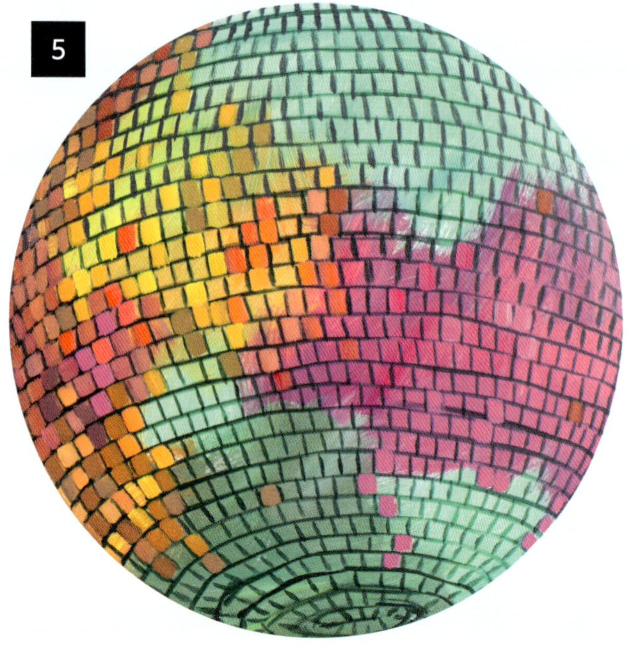

STEP 5

Now, we'll begin layering the actual disco ball tiles. To achieve this, select a flat or bright style brush, ideally one that matches the width or size of the tiles you're painting. This choice of brush will prove tremendously helpful in this step.

Mix colors that closely resemble those on your color map, which you painted back in step 2. Feel free to introduce some variations, as this process allows for a touch of intuition. If needed, refer to a reference photo to aid your visual understanding.

Don't fret about achieving perfection with each individual tile. The allure of disco balls lies in the layering effect and the subtle colors present around the tile perimeters, giving them a realistic tiled appearance. Remember, you're painting miniature mirrors, and in real disco balls, you often observe tiny hints of other colors around the edges of each individual mirror tile. Embrace any mistakes you may make, as they can contribute to this effect in a way that feels organic and effortless.

STEP 6

Moving forward, we continue the process of filling in more disco ball tiles. In this step, you'll notice that I deviated slightly from the darker green color at the bottom of the disco ball, opting instead for more silvery tiles. It's important to remember that you're not bound to adhere strictly to the color map. It serves as a guiding reference for colors, but you have the freedom to explore variations. In fact, I've experienced paintings that deviated significantly from the initial color map.

Remain intuitive in your approach, enjoy the process, and keep in mind that you can always layer over this step if your color experiments don't yield the desired result.

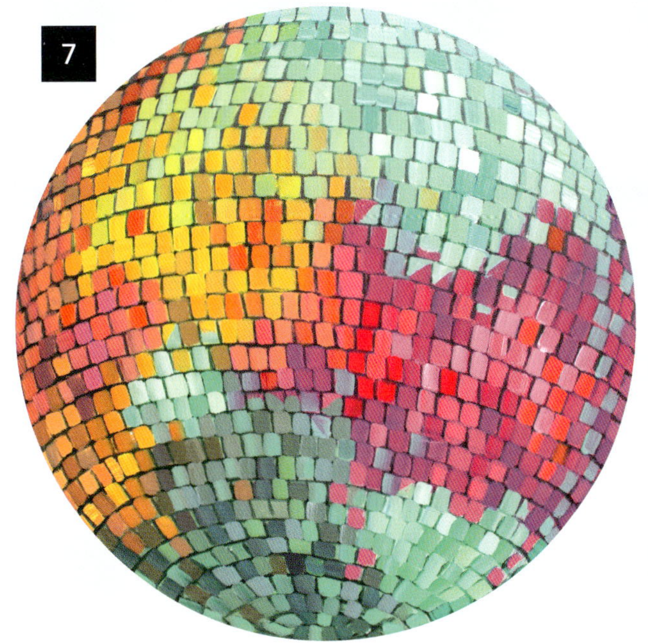

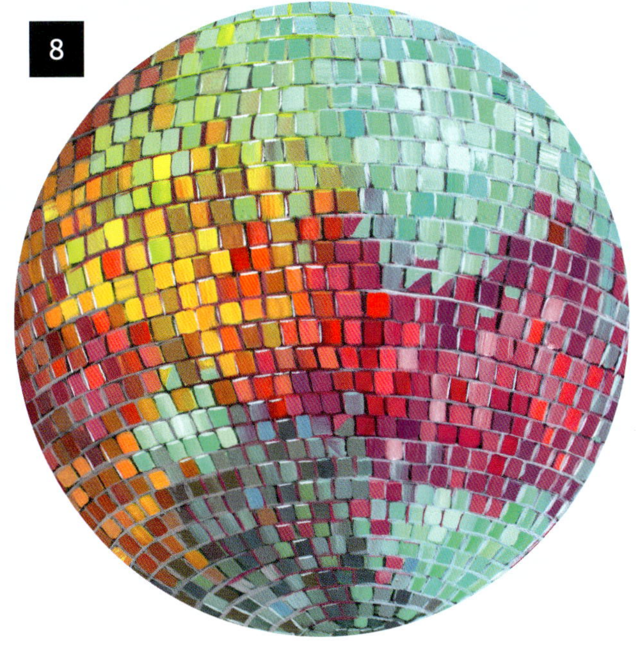

STEP 7

The entire surface of the disco ball has been covered with a layer of tiles. The primary objective in this step is to ensure that the entire painting is comprehensively covered before proceeding to the subsequent round of evaluations, be it in terms of drawing or color choices. It's highly recommended to take a momentary pause at this point and engage in introspection.

STEP 8

Once you have achieved a general sense of satisfaction with the placement, color, and value of all the tiles, it's time to add the final touches to enhance the grouting and incorporate captivating highlights.

In my case, I utilized shades of gray and lighter colors to reinforce the grout lines that may have become somewhat obscured in step 7. Additionally, take a moment to introduce highlights, paying attention to reference photos as they can provide insights into the placement of highlights on various sides of the tiles. Remember, moderation is key when applying highlights. A few well-placed ones can work wonders.

Embrace your mistakes!
They help create a feeling of
organic effortlessness.

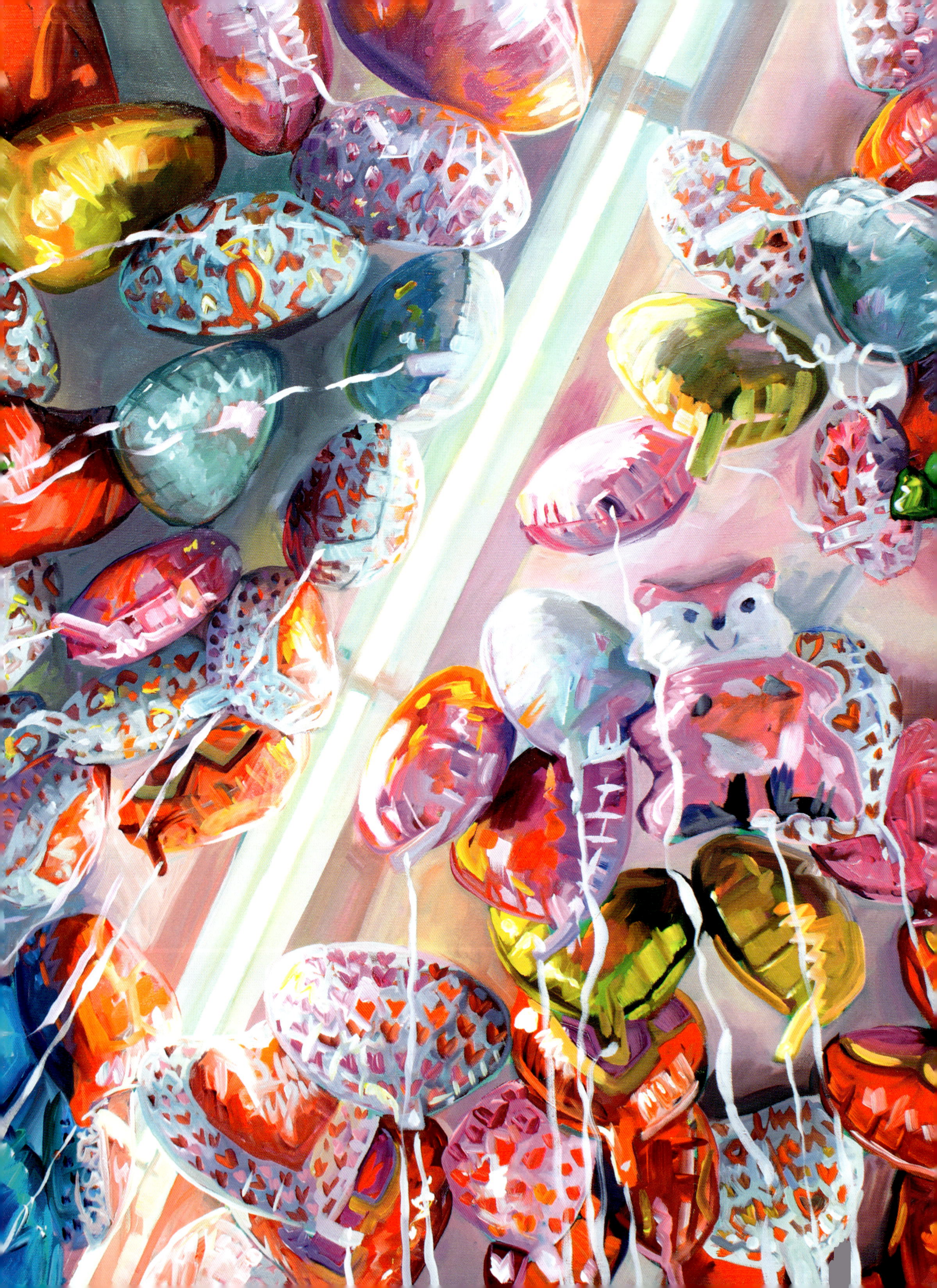

Modern Still Life

(Painting from Life)

WHEN I STARTED writing this painting book, my intention was to merge the traditional skills acquired in college and various professional workshops with accessibility. Admittedly, these elements sometimes conflict. A prime example is the intense debate over the merits of painting from life versus painting from a photograph. This conversation is laden with nuances, and it's crucial for budding artists to understand the compromises made when opting to paint from photographs. However, I believe the trade-offs are justifiable if the alternative between painting from photographs and painting from life is not painting at all, a situation I've experienced.

Choosing to paint exclusively from life is a noble undertaking. This technique was emphasized in college, where painting was a response to our real-world perceptions, and our interpretation held paramount importance—often deemed more important than precise rendering.

In such a student environment, where structure and space were provided, my painting professor highlighted the significance of learning to paint from life. Beyond the underlying philosophy, painting from life offers practical advantages, revealing a broader range of values compared to the constrained values in photos. Additionally, choices of cropping and image selection are inherently predetermined when taking a photograph. While this may seem advantageous, considering our binocular vision, there are subtle changes in perspective that are unattainable when painting from photos, as the camera offers a one-point perspective. Plus, the technological constraints of photography compress the image into pixels, enforcing creative and stylistic limitations due to the inherent limitations of photos. However, this isn't necessarily negative or positive.

For learning purposes, I advocate that students experiment with painting from life to discern the differences. Even if one prefers photo references, trying a few still lifes can illuminate what might be overlooked, providing for more informed decisions in the painting process. In defense of photography, it's an art form in its own right. Photographic references can be manipulated in applications like Photoshop to create more surreal effects. Tools are neutral, and creative pursuits should not be confined by the inability to visualize an image. Reaching a creative outcome is valid no matter how it's achieved, provided it is original and not appropriated from someone else's work.

When incorporating photography into your painting practice, here are several tips to consider:

- **Experience Painting from Life** Even if you predominantly use photos, attempt to paint from life a few times to comprehend the differences, particularly the subtle shifts in value and perspective in compositions. A simple study is a great place to start, focusing on subtle alterations in value and perspective.

- **Comprehensive Photography** When setting up for photography, assume you're preparing to paint from life. Experiment with composistions, sometimes taking up to 100 photos with minor adjustments in objects and perspectives. I've often regretted not spending more time adjusting compositions when painting from photos, as the freedom to modify setups is one of the advantages of painting from life.

- **Consider Your Perspective** Your perception of composition will significantly differ between setting up a photo and sitting down to paint. Something that makes sense photographically can be problematic when painting, like two similar objects losing distinctiveness due to lack of hyper-realistic rendering. Therefore, revisit and potentially modify your requirements for your photograph when switching to a painter's viewpoint.

- **Manage Exposure** To counteract the photo's compression of value, especially with smartphone pictures, create duplicates with varying exposures. This approach ensures the preservation of detail and richness in color and light that might be lost in a standard photograph.

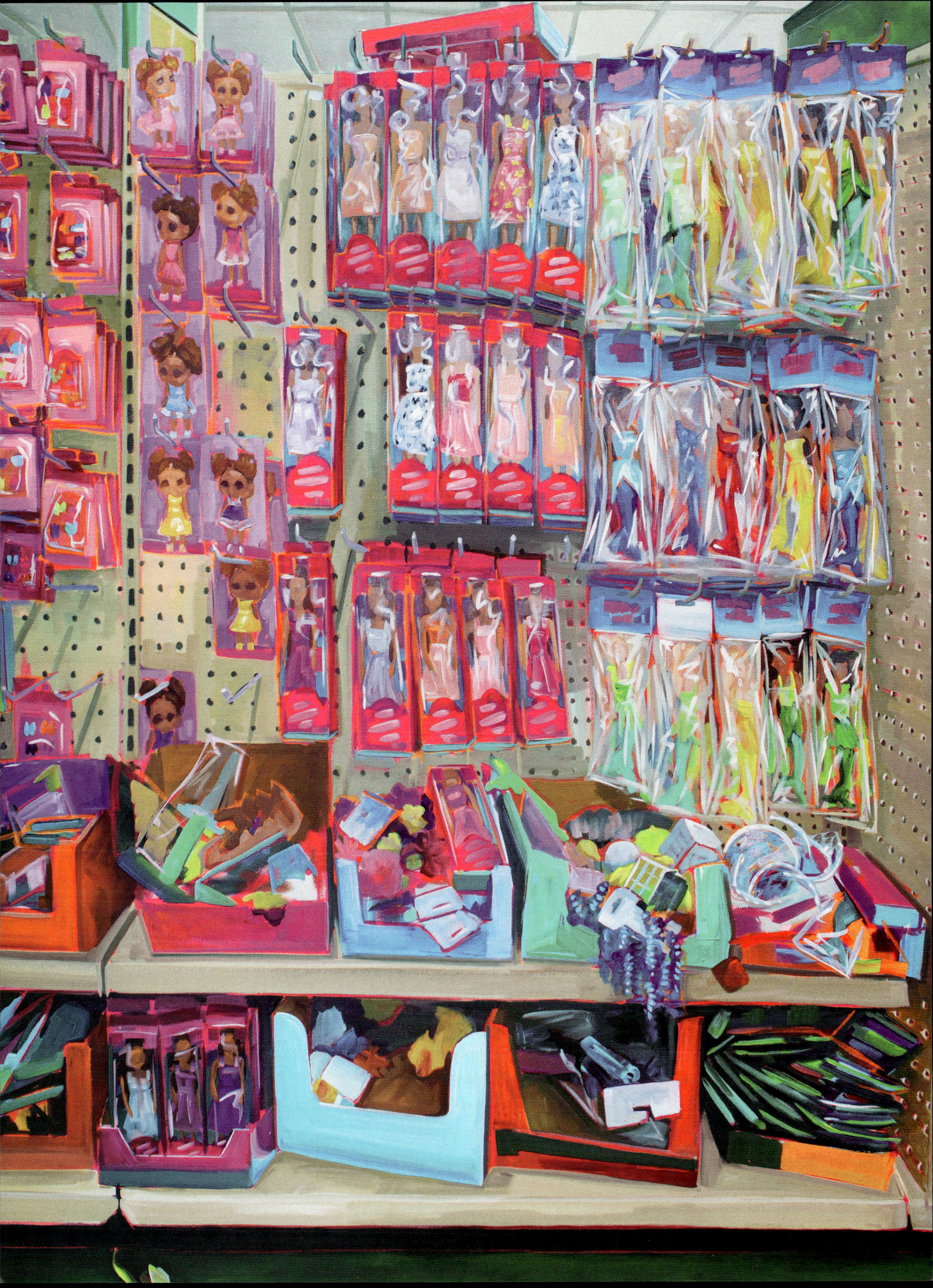

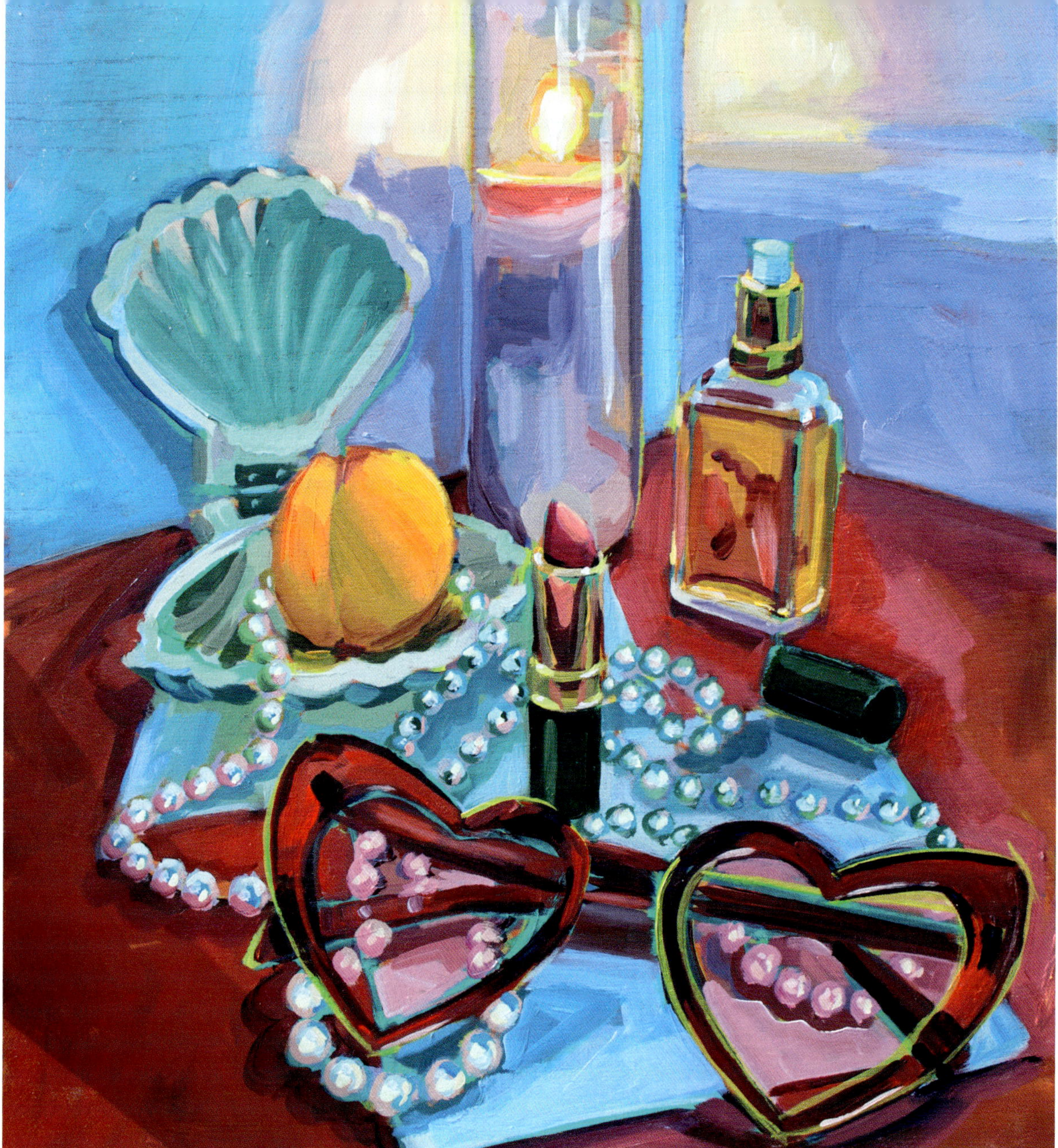

- **Mindful Cropping** Attention to cropping is crucial, not just during photography but also while editing. Use editing apps to adjust crops to match your painting's dimensions, always considering how cropping impacts the composition.

- **Detailed Note-Taking** If possible, record notes about color schemes, light, and other specific elements of the setup that might be lost in translation to photograph. Even a quick sketch or color study from life can be a valuable reference when painting from a photo, providing a richer context and clearer vision for your work.

- **Experiment with Adjustments** Experiencing regret over a photo's composition can be common, but adjusting compositions in real time while painting from life enables more flexibility and satisfaction with the final piece. Consider taking extensive photos and make thoughtful adjustments, focusing on how a painter's needs differ from the photographer's eye.

MODERN STILL LIFE

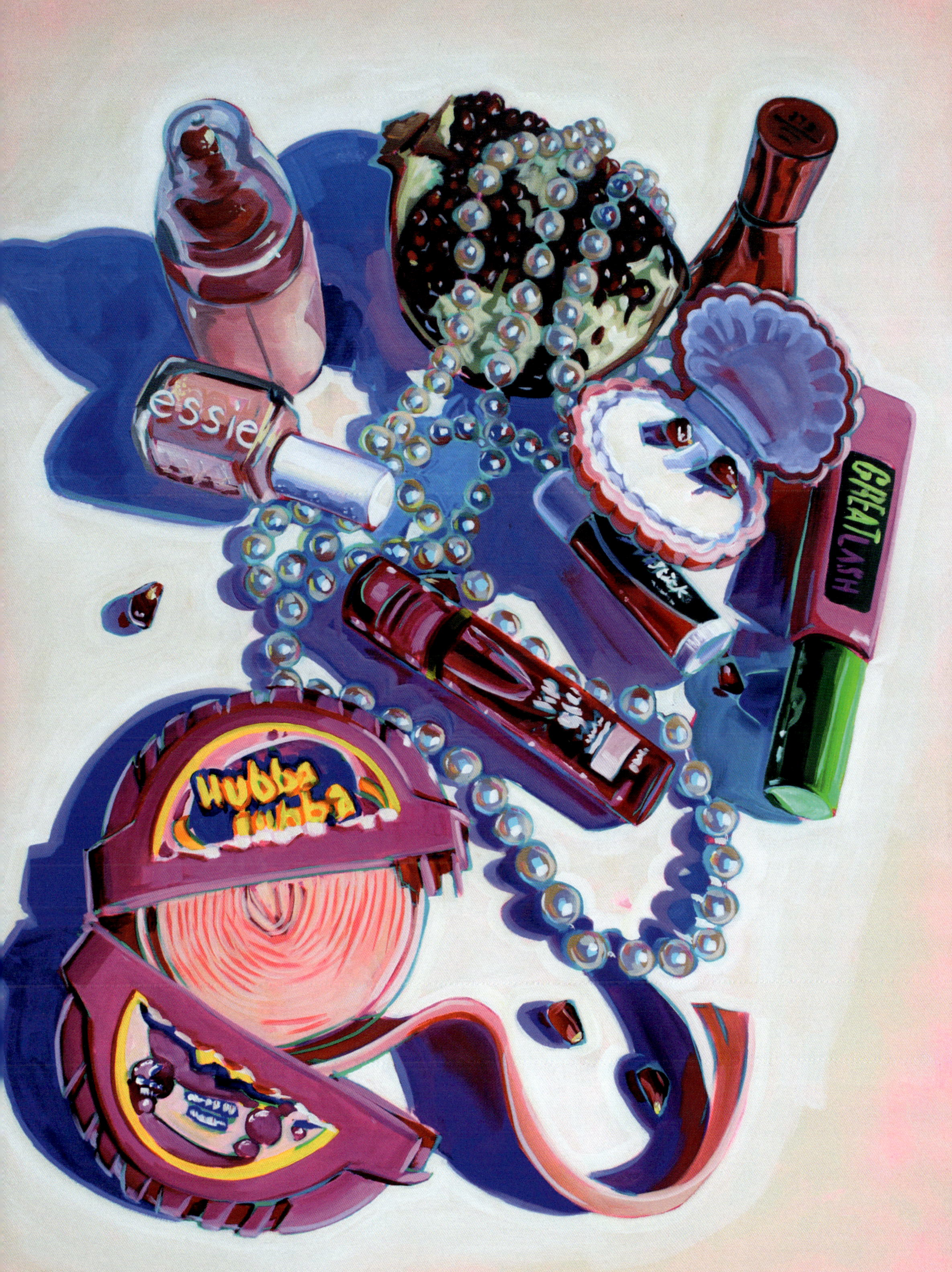

essie
GREAT LASH
Hubba Bubba

SEEING VS. KNOWING

Another important concept is the philosophy of painting what you see, not what you know. This is an art class staple due to its significance, but without proper understanding, it can be confusing.

You might wonder, "Isn't what I see informed by what I know, and vice versa?" To clarify, painting representationally from life best illustrates the stark contrast between these two concepts. When immersed in the act of painting, you realize that "seeing" and "knowing" are, in fact, different. Seeing requires an objective, observational approach, while knowing is shaped by subjective knowledge and preconceived notions. Thus, cultivating the ability to see without the interference of prior knowledge is fundamental in creating art that is a true representation of what is before us.

The process of interpreting visual information starts early in our lives, as we begin to recognize and respond to facial features, and our understanding of the world continually evolves from there. For instance, our innate affinity for recognizing faces develops into a more complex database, enabling us to make judgments and interpret the surrounding world.

Consider a chair: we don't scrutinize every chair to confirm its stability, counting each leg before we sit. From our elevated perspective, we often see only one or two legs, the others obscured by angle and perspective, yet our accumulated knowledge assures us the unseen legs are present and providing support. This is a prime example of the divergence between what we see and what we know, demonstrating how our experiences shape our understanding and expectations of the world around us.

Our brains are conditioned to trust in the unseen, based on prior knowledge and experience, and this ability plays a crucial role in our interaction with the world. Yet, representational painting challenges this fundamental skill, requiring us to bypass our conditioned understandings and see the world anew, interpreting it at face value, unobstructed by preconceived notions and expectations. It demands objectivity, observing the world as it presents itself, free from the interpretations forged by our ingrained experiences.

Developing the ability to bypass our acquired perceptions and paint the world exactly as it appears is fundamental for a representational painter. This isn't just about challenging our judgment, which has been a pivotal survival skill, but also about contesting the visual database encoded in our brains, the mental images that we all can conjure, albeit with varying degrees of clarity and accuracy.

Most often, our internal representations are more akin to cartoons than to realistic depictions. Beginning painters who are struggling might lean on these internal notions as a crutch, substituting them for the demanding task of accurately rendering what is seen. Further complicating this is our brain's propensity to fill in peripheral vision, creating a coherent but not entirely accurate picture of the world around us. This can be likened to a helpful hallucination, where our focus dictates the clarity of our vision, and the peripheries are approximations constructed by our brains. Looking directly and continually at your reference and correlating one look with one brush mark ensures accuracy and avoids the distortion of these helpful hallucinations. This meticulous method may seem extraordinarily labor intensive, but it prevents reliance on our internal, and often inaccurate, visual databases.

I cannot overstate the importance of this practice. It's a central tenet in representational painting. Placing a reminder on your easel to "paint what you see," regardless of your skill level, can be a constant guide to maintain rigorous observational integrity. Mastering this skill is challenging, but it makes painting increasingly exhilarating and rewarding.

Fantasy Still Life Step-by-Step

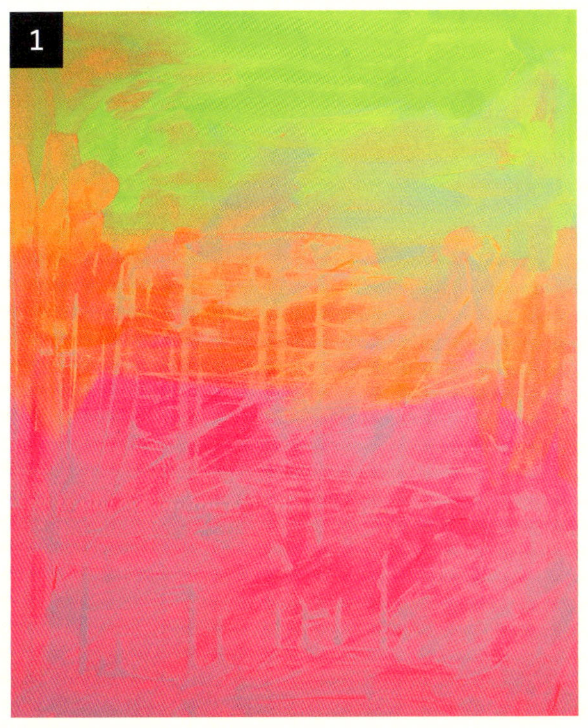

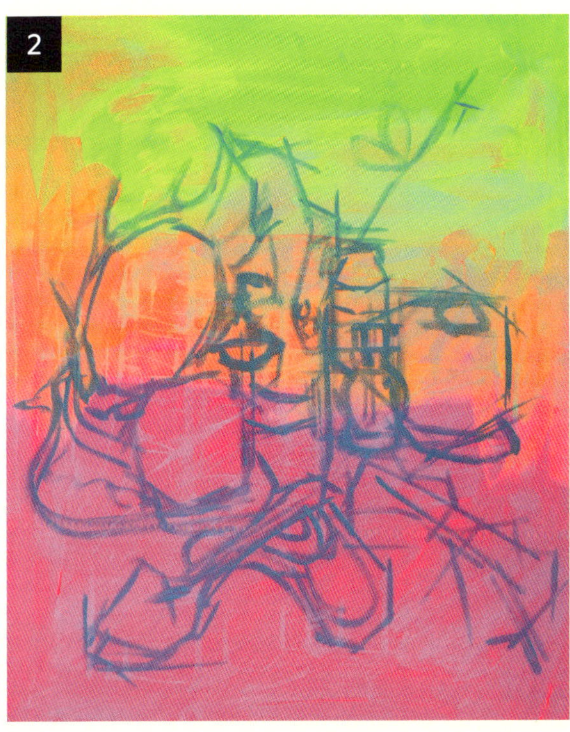

STEP 1

Priming the Canvas I prime the canvas using neon pink and neon yellow. By blending these colors together, we can create a brilliant sunset hue. While I cannot guarantee that this specific color combination will be replicated exactly in the final result, I found it to be an intriguing contrast to the dominant green tone in my reference.

This step aims to demonstrate the freedom and flexibility you have in choosing your starting point. It encourages you to break away from strict guidelines and embrace a more exploratory approach. The key principle to remember is selecting a value that falls within a middle range. If you are a beginner or unfamiliar with working with values, I recommend avoiding bright fluorescent colors for now.

STEP 2

Mapping Out the Image I use a blue color to create a preliminary outline of our image. The primary focus here is on establishing accurate proportions and relationships between the objects. Feel free to utilize a grid or any other tool that aids you in achieving precision. Personally, I rely on a combination of my own drawing skills and a technique where I align the tops of objects with their neighboring and distant objects on the canvas.

Remember to observe how objects align with one another, both vertically and horizontally, and pay attention to how they interact within the composition. This process helps ensure that the overall image remains visually coherent and true to the intended proportions. As you gain experience, you will develop your own abilities to draw with greater accuracy.

(continued)

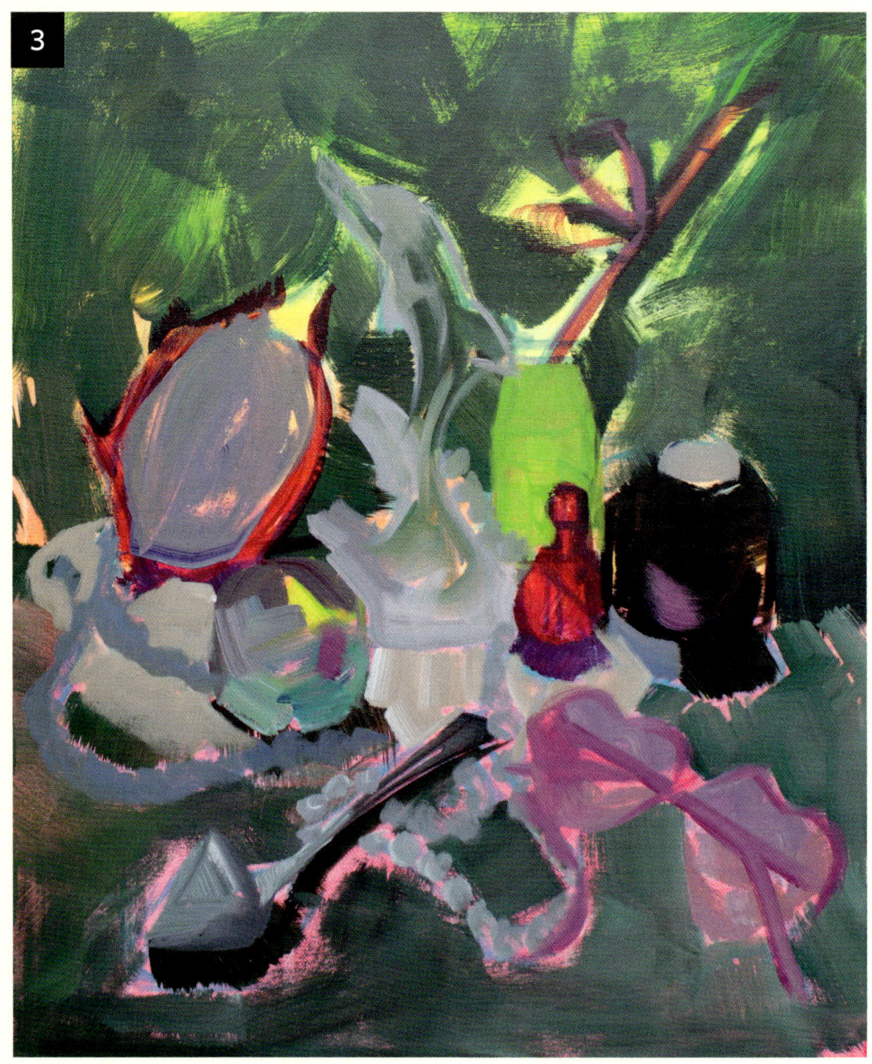

STEP 3

Establishing Base Coverage Our primary objective in step 3 is to cover a significant portion of the canvas or most of the objects within the composition. The focus is not on painting intricate details but rather on achieving approximately 75% completion. We aim to establish the overall value, placement, and color of the elements, understanding that they may not be perfect but are close enough for our purpose.

One key aspect of this step is working with averages. For instance, let's consider a string of pearls. Instead of fixating on the individual specular highlights that create the shiny appearance of each pearl, we concentrate on capturing the average color of the pearls. Rather than painting in all the highlights, we apply a single color to represent the entire pearl. This approach allows us to focus on the larger blocks of form and color, leaving the finer rendering of details for subsequent steps.

While working on circular and shiny objects, such as a disco ball, we can include a few details in different colors. However, at this stage, we avoid painting in each individual tile or specific details. Our emphasis is on capturing the broad shapes and colors, establishing the foundational elements of the artwork.

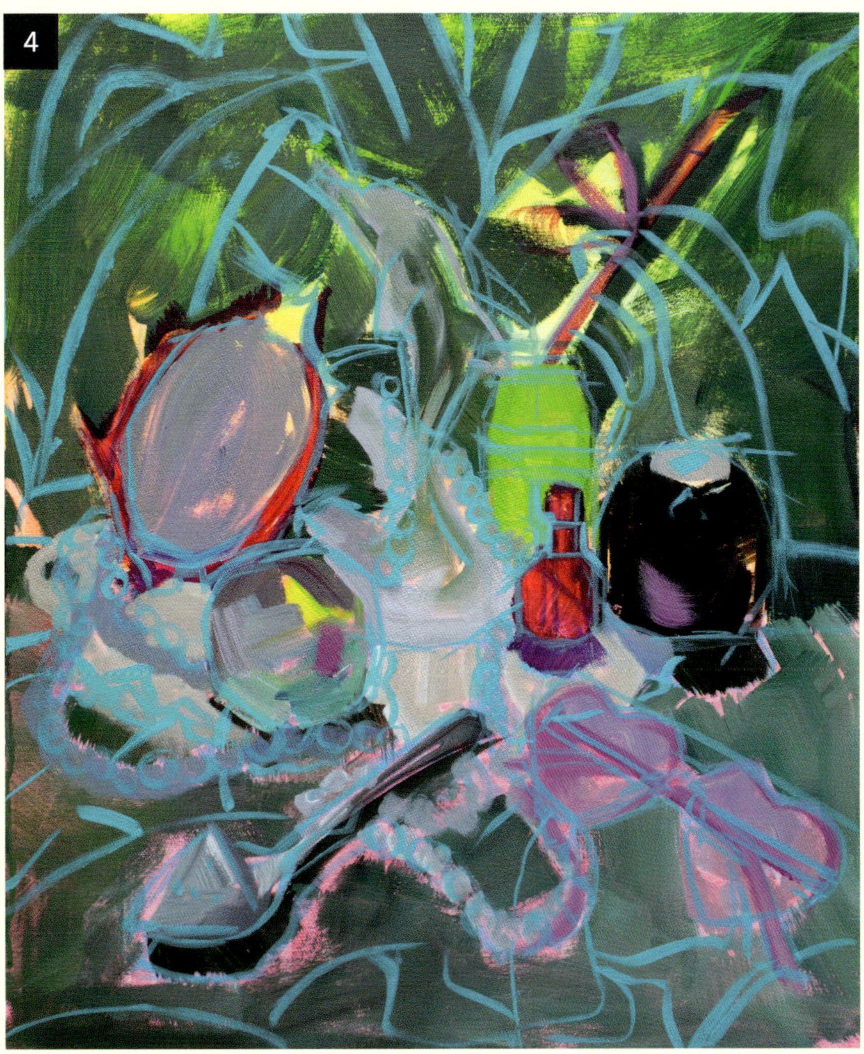

STEP 4

Refining with Teal Redraw Lines Now, we introduce a teal color for our redraw lines. This is the first instance in the painting process where we delve into the finer details and add a second layer of information. With a clearer understanding of the overall composition from the previous steps, we can focus on refining and carving out more specific information.

At this point, the positioning of most of the objects is relatively correct, allowing us to concentrate on adding more intricate details. For example, when working on the pearls, we transition from simply indicating their presence with basic shapes to refining them into distinct individual pearl shapes. This level of detail adds depth and realism to the artwork.

Similarly, with the heart shaped sunglasses, rather than solely focusing on where their edges intersect with other elements, we can now pay attention to the heart shape within the lenses. This heart shape serves as a guide for our next steps, helping us capture the essence of the sunglasses with greater accuracy.

By utilizing the teal redraw lines, we refine our initial drawing, incorporating more nuanced information and enhancing the overall intricacy of the painting. This step allows us to bring the objects to life and move closer to achieving the desired level of detail and realism in our artwork.

(continued)

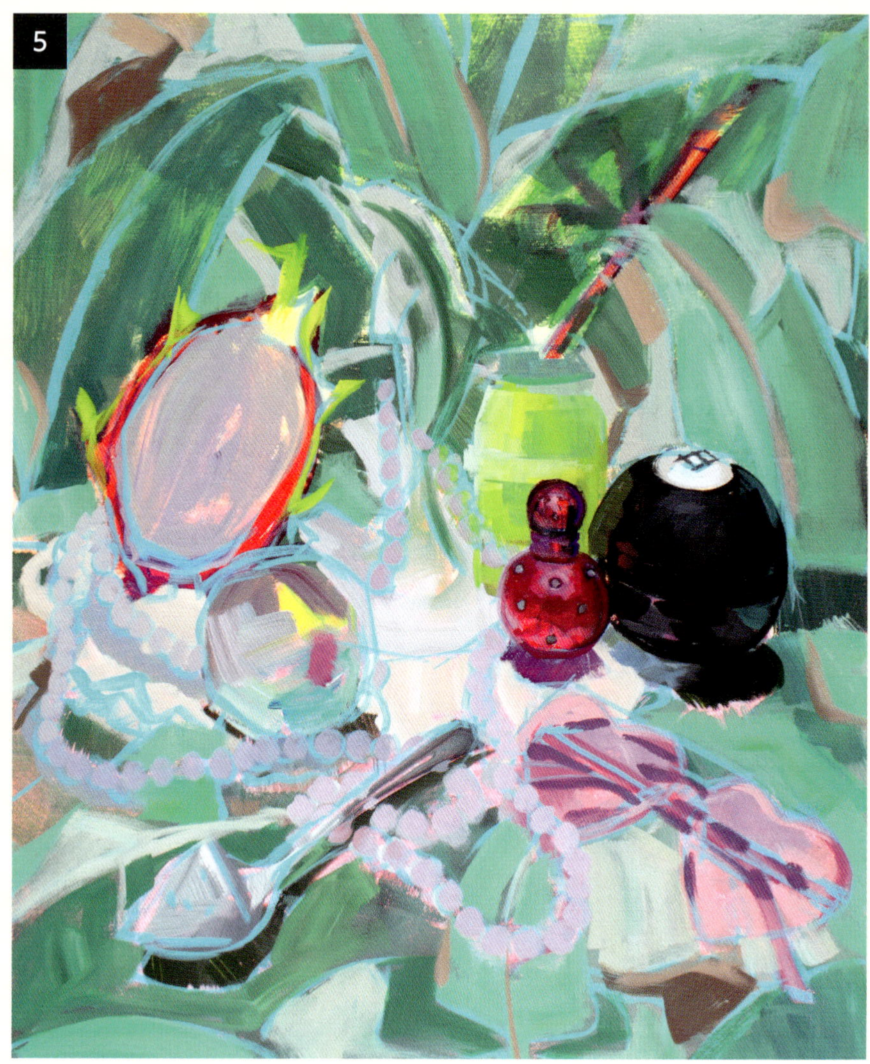

STEP 5

Adding Background Details Our focus shifts to blocking in more background information in step 5. In the previous step, we established a basic representation of the banana leaf print pattern, opting for an average color slightly leaning towards darker tones. This served as a holding space for future development and detail work. It's important to note that, at this stage, the pattern might feel somewhat inverted and distracting since only a few objects have been rendered in detail. However, trust the process, as we know that as we render more foreground objects and the main subject, the pattern will recede further into the background, creating a sense of flatness and emphasizing its nature as a pattern rather than actual banana leaves.

Additionally, we've dedicated more attention to rendering the Magic 8 Ball and the pink perfume bottle with a higher level of detail. Sometimes during the painting process, it can be beneficial to render certain objects to a particular level of detail before moving on to others. This selective approach allows for a more balanced development of the painting, ensuring that each object receives the necessary attention and refinement.

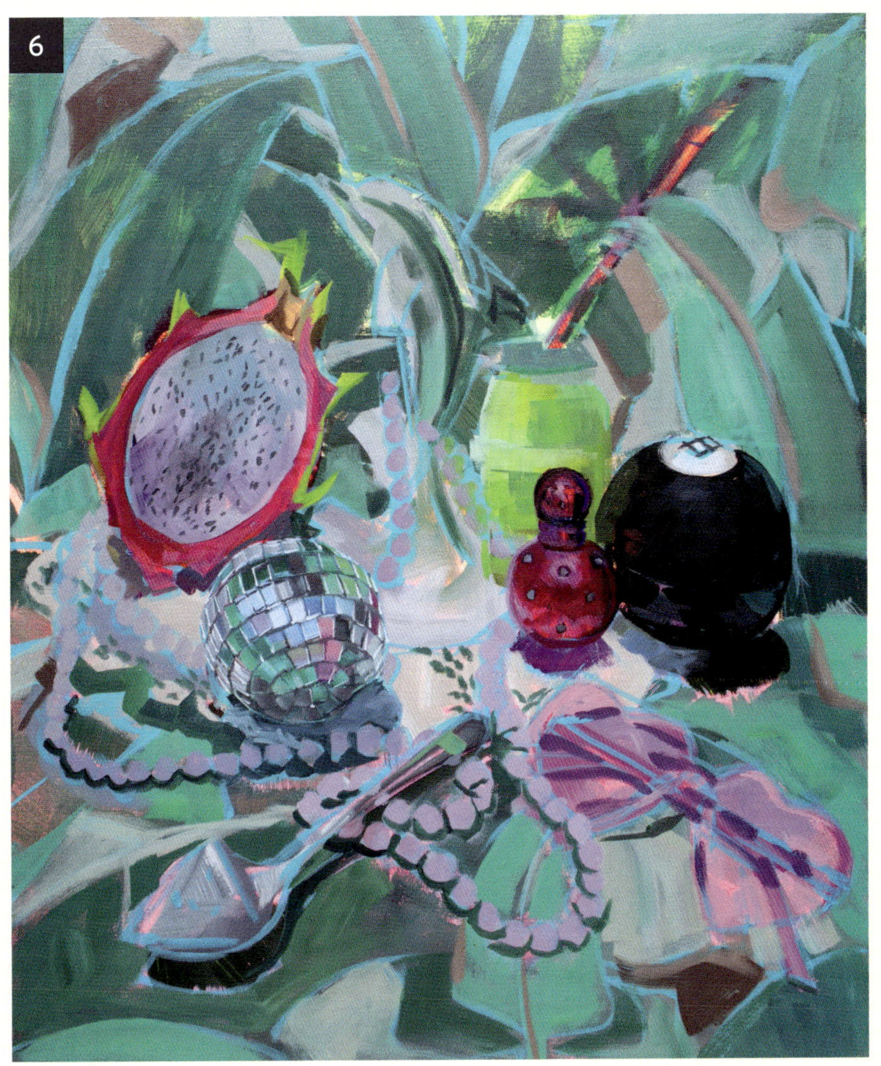

STEP 6

Adding Detail to Various Elements Now, we begin to introduce more information to different parts of the composition, specifically focusing on the disco ball, dragon fruit, and enhancing the shaping of the pearls and sunglasses by incorporating darker elements. As we navigate through the various objects, we strive for a balanced approach, ensuring that no single element receives full rendering before others.

The complexity of objects like the disco ball, dragon fruit, and pearls necessitates a careful understanding of their intricacies. Consequently, it may be necessary to render specific objects with a slightly higher level of clarity. However, it's crucial to maintain a disciplined approach by stopping short of fully rendering them, allowing for an even development of the composition as a whole.

By moving around and working on different objects in a systematic manner, we achieve a sense of balance and coherence across the artwork. While providing additional detail to specific elements, we keep in mind the importance of maintaining an overall even progression throughout the composition.

(continued)

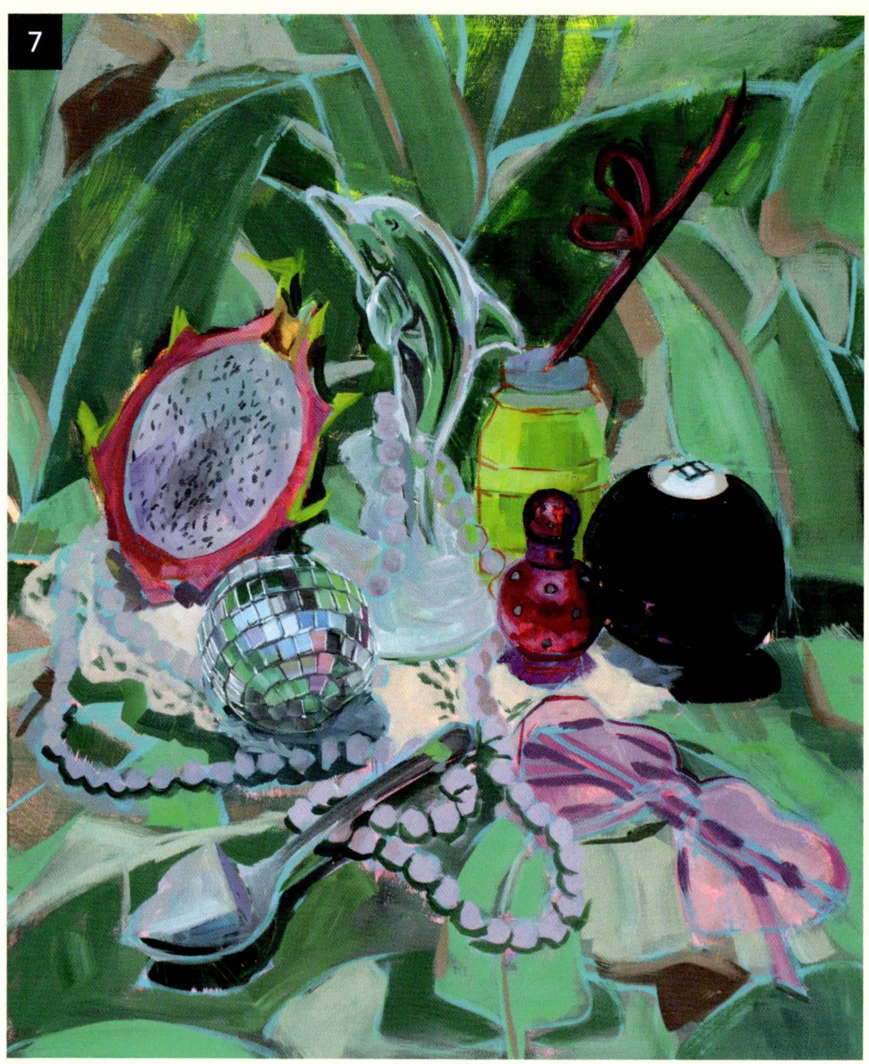

7

STEP 7

Further Redraw and Rendering I am employing another redraw to refine specific elements within the composition. This is particularly noticeable in the yellow green jug in the background, as well as the straw, and to a lesser extent, the dolphin. While I invest more effort in rendering details for the dolphin and straw, the jug and some of the previously carved-out pearls still require attention.

Remember, the redraw line can be utilized at various stages of the painting process. Not every stage necessitates a complete and total redraw. In this instance, only a small portion of the painting in this step required a redraw, while other objects remained untouched. This approach allows for a focused and efficient use of time and effort.

By engaging in a redraw, I was able to overcome confusion regarding the proportions of the jug. The presence of the background elements had previously obscured its form. However, through the redraw, I found clarity and a better understanding of its shape. Similar to the jug, the redraw also helped me refine the form of the straw.

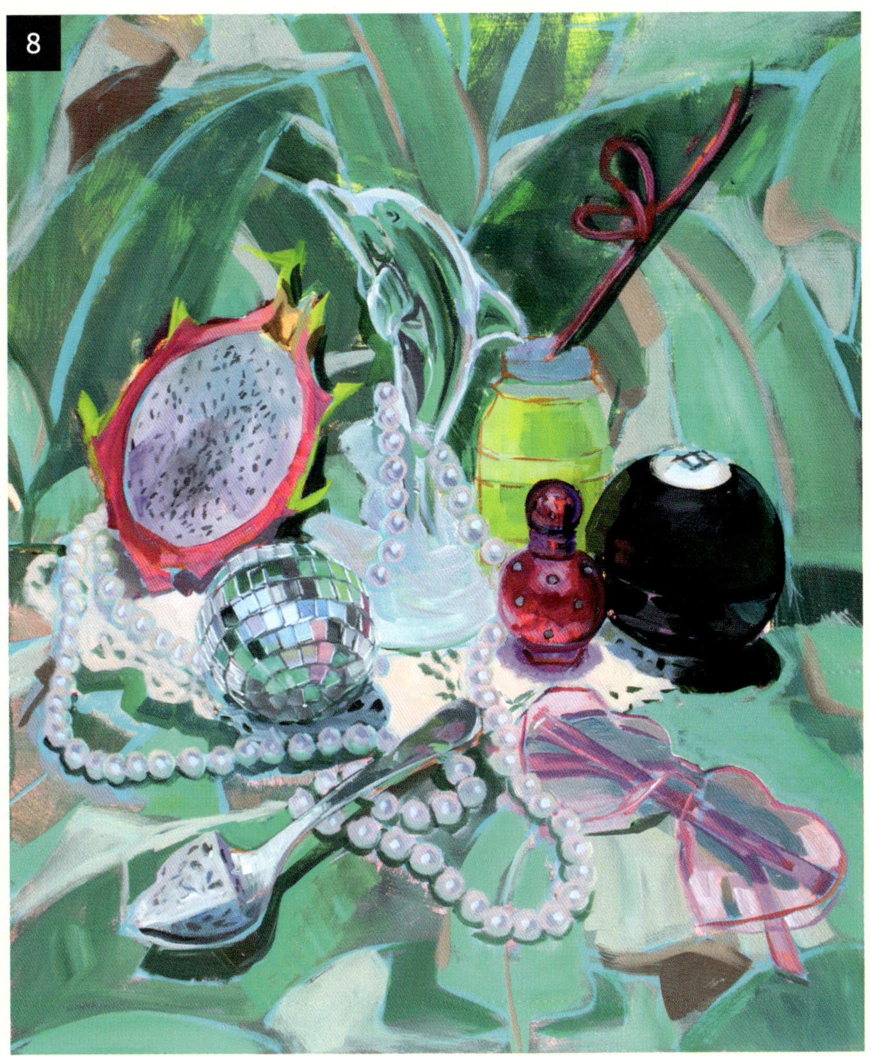

STEP 8

Adding More Detail We're continuing to add more information and detail to the pearls, sunglasses, spoon with the dragon fruit flesh, and certain areas of the banana leaf print background. By now, most of the objects in the painting have reached about 80% completion in terms of rendering.

As we prepare to transition to step 9, this stage allows us to make informed decisions about the level of information and detail we want to give to each object. The amount of attention and detail given to each object contributes to the overall style and visual impact of the image. For example, if we were to paint everything in perfect realism,

including individual images reflected in each tile mirror of the disco ball, it would result in a hyper-realistic representation. In contrast, by incorporating a painterly approach and focusing on color averages, we can achieve a realistic yet expressive rendition of the disco ball.

Maintaining control over the level of detail provided to each element is crucial. By working circularly throughout the painting, systematically addressing different areas, we can ensure a cohesive and balanced distribution of attention and detail across the composition.

(continued)

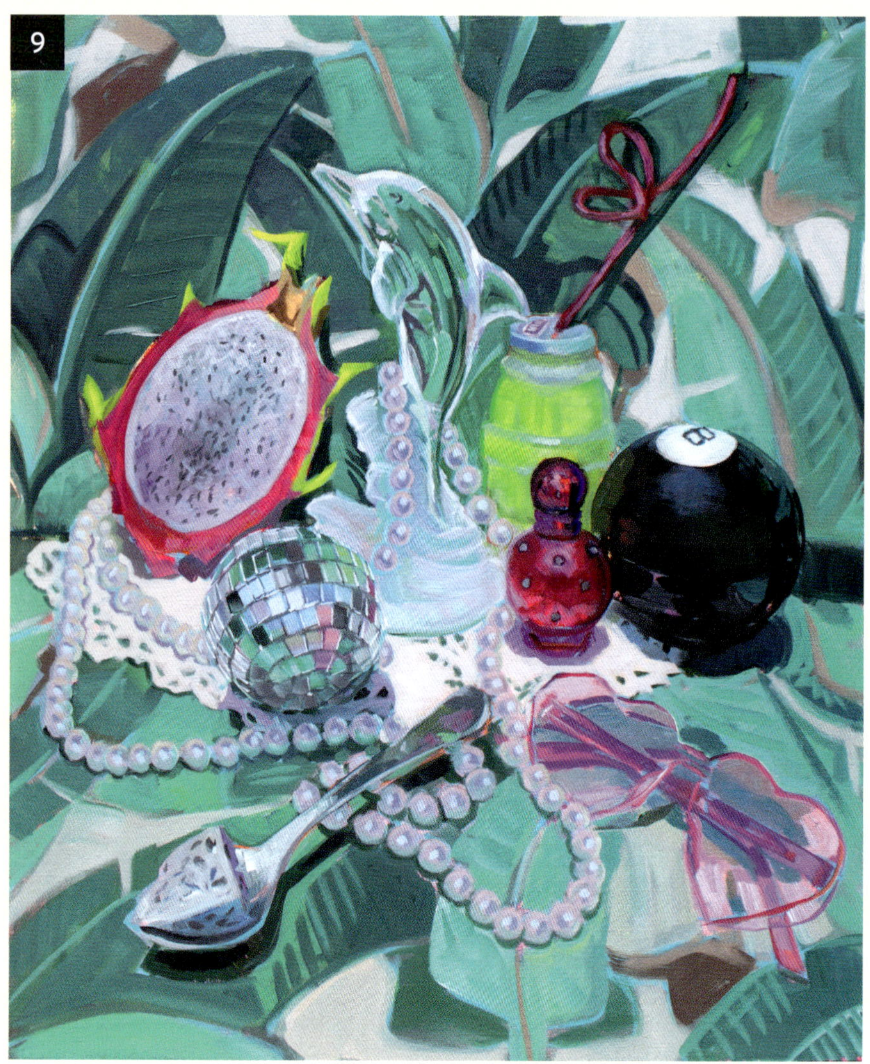

STEP 9

Resolving the Painting In the penultimate step, our focus is on resolving the painting to a relatively complete state. However, we have not yet added the final highlights to most of the objects. While there are lightest values present without the highlights, such as the finish on the pearls, an additional level of highlight will be incorporated. Similarly, reflections on the black surface of the Magic 8 Ball have been included, but the uppermost highlights have yet to be added. This deliberate approach allows for better control and ensures that the painting remains coherent and meaningful even without the presence of highlights.

It's important to note that the chosen complex pattern in this image, specifically the banana leaves, has been resolved to a point where they are recognizable but not overly rendered. The values have been flattened to maintain a clear distinction between the background print and the objects in the foreground. By striking a balance and avoiding excessive rendering of the banana leaves, we create visual separation, distinguishing the flat pattern from the three-dimensional objects that exist in a more realistic space.

While the pattern may be visually busy, the deliberate approach to rendering allows for clear differentiation and a cohesive portrayal of the objects in the foreground and the pattern in the background.

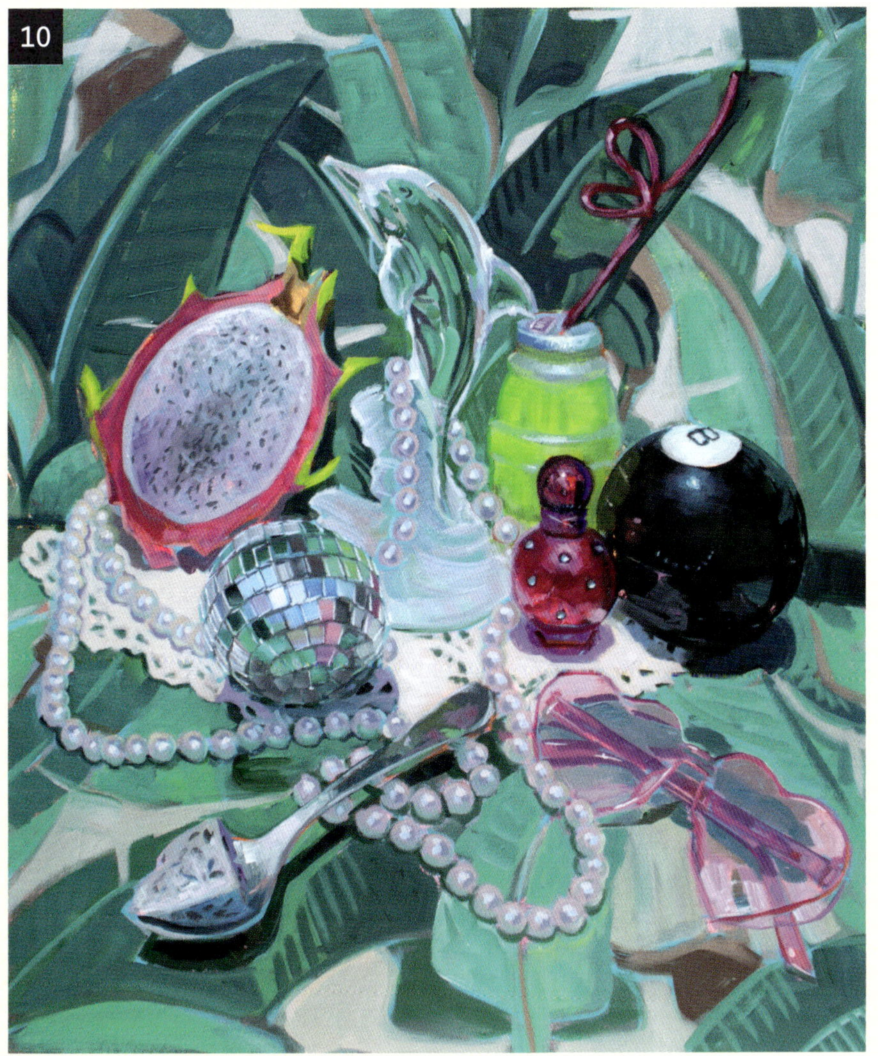

STEP 10

Finalizing the Painting Here, we carefully analyze the artwork to ensure that we are satisfied with the order of values and the overall color harmonies at play. If everything meets our expectations, we proceed to add finishing details and highlights.

Finishing details, while not carrying significant weight in the overall composition, play a crucial role in achieving a realistic look. For instance, we focus on adding highlights to specific areas, such as the Magic 8 Ball, sunglasses, disco ball, and pearls. These highlights bring a sense of luminosity and dimensionality to the painting, enhancing its visual impact.

During this stage, it's also important to conduct a thorough check for any drawing errors or inconsistencies. Often, with a fresh perspective, small errors that may have been overlooked before become apparent. It's beneficial to allow a day of rest between the last two steps to approach the painting with the freshest eyes possible.

The addition of highlights and meticulous attention to detail in this final step help bring the painting together and make it shine. It adds the final touches that complete the artwork and enhance its overall realism and appeal.

(continued)

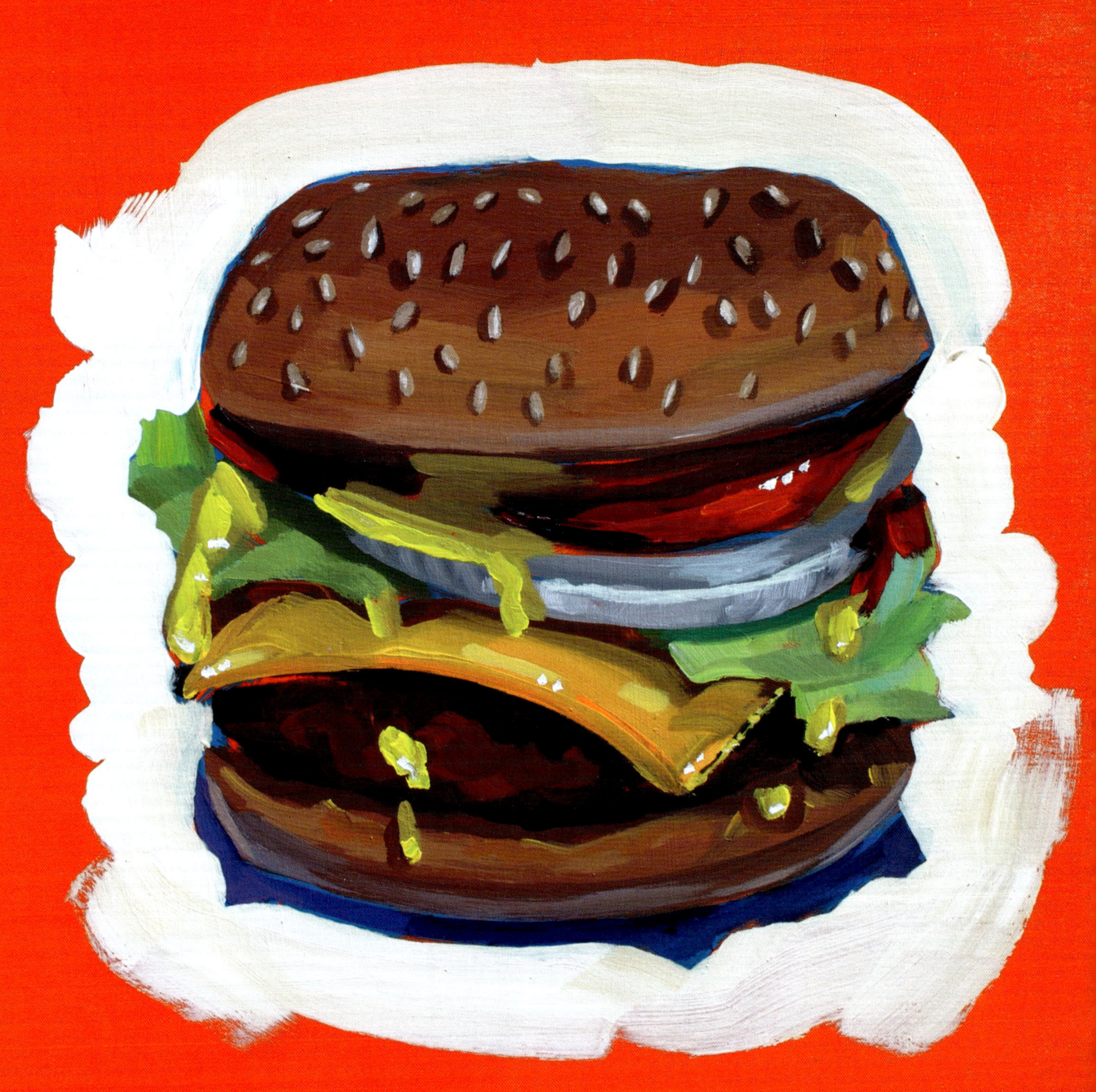

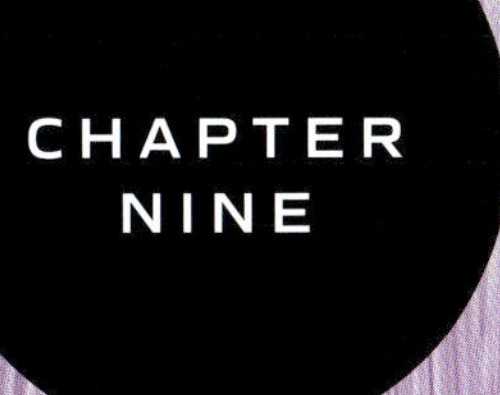

Style Sandwich

DISCUSSING STYLE can be challenging. In painting, the narrative often goes something like, "You don't find your style; your style finds you." That's true, but it's not necessarily helpful, especially for new painters or those exploring new styles like representational painting.

If there's one piece of advice I can give to new and emerging painters, it's to not only learn to accept your mistakes, but to treasure them.

I don't simply mean tolerate your painting mistakes. I want you to really lean in and embrace them. I remember when I started to get some podcast interviews early in my career, the question about how I found my style always caught me off guard. At the time, I was trying my best to make realistic paintings, so any "style" that was showing through was simply me falling short of my intention.

My colors were exaggerated, I probably could have found a few more levels of value with my objects, and my drawing has always been a little "off." Believe me, if at the beginning of my career I could have easily corrected those perceived issues, I would have. But in hindsight, I know if I had done that I wouldn't be the painter I am today.

For those needing reassurance and guidance in discovering style, consider my analogy: I think of style like a sandwich. The top bun represents our strengths, and the bottom bun represents our perceived weaknesses. For instance, Alice Neel, a renowned twentieth-century American figurative painter, seemingly defies traditional anatomical representation by choosing expression and uniqueness over accuracy. Some might view this as a weakness, but it's arguably her greatest strength.

Similarly, what we perceive as strengths and weaknesses in art can often be interchangeable, just like the buns of a sandwich. The fillings of your sandwich are your influences: other artists you admire, your chosen techniques and colors, media forms, workshops attended, and any other creative practices influencing your painting. Over time, as you accumulate diverse influences, your style sandwich evolves from one-dimensional to rich and complex, becoming distinctly yours. There's no need to strive deliberately for uniqueness. Every artist, influenced by their unique set of strengths, weaknesses, and experiences, will naturally develop a distinctive style, even when working with similar subject matter and mediums.

Your unique sandwich is constructed by your craftsmanship and the myriad of ingredients that influence how you perceive and translate the world around you. Remember, developing style doesn't necessitate an immediate, profound uniqueness. Many start by emulating the style of an artist they admire, finding their entry point into the vast ocean of interpretational possibilities, before eventually swimming to their unique spot in the expanse of artistic interpretation.

When conducting a master study to learn from an accomplished artist, the emphasis should be on learning how they perceive the world, not just replicating their work. Proper credit must be given to the original artist to protect the creative labor and intellectual property of fellow artists. This ensures respect and ethical conduct within the artistic community. However, don't be deterred by this delicate balance. Master studies are a normal and invaluable part of learning, offering insight into the creative processes of other artists and helping you develop your unique style sandwich. So, keep painting, enjoy learning, and remember, your style will find you.

There's no need to
strive deliberately for uniqueness.

HOW TO UNDERSTAND GROWTH AS A PAINTER

One of the aspects I cherish about painting is its seemingly low stakes. To my knowledge, no one has ever faced dire consequences due to a poorly executed painting. Yet, this seemingly harmless activity often creates fear, uncertainty, and an urge towards perfectionism for many.

It's this curious juxtaposition of apparent triviality with deep emotional vulnerability that fascinates me. While painting is often equated with bravery, most people reserve that word for actions like skydiving, bungee jumping, or facing life-altering challenges. Comparatively, approaching an easel seems much less daunting. However, it's this very understatement that often prevents us from addressing the genuine courage painting demands.

Unfortunately, the Western teaching surrounding visual arts seems flawed. From a young age, children are encouraged to pick up crayons and express themselves. However, as they progress through early education, a divisive hierarchy emerges. A select few are labeled as *artists*, while the rest, perhaps those whose skills develop at a slower pace, are dismissed as *non-artists*. This division isn't a testament to inherent talent but rather an unfortunate labeling system. Contrary to popular belief, no one is born an artist. While some may seem preternaturally talented, the majority, including myself, rely on persistence and passion. This ill-conceived labeling often leaves individuals feeling they must validate themselves as artists.

For many, there's a looming pressure to monetize their art quickly to justify the investment of time and energy. In my experience teaching painting, I've observed common self-doubt themes: not being good, skilled, talented, quick, or dedicated enough . A pertinent quote I've come across encapsulates this sentiment: "The harshest criticism you've ever heard is likely something you've already told yourself." It underscores the idea that our internal narratives, often established in childhood, are the primary culprits behind our artistic anxieties. Thus, my top advice for understanding growth as a painter is to shift focus from producing a "good painting" to seeking intrinsic goals and motivations. Instead of relying on external validation, anchor your journey in personal milestones and self-awareness.

So, how do we truly understand growth as a painter? At its core, you must reconcile with a gulf—the gap between your current skills and where you aspire to be artistically. For many, this gap appears daunting at first. We approach our initial artwork with enthusiasm, guided by a step-by-step process. However, reality often diverges from our expectations. Painting is intricate, requiring a delicate balance between conceptual understanding and physical skill. Over time, as your proficiency improves, this gulf narrows. But be warned—it never disappears entirely.

Despite years of dedication and countless hours at the easel, I too still find areas of improvement. This perpetual push for improvement is something every painter must grapple with. In these early stages, when the divide between aspiration and reality is widest, you need motivation to persist. It's essential to find comfort in discomfort and set manageable, internally driven goals. Instead of aiming solely for a "good painting"—a subjective target influenced by external perceptions—focus on smaller, specific milestones.

For instance, challenge yourself to utilize a larger brush than usual or achieve a specific lighting effect. These tangible targets not only provide direction but also offer genuine satisfaction when achieved.

A constructive approach I recommend involves pre-planning before painting. Begin by jotting down aspects of your subject that captivated you. This preserves your initial inspiration, preventing it from being overshadowed by the subsequent hours of scrutiny and

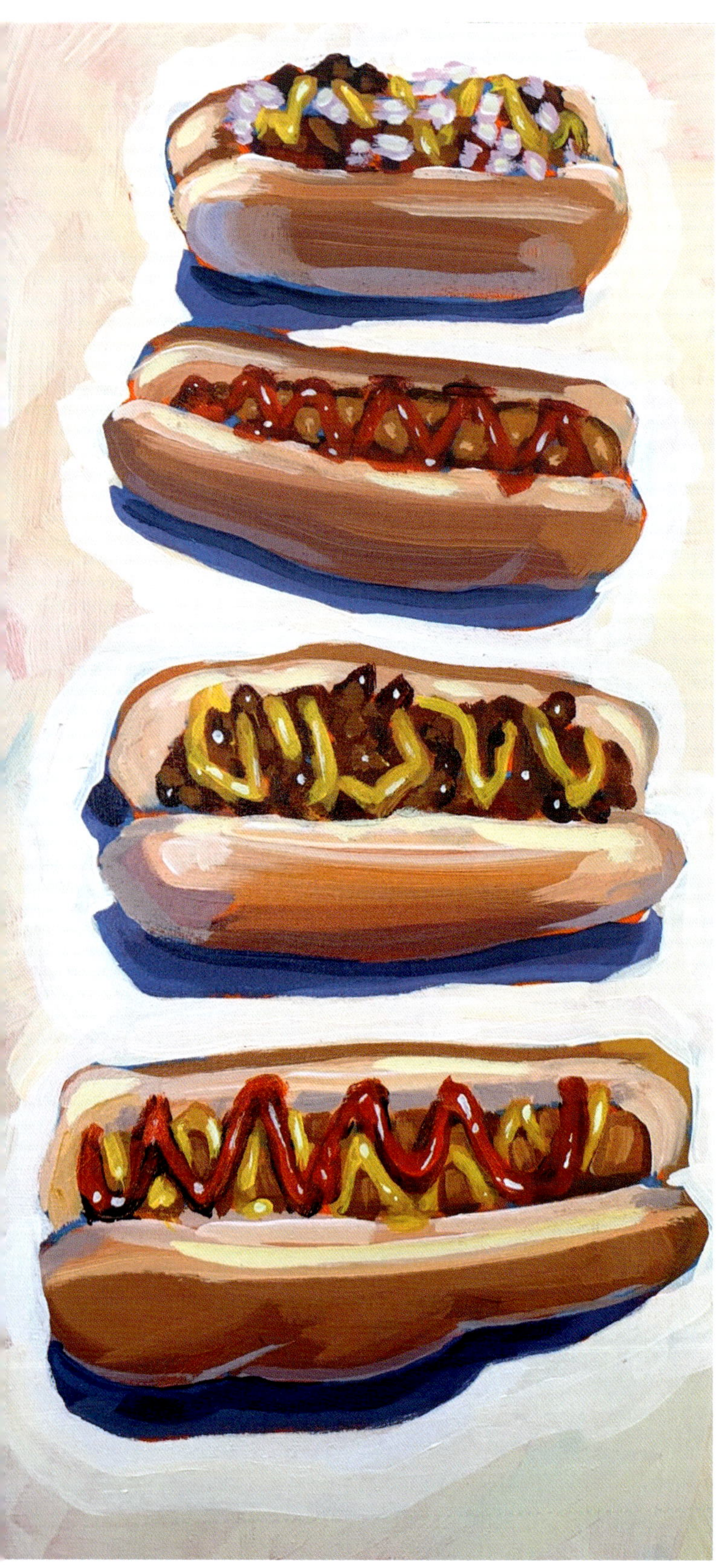

the urge for realism. Establish a set of goals for the painting, technical or emotional, ensuring they're achievable and true to your intent. When you're finished, assess whether you've met these objectives or gleaned insights to enhance future paintings. Remember, growth is a continuous journey. Every painting doesn't need to be a masterpiece. Sometimes, it's essentially about accumulating experience.

Drawing an analogy from my time as a collegiate cross-country runner: not every run is a record-breaker. Most runs are foundational and unexciting, preparing you to run your fastest for the moments that count. Similarly, most paintings serve as studies, building your expertise bit by bit. The other facet of growth is embracing discomfort. Pop culture often romanticizes painting as a serene activity. But for many, especially those honing their representational skills, painting is more of an emotional battle. There are highs and lows, periods of doubt, and moments of revelation. Understand that it's natural for something to be challenging and gratifying simultaneously. Exercise patience, take breaks, and most importantly, be kind to yourself.

It's essential to find comfort in discomfort and set manageable, internally driven goals.

MODERN STILL LIFE

Style Sandwich Step-by-Step

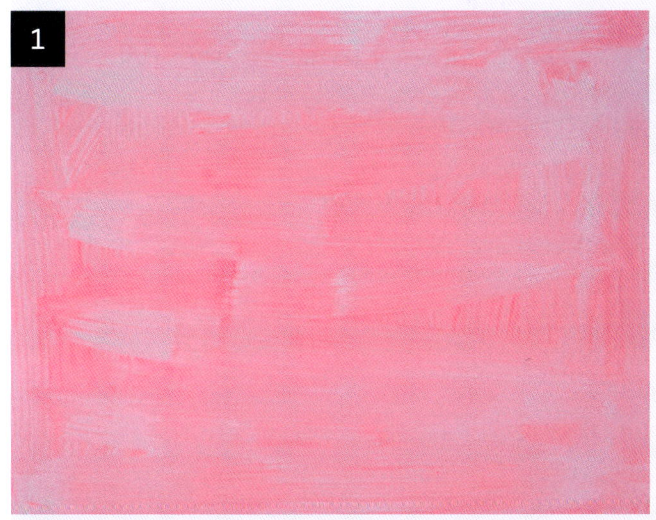

STEP 1

To start, I primed my canvas with a bright pink color. Knowing the painting would feature a lot of greens—both in the ketchup and the bottle or cup of green soda—I chose pink as a complementary backdrop.

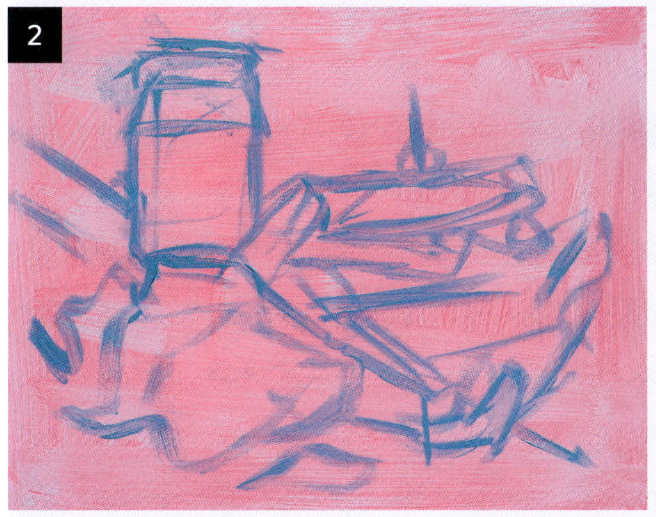

STEP 2

I use a mixture of Phthalo Blue (Green Shade) and Titanium White to block in the general composition. Given that there are only about three objects and their shadows, the composition isn't too intricate.

Therefore, I opt for a looser, more impressionistic blocking-in style. This approach works well for simpler compositions and lends itself to a more brushy, less measured look.

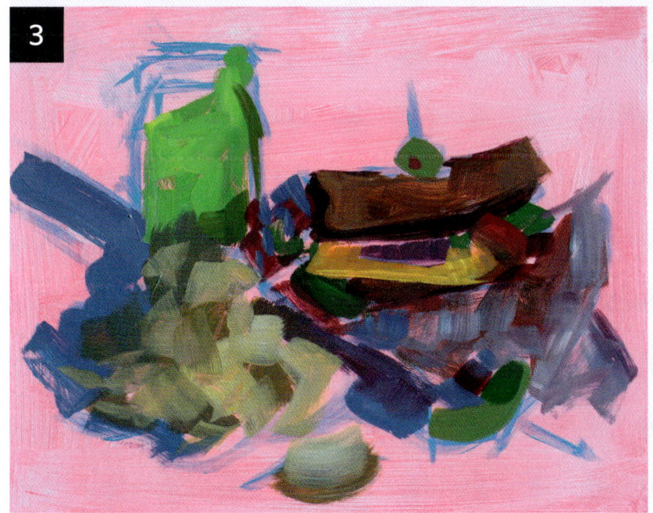

STEP 3

Using a larger brush, I block in the general forms and colors based on the initial drawing lines. While I leave out the background color for now, I do include the shadows. To effectively convey lighting, it's crucial to treat the shadows with the same level of intensity and focus as the main objects in the painting, such as the sandwich, the chips, and the drink.

(continued)

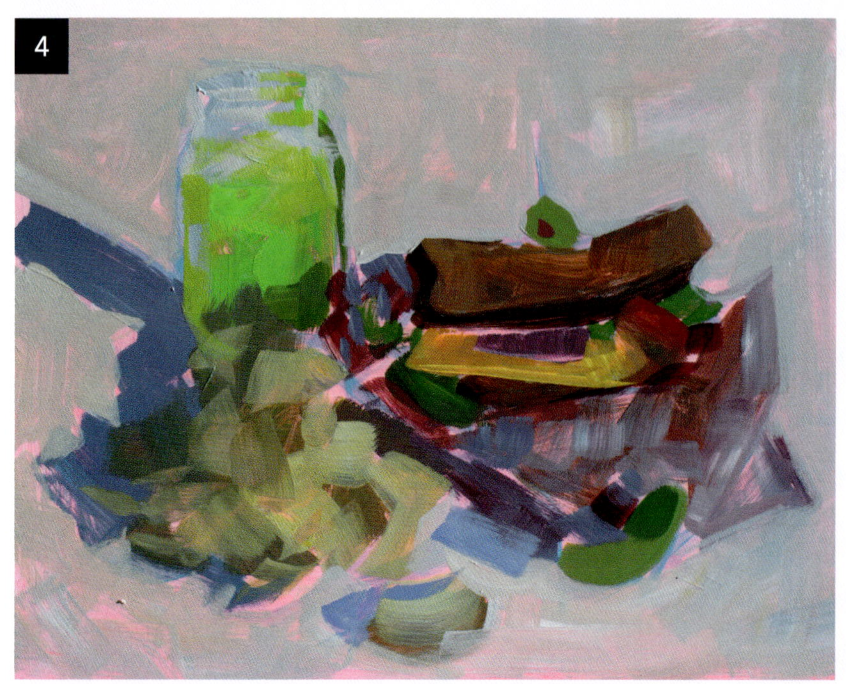

STEP 4

I use a creamy off-white color for the background, mirroring the white board I set the still life on. While the main aim is to cover the canvas, I let bits of the pink underpainting peek through. Initially, this was done for expediency, but it evolved into a stylistic choice I now embrace. Often, choices made to solve problems quickly—or even unnoticed details—can contribute to our unique style. Being a bit looser allows for the emergence of personal style and fosters a more compassionate painting mindset.

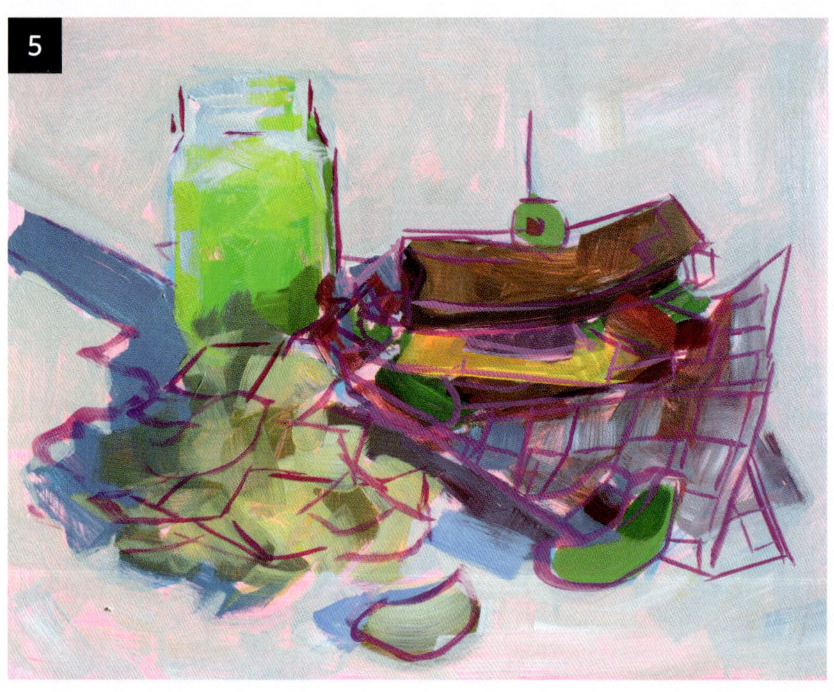

STEP 5

I use Quinacridone Magenta as a redraw color to focus on details omitted during the initial block-in. For example, the pattern on the napkin and the paper in the sandwich basket were left out earlier. The larger brush I initially used was great for quickly blocking in forms but too large for rendering details. So, I chose a color that sits between the checkered red and white, planning to refine it later. It's worth noting that redrawn lines serve a technical purpose, guiding you as you refine your painting. However, if they're not entirely covered, they can contribute to your style.

MODERN STILL LIFE

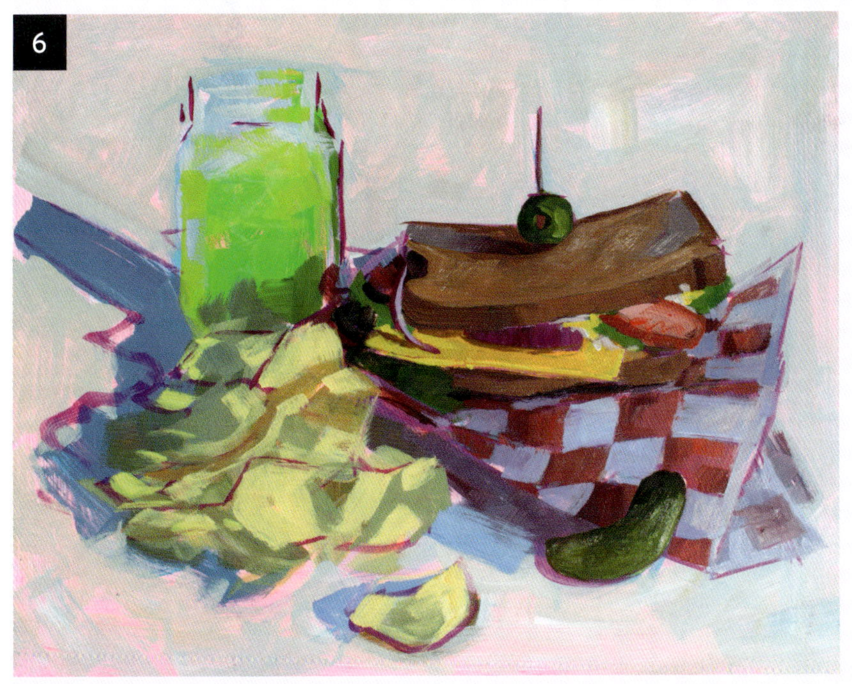

STEP 6

I switch to a smaller brush to add more details and bring the painting into clearer focus. This includes the checkers on the paper under the sandwich basket, the lighting and coloring on the chips, and details like the sandwich ingredients and the pickle. It's important to note that this step isn't about rendering anything to completion. It's about advancing the painting toward its final form. I view this as establishing a solid structure, which provides the information needed for making more detailed decisions later on.

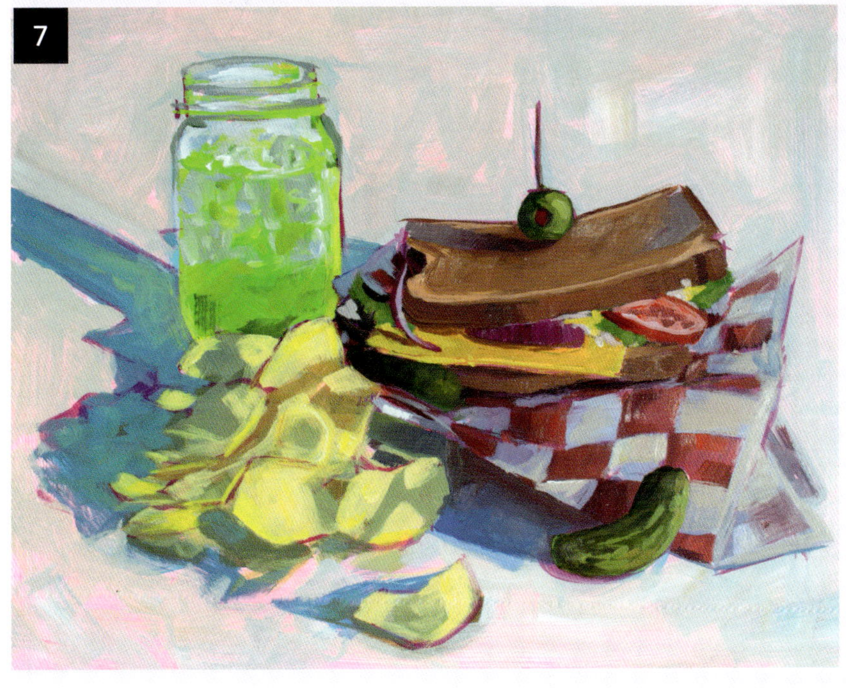

STEP 7

I focus on rendering the ice details in the glass of green soda and adjust the color in its shadow. The glass is translucent, and the sunlight shining through it casts a greenish tint onto the shadow, along with reflected light making the bluish shadow more green. This highlights the importance of observing how light interacts with shadows, rather than simplifying them into a generic bluish gray. Shadows often differ in hue based on the objects casting them, so it's crucial to pay attention to these nuances. I also refine some details in the pickle, chips, and sandwich.

(continued)

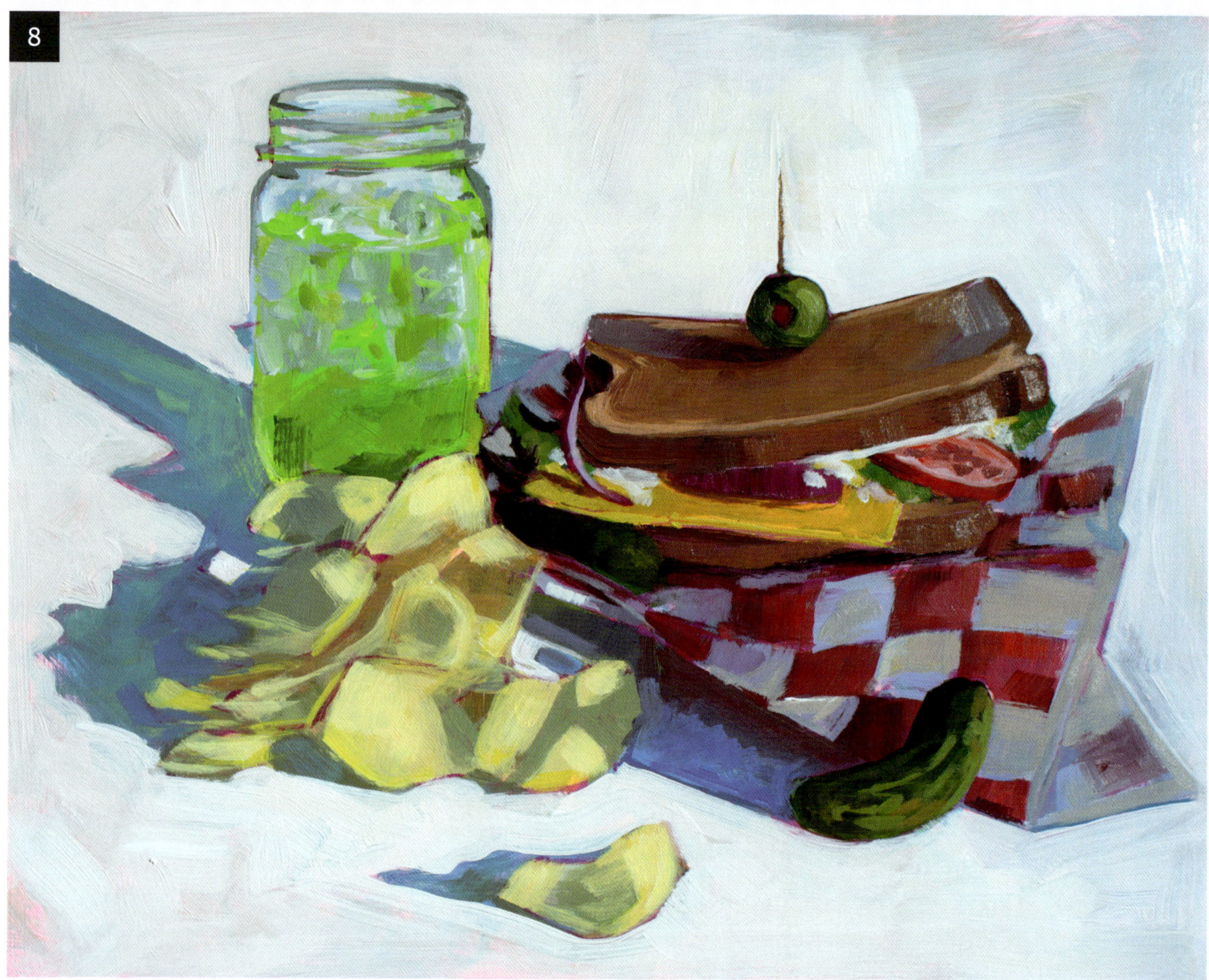

STEP 8

I use the white background to sharpen object edges, particularly the toothpick. For narrow details like this, I recommend the "carving out negative space" approach mentioned in earlier chapters, as it allows for straighter, finer lines—which is especially useful if you have a less steady hand. I also refine the shadow and add more details to the checkered pattern under the sandwich, as well as the sandwich ingredients.

At this point, the painting should make sense even without highlights. If an object relies solely on highlights for clarity, it likely means the form building hasn't been sufficient in creating volume and texture. By now, the painting should have that sense of volume and texture, preparing it for the final step.

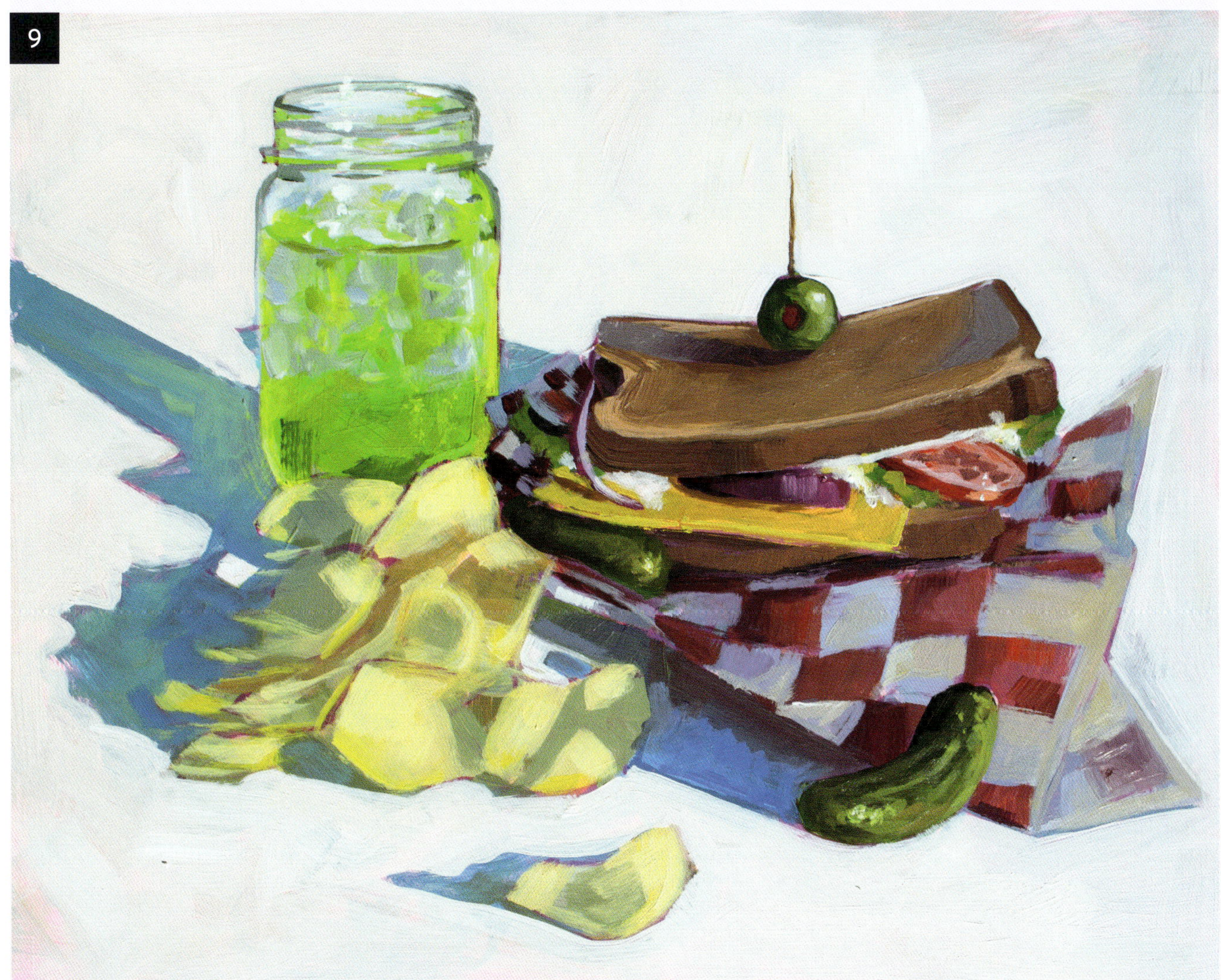

STEP 9

I use highlights and final touches to add a last layer of texture, rather than merely embellishing the painting. It's important to note that not all objects warrant highlights. Some are not reflective enough to merit them. Selectively applying highlights to certain elements, like the pickle and specific points on the glass where light reflects, enriches the overall texture of the composition. This nuanced approach to highlights contributes to a more life-like and compelling final piece.

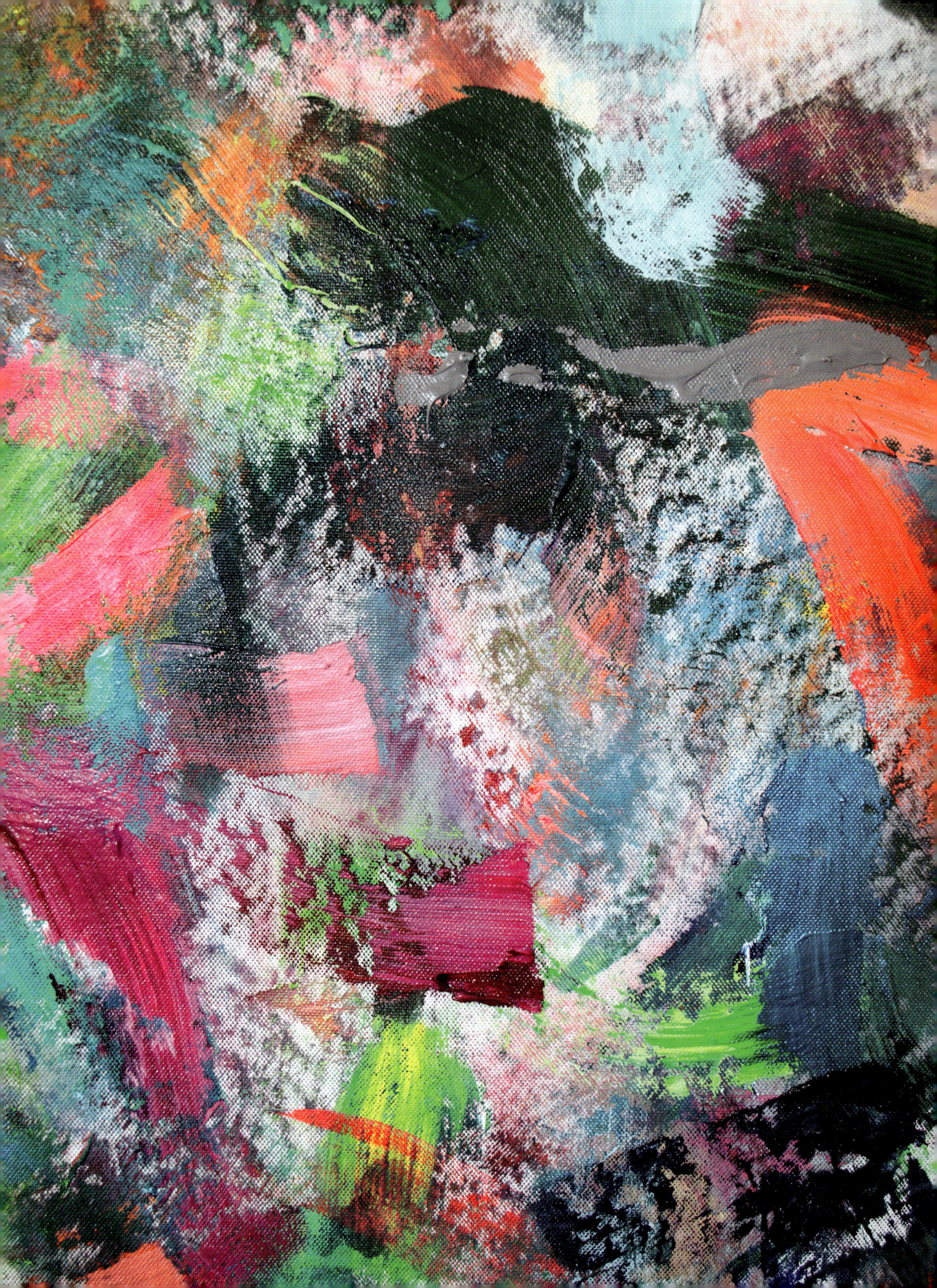

Cleanup & Closure

EFFECTIVE CLEANUP in painting involves two crucial components: responsible water disposal and maintenance of supplies.

I am fond of acrylic paint due to its opacity, user-friendliness, low toxicity compared to oil paint, and comparable vibrancy. However, its significant drawback is its composition: it's constructed of a mixture of pigment and plastic, leading to concerns about microplastic contamination in our soil and water supplies.

Given its potential impact on the environment and plumbing systems, proper water disposal is critical. I advise that you consult with your local municipal water supply on appropriate disposal methods, as guidelines can vary significantly, even within the same state or country. However, I will share my strategies and best practices for water cleanup, but remember, these may not be applicable relative to your local regulations.

Your cleanup strategy might also be influenced by factors such as your climate and available tools. I utilize the evaporation method, which converts paint water into solid waste to prevent contamination of water supplies. I place multiple five-gallon (19 L) containers, equipped with fine metal strainers, under clear corrugated plastic beside my studio, allowing for evaporation while keeping rainwater out.

Given the warm climate of central Texas, this method is quite effective, typically leaving behind solid, disposable paint residue by the end of summer. When evaporation rates decrease in winter, I sometimes resort to the GOLDEN Crash Paint Solids Waste Water Cleaning System, which involves a chemical solution that separates water from paint solids. Although costlier than evaporation, this method allows for the reuse of the separated water in painting and minimizes the environmental impact.

Other alternatives include absorbent materials like cat litter to solidify the paint or paint hardeners, but again, always confirm their acceptability with your local municipality. Responsible and efficient cleanup is a vital aspect of the painting process, contributing to environmental preservation and sustainable painting practices.

Responsible and efficient cleanup is a vital aspect of the painting process.

EFFICIENT WATER & BRUSH MANAGEMENT

Starting with arguably the most critical part of the cleanup process, we address water and brush management. The objective is to minimize water contamination, given that water is essential for cleaning brushes. I prefer olive oil soap for cleaning, avoiding harsh chemicals to maintain the integrity of the brushes, similar to hair care. It's crucial to clean brushes frequently, ensuring they are not left in water unnecessarily, especially overnight.

Mitigating Water Contamination

The first step is keeping paint out of the water as much as possible. One method I use involves having a drop cloth setup in my studio, which includes a plastic cloth as a non-permeable layer and fabric cloths to absorb excess paint. Excess paint from brushes is pressed against these cloths before dipping them in the water bucket, reducing the amount of paint entering the water.

Structured Water Cleaning

For further mitigation, structured water cleaning involves using multiple water cups or a segmented bucket, designated as dirty, intermediate, and clean water sections. This staged cleaning minimizes the transfer of paint into the clean water. Over time, the cleanest water may become contaminated, requiring a reshuffling of the water designation. Even with this structured approach, a final thorough cleaning of the brushes is necessary.

Simplifying the Process

While these processes might seem complex initially, they are inherently straightforward: aim to minimize paint in your water. Multiple methods exist, and adaptability and creativity are encouraged in finding the best approach for individual practices. Balancing effective cleaning with environmental consciousness is the key to responsible and sustainable painting practices.

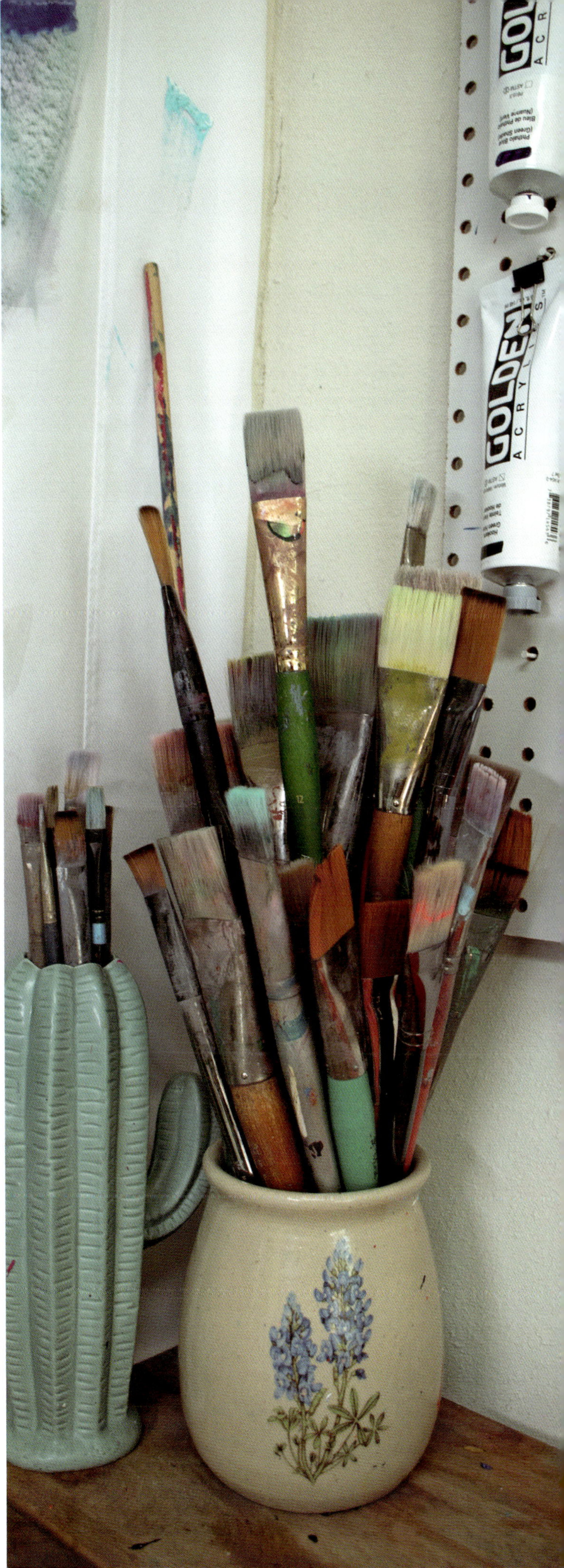

PALETTE PRESERVATION

The palette cleanup is quite varied, depending on the type of palette you are using. Whether you're using a Sta-Wet Palette or a flat glass palette, each requires different preservation methods:

- **Sta-Wet Palette** For Sta-Wet palettes, simply secure the lid properly, ensuring it's sealed, and your job is done.

- **Glass/Flat Palette** Using Glad Press'n Seal Cling Film can be effective in preserving paints on these palettes. If the palette is sealed properly, it can be placed in a cool and dry location to extend the life of the paints.

Getting Ready for the Next Day

I find it helpful to prepare for the next painting session during the cleanup. I tidy up the palette, place the brushes to dry, and organize other supplies to ensure a smooth start for the next day. This also means turning off the lights, music, and making sure everything is in place.

Conclusion

The preservation of your palette is crucial and varies with the type of palette in use. Adopting the right techniques can extend the life of your paints and ensure a seamless start for the next session. Whether it's securing a lid or using cling film, proper preservation can make your painting journey more enjoyable and less wasteful.

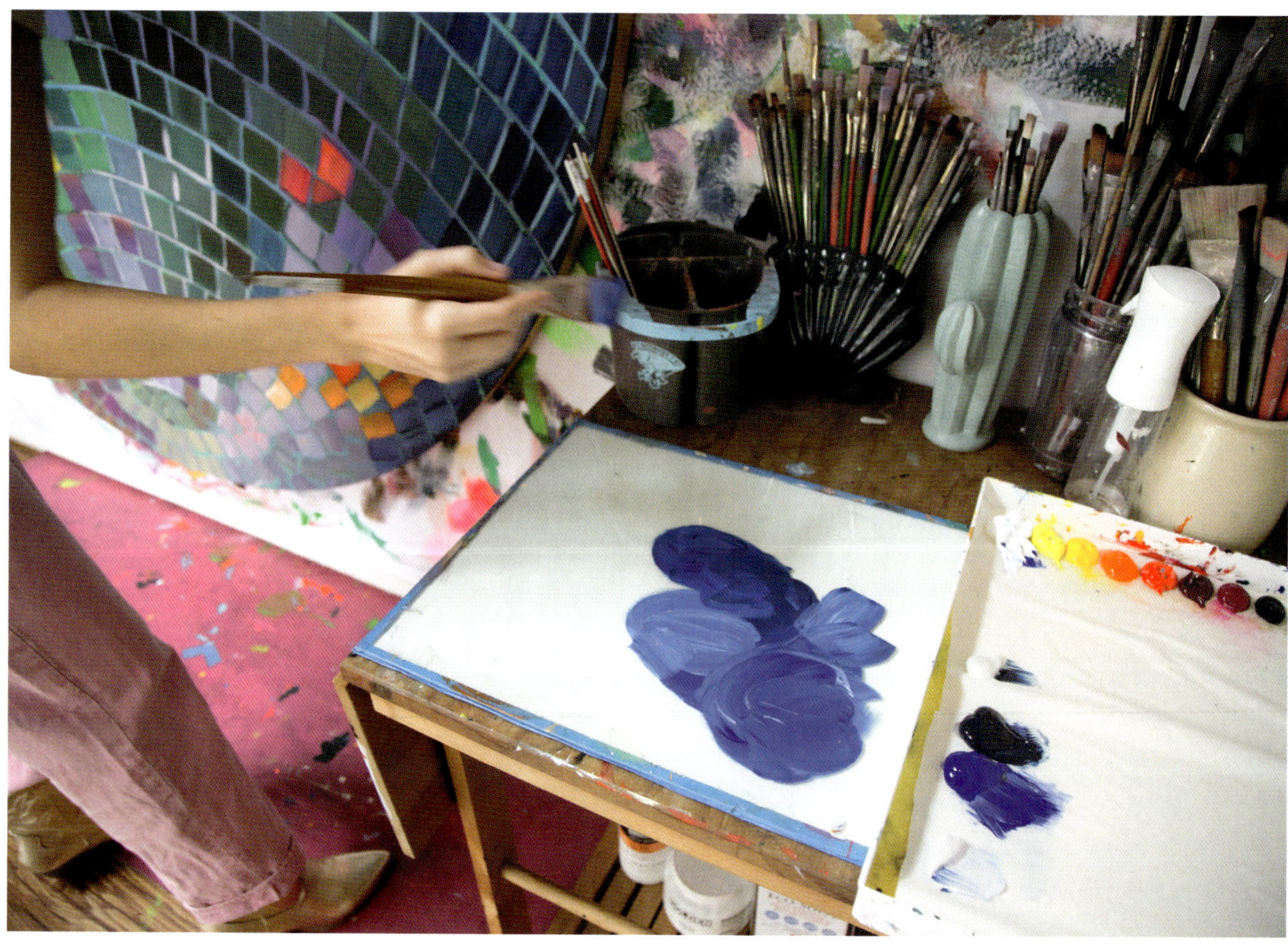

COMPLETING YOUR PAINTING

Admittedly, determining when a painting is complete can be challenging. Leonardo da Vinci is known to have revisited his paintings for years, continually applying little glazes. I give you my full permission to allow your paintings to simmer in that not-quite-finished zone. In fact, there's a wall in my home that has paintings constantly rotating in and out. Nestled in a corner that receives ample light, I call it *my thinking spot*. A painting I presume is finished, but am uncertain about, often resides on this wall—sometimes for a day or two, other times for months until I feel genuinely content with it.

Initially, "finished" often meant I felt I was making more mistakes than progress. This was a common sentiment at the outset of my painting career before I honed the skill of discerning a painting's completion. Now, further along in my journey and with a measure of confidence, I trust my ability to gauge a painting's doneness. It's vital not to conflate the notion that more painting equals greater skill with the idea that extra work on a current painting will always lead to improvement.

Theoretically, you could perpetually refine your student paintings, gradually developing the skills to truly complete work. However, I advocate for finding a sense of closure within each painting, trusting that with each new piece, your mastery over all painting aspects will grow. Remember, a painting doesn't have to serve as a grand testament to your skill level but rather as a thought carried to fruition. I often ask myself, "Have I articulated everything there is to say about this painting to the best of my ability at this moment?" Generally, if the answer leans more towards *yes*, I consider that a completed painting. It's rare to feel a strong, unyielding certainty that a painting is complete. It's usually a gradual conclusion, a series of self-assurances that next time it'll be better, and an acknowledgment of both the strengths and weaknesses present in the painting.

I often find that, months later, with the memory of the painting's struggles faded, I can appreciate the merits of my work. Determining the completion of a painting can be elusive, but if you feel at ease, if you believe you've made the most coherent statement possible with your current skill set, then congratulations—you've completed a painting.

Upon deciding a painting is finished, there are a few final tidying up tasks to consider: varnishing, signing your painting, and addressing the edges, to name a few. While these steps are advisable, remember there's no definitive way to conclude a painting. Thus, the conclusion of your painting can be as unique and personal as every other aspect of it.

Here's how I close out my paintings:

Varnishing Acrylic Paintings

Varnishing isn't a strict requirement for acrylic paintings as it is for oil, given that high-quality acrylics often contain built-in varnish. However, varnishing can enhance the aesthetic and longevity of your work, especially if you're aiming beyond student-grade pieces.

Aesthetic Uniformity

Different pigments have varied levels of sheen. Earth pigments might be matte, while synthetics could be glossy. Varnishing can harmonize the surface sheen across your painting, offering options like matte, glossy, or satin finishes. Satin, a blend of glossy and matte, is favored for preventing glare without compromising the piece's values. However, the choice of finish largely depends on individual preference.

Longevity, Preservation, and Cleaning

An isolation coat between the painting and the varnish can facilitate future archiving and restoration. Some artists swear by this method, and others opt not to varnish at all. Varnishing is particularly helpful for textured paintings, where it can smooth out the surfaces, preventing the accumulation of dust and dirt and making cleaning easier for collectors.

Conclusion

The decision to varnish acrylic works hinges on personal preferences and the artist's vision for the piece. Whether it's for aesthetic uniformity, preservation, or ease of cleaning, each artist must weigh the benefits against their desired outcome for the painting.

Painting the Edges

Painting the edges of your artwork is a stylistic choice and there are numerous ways artists go about it, each adding a unique flourish to the final piece.

Continuing the Front Image

Some artists opt to extend the painting from the front surface onto the edges, creating a continuous flow.

Abstract Edge Painting

Others prefer using their excess paint on the edges, giving the artwork abstract congruence with the colors used within the painting.

Preserving the Base Material

Many artists choose to tape off the edges to preserve the original canvas or wood panel finish, emphasizing the material used.

Distinct Colors

Using colors that correspond with the main elements of the painting on the edges can create intriguing effects, such as a glowing effect against certain wall colors, adding an extra dimension to the work. This is the style that I've adopted in recent years for my original work.

Consideration of Timing

Whether to paint the edges first or last is again a matter of preference. Painting them first can avoid the risk of contaminating the main painting, but painting them last can also be a rewarding challenge for those who aren't afraid of taking risks.

Color Choice

Color choice for the edges can range from neutral, like matte black, to more vibrant colors that align with the painting's theme. For instance, a painting with prominent red elements might have edges painted in bright red, adding a distinctive visual impact.

Conclusion

Ultimately, how you choose to paint the edges is your stylistic statement. From the timing to the color choice, each decision is a brush stroke in your artistic expression. Whether you want a seamless extension, a striking frame, or to emphasize the base material, there's no right or wrong—only what resonates with your vision for the piece.

The Art of the Signature

The signature on a piece of art might seem a simple matter, but it involves several considerations, each affecting the artwork's final presentation and its authentication.

Signature Placement

Artists have differing opinions on whether to sign the front, the back, or at all. I prefer signing the back to avoid interference with the composition, ensuring that the painting is sold with my signature without compromising its aesthetic integrity.

In contrast, some artists find joy in adding a stylistically scrawled signature on the front, feeling their piece is incomplete without it.

Signature Style

Whether you use your full name, initials, or even a unique symbol, finding and maintaining a consistent signature style is crucial. It becomes an integral part of your artistic identity, a recognizable symbol of your work.

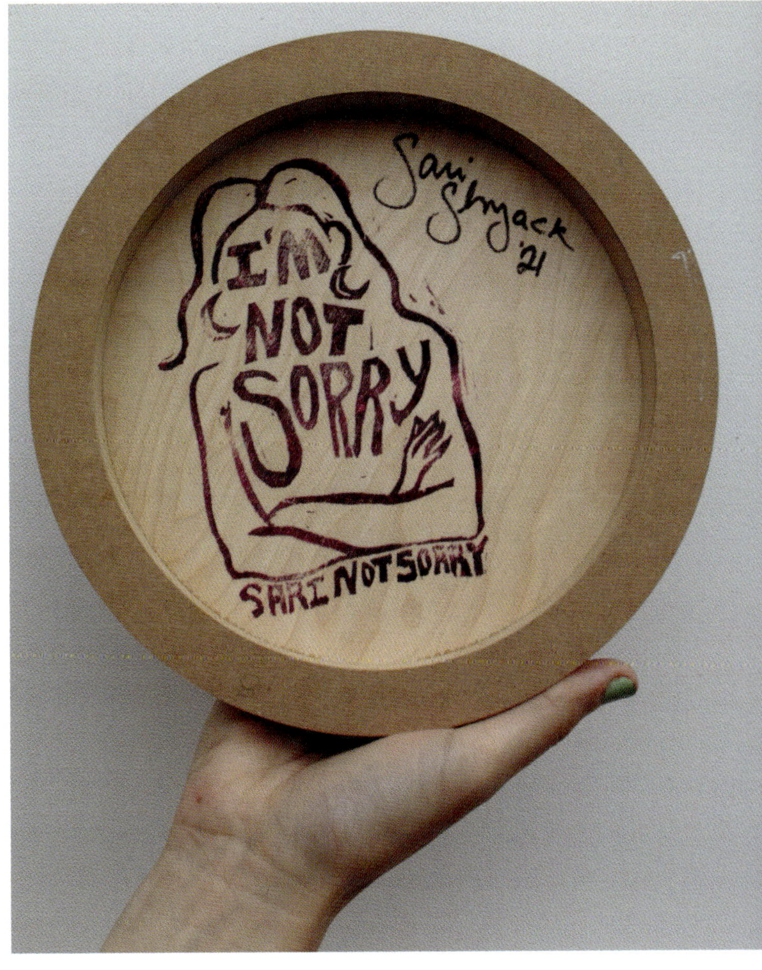

Authentication

Providing a letter of authentication can be beneficial, particularly for collectors. Such a document typically includes a color photo of the painting, title, dimensions, date of completion, and the artist's signature. Even if you opt not to sign the painting itself, offering a letter of authentication can fulfill the desire for signature validity among collectors.

Accommodating Preferences

While many artists have a steadfast preference for signature placement and style, it's also important to be accommodating when dealing with commissions. Some collectors may have specific requests regarding the presence and placement of your signature on the piece, and obliging such requests can contribute to a satisfactory commissioning experience for the collector.

Conclusion

The simple act of signing your artwork involves nuanced decisions about placement, style, and additional methods of authentication. Balancing your artistic preferences with the expectations and desires of collectors ensures that your signature complements your work while also serving as a seal of its authenticity and originality.

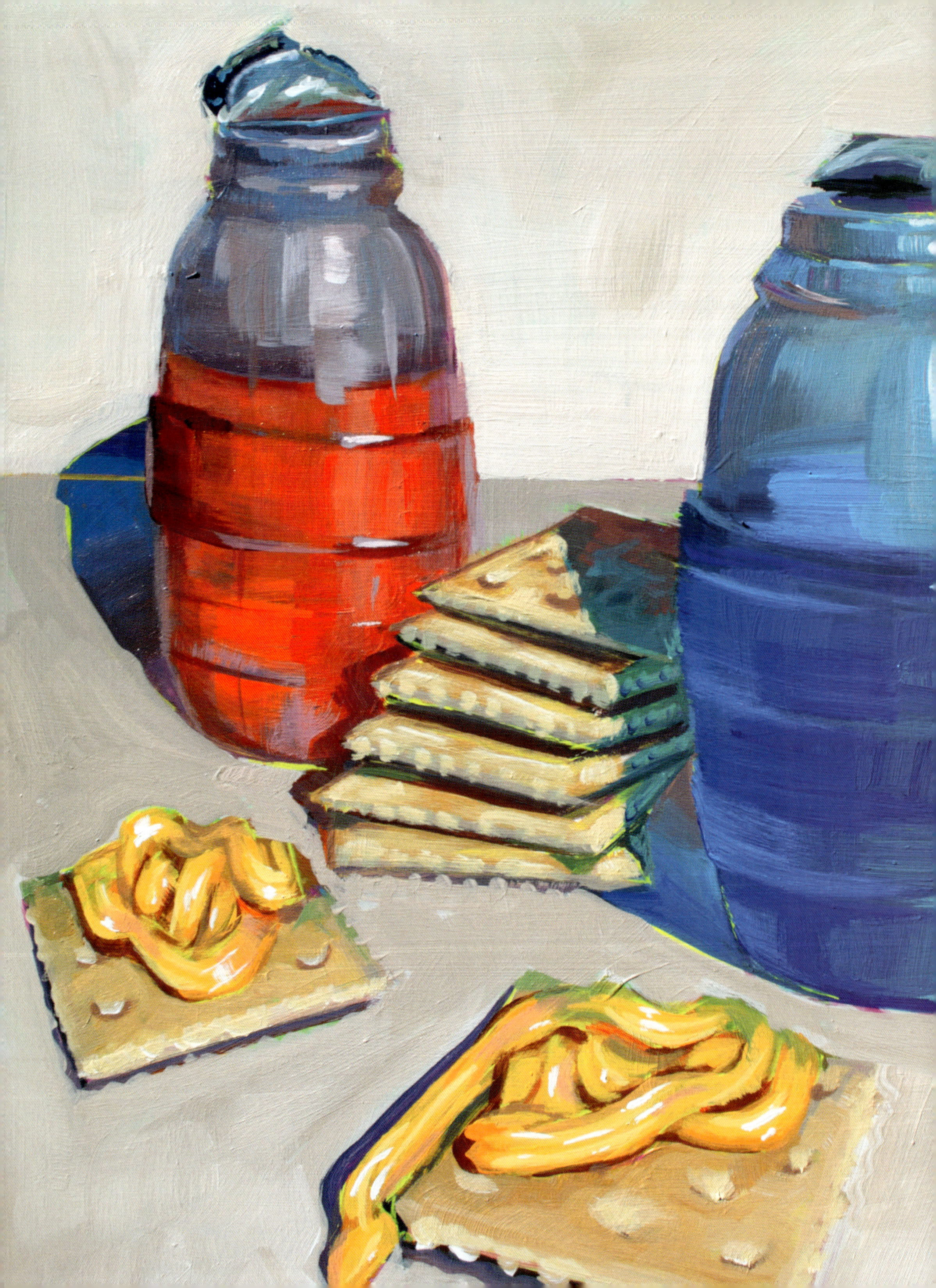

Conclusion

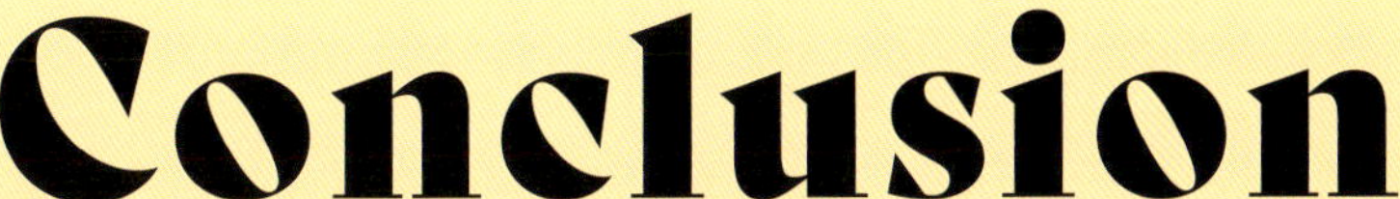

EMBARKING ON the painting journey, especially in representational styles, involves more than mastery of technique. It's about sustaining joy and passion in the practice, about learning to paint what resonates with your soul.

Developing a joyful practice is key. The mistake often made by beginners is the belief that one needs to paint "really well" to be worthy of a painting practice. The concept of painting "well" is subjective. The intrinsic human desire to create, to leave a mark, is the very essence of art.

Painting is not a privilege earned by mastery but a fundamental human expression. Progress and refinement in painting doesn't come overnight. It takes years of dedicated practice, fueled not by the pursuit of perfection but by the joy derived from the act of creating. The principles laid out in this book are not rigid rules but stepping stones, evolving with every brushstroke, developing into second nature.

Sometimes, diverging from the well-trodden path can lead to extraordinary discoveries. For me, the shimmering disco balls were a detour, a blend of abstraction and reality, color, and light that resonated with many and became a phenomenon in the art world. It was a reminder to listen to my creative voice and pursue that intuition to its completion.

Be patient with yourself, honor your unique expression, and above all, keep showing up. Painting is as much about representation as it is about conveying the unseen, the emotions, and following your instincts. Whether your message is about rendering the seen world or expressing the unseen one, remember to dance to your rhythm, to find joy in the journey, and to keep painting your story.

Thank you for joining me in this journey through the pages of this book. I hope the lessons and experiences shared here help guide you to explore, to create, and to find joy in each brushstroke. Keep painting, keep exploring, and remember, the world is better with your art in it.

Index

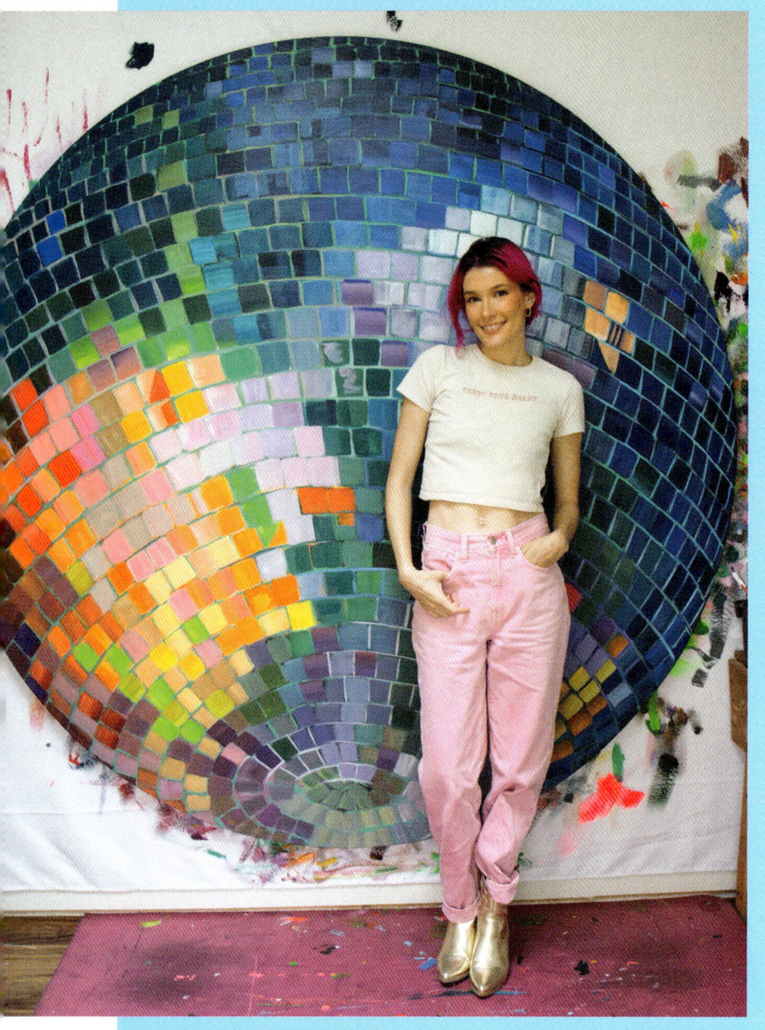

ABOUT THE ARTIST

SARI SHRYACK is an acrylic and oil painter from Austin, Texas. Her work is as colorful as it is wide-ranging in subject matter, and Sari brings her distinct bright style to everything from still life, portraits, landscapes, botanicals, disco balls, and much more.

Themes of her childhood, class consciousness, femininity, and motherhood are some of the strands that tie all of her paintings together to make a cohesive body of work.

Experiencing persistent poverty growing up in southwest Missouri has informed much of her world view, and it's through art that Sari is able to communicate structural class issues that are often left unaddressed to harmful effect.

Teenage girlhood from the 1990s and early 2000s is repositioned and re-examined in Sari's artwork as well, with era-specific products, candies, and toys from advertisements and thrift stores recast for their inherent beauty regardless of monetary value and utility.

Sari achieves this effect with still life as her guide, and this process is explained in thorough detail in these pages.

Sari found her love for painting in college with the help of a passionate art professor at Drury University in Springfield, Missouri, named Todd Lowery. His approachable technical lessons and steady belief in his students' ability informs Sari's teaching style, and his impact appears throughout the lessons of this book.

Sari was born in 1991 in Clearwater, Florida, and grew up in Missouri. She lives in Austin with her husband and two young children.